This volume comprises a timely and strategic contribution to a field that has so far remained neglected in India despite its crucial importance and role in enabling massive changes to take place without being noticed as such. The use of 'quality' as a term has permitted an alliance to emerge between the state and the market. Readers will find in this volume both conceptual and empirical writings that help to recognize and analyze the 'quality' discourse with pointers to the political economy in which this discourse grew without drawing attention to itself.
– **Krishna Kumar**, Honorary Professor of Education, Punjab University; Retired Professor, Department of Education, University of Delhi; and former Director, National Council of Educational Research and Training, India

This is an important book. India's school system is significant for international education debates not only as one of the world's largest but also as a site of many experiments, particularly regarding the roles of markets and states. This collection engages critically and thoughtfully with what is happening in Indian schooling and offers new insights for the international education community.
– **Simon McGrath**, Professor and Associate Head of School, School of Education University of Nottingham, UK; and UNESCO Chair in the Political Economy of Education

An exceptionally rich volume that ruthlessly challenges the contemporary concepts and theories that have shaped policy on education in India! Its fresh theorisation and nuanced conceptualisation blends long forgotten philosophical aims of school education and notions of equity in India. Must be read.
– **Shantha Sinha**, former Professor, University of Hyderabad; and former Chairperson, National Commission for Protection of Child Rights, India

School Education in India

This volume examines how the public and private domains in school education in India are informed and mediated by current market realities. It moves beyond the simplistic dichotomy of pro-state versus pro-market factors that define most current debates in the formulations of educational reform agendas to underline how they need to be interpreted in the larger context. The chapters in the volume present a series of conceptual and empirical investigations to understand the growth of private schools in India; investigate the largely uncontested claims made by the private sector regarding provision of superior quality of education; and their ability to address the educational needs of the poor. Further, the book looks at how the private–public dichotomy has been extended to professional identity of teachers and teaching practices as well.

Rich in primary data and supported by detailed case studies, this volume will be of interest to teachers, scholars and researchers dealing with education, educational policy, school education and public policy. It will also interest policy makers, think tanks and civil society organisations.

Manish Jain is Associate Professor at the School of Education Studies, Ambedkar University Delhi, India. He had been a school teacher prior to this for 10 years. His teaching and research interests lie at the intersections of history, politics and sociology of education.

Archana Mehendale is Professor at Tata Institute of Social Sciences, Mumbai, India, and leads the research programme of the Connected Learning Initiative. She has researched and published in the area of child rights, but more specifically on education law and policy, inclusive education and early childhood education.

Rahul Mukhopadhyay is Visiting Faculty with the School of Education, Azim Premji University, Bengaluru, India. His research interests are sociology of education, educational policy, sociology of organisations and anthropology of the state.

Padma M. Sarangapani is Professor of Education, Tata Institute of Social Sciences, Mumbai, India. Her current areas of work and research include teacher education, quality in education, culture and education and school systemic change at scale.

Christopher Winch is Professor of Educational Philosophy and Policy in the Department of Educational Studies at King's College London. He researches in the areas of philosophy of education, professional knowledge and qualifications and European VET policy tools. He has a long-standing interest in policy issues in education in India.

School Education in India
Market, State and Quality

Edited by
Manish Jain, Archana Mehendale,
Rahul Mukhopadhyay,
Padma M. Sarangapani and
Christopher Winch

LONDON AND NEW YORK

First published 2018
by Routledge
2 Park Square, Milton Park, Abingdon, Oxon OX14 4RN

and by Routledge
711 Third Avenue, New York, NY 10017

Routledge is an imprint of the Taylor & Francis Group, an informa business

© 2018 selection and editorial matter, Padma M. Sarangapani; individual chapters, the contributors

The right of Manish Jain, Archana Mehendale, Rahul Mukhopadhyay, Padma M. Sarangapani, and Christopher Winch to be identified as the authors of the editorial material, and of the authors for their individual chapters, has been asserted in accordance with sections 77 and 78 of the Copyright, Designs and Patents Act 1988.

All rights reserved. No part of this book may be reprinted or reproduced or utilised in any form or by any electronic, mechanical, or other means, now known or hereafter invented, including photocopying and recording, or in any information storage or retrieval system, without permission in writing from the publishers.

Trademark notice: Product or corporate names may be trademarks or registered trademarks, and are used only for identification and explanation without intent to infringe.

British Library Cataloguing-in-Publication Data
A catalogue record for this book is available from the British Library

Library of Congress Cataloging-in-Publication Data
A catalog record for this book has been requested

ISBN: 978-1-138-49474-9 (hbk)
ISBN: 978-1-351-02566-9 (ebk)

Typeset in Sabon
by Apex CoVantage, LLC

Contents

List of tables ... ix
List of contributors ... x
Acknowledgements ... xiii
List of abbreviations ... xvi

Introduction: Education in India between the state and market – concepts framing the new discourse: quality, efficiency, accountability ... 1
RAHUL MUKHOPADHYAY AND PADMA M. SARANGAPANI

PART I
Conceptual papers ... 29

1 Public, private and education in India: a historical overview ... 31
  MANISH JAIN

2 Markets, state and quality in education: reflections on genuine educational markets ... 67
  CHRISTOPHER WINCH

3 Normative articulations of the aims of education: an exploratory analysis ... 83
  ARCHANA MEHENDALE

4 Regulatory state and the diversified private ... 104
  ARCHANA MEHENDALE AND RAHUL MUKHOPADHYAY

5	Recovering the practice and profession of teaching PADMA M. SARANGAPANI, RAHUL MUKHOPADHYAY, PARUL AND MANISH JAIN	123
6	Notes on quality in education PADMA M. SARANGAPANI	139

PART II
Empirical studies 159

7	Hyderabad's education market PADMA M. SARANGAPANI	161
8	Schools, market and citizenship in Delhi MANISH JAIN	191
9	Curriculum as a dimension of quality: its production and management in schools in Hyderabad SAKSHI KAPOOR	227
10	Management of home–school relationship: role of school principals in low-fee private schools POONAM SHARMA	244
11	School quality: parent perspectives and schooling choices ELEANOR GURNEY	260
12	Teaching because it matters: beliefs and practices of government school teachers NIHARIKA SHARMA AND PADMA M. SARANGAPANI	281

Index 299

Tables

3.1	Normative frameworks on aims of education examined	86
4.1	Multiple regulatory agencies for school education and their functions	113
6.1	Comparison of quality frameworks	148
6.2	Education quality and indicators	150
7.1	Schools in Mandal A, B and C and year of establishment	166
7.2	School enrolment size and growth status	169
7.3	Management types and sources of funding	171
7.4	Occupational profiles of parents	174
7.5	School clientele	175
7.6	Pedagogic forms by funding type and clientele groups	181
8.1	Classification of schools covered in Delhi	195
8.2	School clientele profiles	199
8.3	School type and clientele	200
8.4	School type and spaciousness	201
8.5	Clientele and spaciousness	202
8.6	School type, spaciousness and maintenance	203
8.7	Pedagogy in classes	207
8.8	Pedagogic forms across school type	209
8.9	Clientele type and pedagogic forms	212
9.1	Basic profile of selected schools	229
11.1	Number of parent interviews by location	261
12.1	General profile of teachers	285

Contributors

Eleanor Gurney is a doctoral research student and Lecturer in International Education at King's College London, United Kingdom. Her research interests include processes of education reform, and issues of equality and social justice.

Manish Jain is an Associate Professor at the School of Education Studies, Ambedkar University Delhi (AUD), India. He has taught in a school for about a decade. His teaching and research interests lie at the intersections of history, politics and sociology of education, and he uses this lens to engage with education policies, urban education, comparative education and social science curriculum and citizenship education. His doctoral research was a comparative historical study of civics curriculum and citizenship in India and Canada since late nineteenth century. Manish writes in both Hindi and English and has most recently published in *Curriculum Studies in India* (Palgrave Macmillan, 2015).

Sakshi Kapoor is a doctoral student at Tata Institute of Social Sciences, Mumbai, India. Her research interests include education quality, accountability, school leadership and management, education policy, school organisations and institutional systems of education. She is currently working at the New York City Department of Education.

Archana Mehendale is Professor at Tata Institute of Social Sciences, India, since 2015 and leads the research programme of the Connected Learning Initiative. She has earlier worked in various capacities with Centre for Child and the Law, National Law School of India (1998 to 2014). She has researched and published in the area of child rights, but more specifically on education law and policy, inclusive education and early childhood education.

Contributors xi

Rahul Mukhopadhyay is a Visiting Faculty with the School of Education, Azim Premji University, Bengaluru, India. His doctoral work was on Anthropology of Education Bureaucracy. His research interests are sociology of education, educational policy, sociology of organisations and anthropology of the state. He has researched and published in the areas of elementary education in India, Right to Education, educational institutions and policies and quality in education.

Parul is presently working as Assistant Professor in Department of Elementary Education, Gargi College, University of Delhi, India. She is a PhD scholar from Tata Institute of Social Sciences, Mumbai, India, and pursuing her doctorate in the area of teachers' professionalism in context of policy changes. Her research interests include teachers' professional development, gender and education, policy studies and curriculum studies.

Padma M. Sarangapani is Professor of Education, Tata Institute of Social Sciences, Mumbai, India. Her current areas of work and research include teacher education, quality in education, elementary education and the use of ICTs in curriculum and teacher professional development and education and culture/indigenous education. She was a member of the Steering Committee of the National Curriculum Framework 2005 and the National Council of Teacher Education (2013–2016). She was a member of the founding editorial collective of *Contemporary Education Dialogue* between 2002 and 2012 *(SAGE)*, and is on the international editorial boards of the *British Journal of Sociology of Education* and the *International Journal of Sociology of Education*. She is author of *Constructing School Knowledge* (SAGE, 2003), and contributing editor of *Improving Government Schools: What Has Been Tried and What Works (Books for Change, 2003)*.

Niharika Sharma is presently working as an elementary educator in Canada. She is a BElEd graduate and has MA Education (Elementary) and MPhil in Education degrees from Tata Institute of Social Sciences. She has worked as an elementary educator, curriculum consultant, school leader and researcher in the field of elementary education. Her research interests include pedagogy, teachers' beliefs and practices, children's beliefs and understanding and teacher education.

Poonam Sharma is a doctoral student at the Tata Institute of Social Sciences, Mumbai, India. Her research interests include childhood studies, ethnography, family–school relationships and school management. She is presently associated with Save the Children, India. Previously she has worked as teacher educator at the Amity University, NOIDA and as a primary school teacher at the Heritage School, Gurgaon.

Christopher Winch is Professor of Educational Philosophy and Policy in the Department of Educational Studies at King's College London, United Kingdom. From 2008–2012, he was head of the department. He was Chair of the Philosophy of Education Society of Great Britain from 2008–2011 and is now an honorary vice-president of the society. Christopher Winch researches in the areas of philosophy of education, professional knowledge and qualifications and European VET policy tools. He has a long-standing interest in policy issues in education in India.

Acknowledgements

This book is the culmination of a collaborative effort over seven years during which this group of editors and their students (also authors of chapters in this collection) worked together to problematise 'quality' of education and understand the nature of the diversity of schools that are available to children in India, and the education 'market'. This multidisciplinary team was formed to be able to examine conceptual matters and draw on this to undertake a few empirical studies. Some of our students also undertook their MPhil and doctoral research work in these locations and around related themes. This book brings together and presents the outcomes of the collaborative endeavour and the scholarship it has fostered.

We were fortunate to secure the support of a series of small grants to enable us to more or less proceed as we had planned. The Sir Ratan Tata Trust and ICICI-Social Initiatives Group supported a grant to the MA Education (Elementary) programme at the Tata Institute of Social Sciences through which we were able to secure a small grant for 'Conceptual Work Relating to Quality in Education' (2009–2010). The ICSSR-ESRC scholar exchange provided us with a grant, 'Conceptual Enquiry for the Design of a Survey of Schools (School Quality, Teachers and Parents)' to support international travel (2011–2012). The EdCIL, Ministry of Human Resource Development, Government of India, New Delhi, provided us with a crucial grant to undertake our major study of three cities, 'Baseline Survey of the School Scenario in Some States in the Context of RTE: Study of Educational Quality, School Management, and Teachers. Andhra Pradesh, Delhi and West Bengal' (2010–2011). We are grateful to the late Ms. Anita Kaul, IAS, who was Joint Secretary, MHRD at that time, for her positive response to our proposal and request for government support for the core empirical work that is presented in this book. Subsequently we benefited from two rounds of grants for collaboration, the conduct

xiv *Acknowledgements*

of short courses and workshops and exchange of faculty of students between the Tata Institute of Social Sciences, Mumbai and King's College London. The British Council awarded us with a grant for 'Collaborating for Quality' (2012) and subsequently the UGC-UKIERI thematic partnership grant with University Grants Commission India, for the project 'Changing Nature of the Public and the Private in School Education' (2014–2017). These grants enabled us to organise several meetings, workshops and summer and winter schools, and to undertake field work, and student exchanges, through which we were able to develop our ideas, and present data, emerging analyses and working papers to advanced research students and colleagues. We are grateful to these various funders whose grants allowed us to carry forward our work in stages over the years.

We organised four major workshops/schools related to this work: 'Workshop on Comparative Study of Schools' (17–18 December 2010, Mumbai); 'Quality in Education' (16 January–28 March 2012, Hyderabad and London); 'Changing Nature of the Public and the Private in School Education' Regulation in Education (15–20 June 2015, Bengaluru) and 'Conducting Research in Developing Countries: Thematic Case Studies and the Use of Primary Data' (23–26 November 2015, London). We are grateful to the resource persons and participants of these workshops who enabled us to reflect on and develop many of our ideas.

The core empirical research – the survey of schools – was possible only because of the co-operation of heads and teachers of schools who allowed us entry in their schools and classes and spent considerable time with us for interviews. We are grateful to the Education Department of the Municipal Corporation of Delhi (MCD) for giving us permission to carry out this research in MCD schools. Nargis Panchapakesan guided us to Najma Siddiqui and Nasim Siddiqui who helped us contact various MCD officials. We are grateful to Upender Reddy, Professor at SCERT, Andhra Pradesh, and the Deputy Education Officer Hyderabad for giving us permission to conduct the study and for facilitating our work in the chosen Mandal. We are grateful to the Department of School Education, Government of West Bengal and the Sarva Shiksha Abhiyan Office, West Bengal for facilitating permissions for this study. We are grateful to the Vikramshila Education Resource Society for extending support for the fieldwork pertaining to the study and other processes, and particularly to Shubhra Chatterji and Kanupriya Jhunjhunwala. We benefited from interactions with Geetha Nambissan, Manabi Majumdar, Rohit Dhankar, G. Nagaraju and Amita Bhide in the early phases of this work.

Acknowledgements xv

We are grateful to all the members of the research teams in the cities of Hyderabad, Delhi and Kolkata, for their amazing commitment and rigour in research and insights, and for the enthusiasm with which they participated in the research, collected data amidst all adversities that included repeated refusal, weather and considerable travel: Rekha Pappu, Anuradha P., Ramgopal Koneripalli, Sakshi Kapoor, Bhagyalakshmi V., Amar, Praveen Reddy, Saroj Bangaru, G. Sreeramulu in Hyderabad; Poonam Sharma, Parul Kalra, Niharika Sharma, Yuveka Singh, Ridhi Pathak, Manoj Kumar Chahil and Kriti Srivastava in Delhi and Shruti Jain who tabulated the data; Kanupriya, Proma, Shinjini, Shubhomita, Jayanta, Mustafiz, Pritha, Srabanti, Manjula, Rejaul, Saurabhi, Babita, Sarmishtha, Jhuma, Nazneen, Arun, Partho, Palash, Sujata, Samima, Rozina, Shibani, Namrata, Sutapa, Atanu, Soma, Sariful, Nibedita, Ahana, Ajanta, Riti and Atri from Vikramshila and Sahana Sen, in Kolkata.

We are grateful for assistance received from our universities to enable us to engage with this work and support to conduct various workshops, schools and events: Ambedkar University, Delhi, Azim Premji University, Bengaluru, King's College, London and the Tata Institute of Social Sciences, Hyderabad and Mumbai. The Accounts Department of Tata Institute of Social Sciences, Mumbai, in particular Rajee Menon and Joycie Dias assisted in managing various grants that we received over the years. We are grateful to them for this assistance and enabling us to meet numerous reporting requirements admirably.

Abbreviations

ASER	Annual Status of Education Reports
BEd	Bachelor of Education
BElEd	Bachelor of Elementary Education
CBSE	Central Board of Secondary Education
CCE	Continuous Comprehensive Evaluation
CCS	Centre for Civil Society
CED	Contemporary Education Dialogue
CfBT	Centre for British Teachers
CSF	Central Square Foundation
CSR	Corporate Social Responsibility
DEd	Diploma in Education
DCB	Delhi Cantonment Board
DDA	Delhi Development Authority
DEO	Department of Education
DISE	District Information System for Education
DoE	Directorate of Education
DPEP	District Primary Education Programme
DSW	Doon School Weekly
EC	Education Commission
EIC	East India Company
EWS	Economically Weaker Sections
GNCTD	Government of the National Capital Territory of Delhi
GoI	Government of India
ICESCR	International Covenant on Economic, Social and Cultural Rights
ICSE	Indian Certificate of Secondary Education
IHDS	Indian Human Development Survey
JEE	Joint Entrance Examination
KCF	Karnataka State Curriculum Framework
KV	Kendriya Vidyalaya

LFP	Low-Fee Private
MCD	Municipal Corporation of Delhi
MDL	Middle
NCERT	National Council of Educational Research and Training
NCF	National Curriculum Framework
NCTD	National Capital Territory of Delhi
NCTE	National Council for Teacher Education
NDMC	New Delhi Municipal Council
NPE	National Policy on Education
NPM	New Public Management
PCF	Punjab Curriculum Framework
PP	Pre-primary
PPPs	Public–Private Partnerships
PSTE	Pre-Service Teacher Education and Training
PTA	Parent-Teacher Association
PUA/PUR	Private Unaided Recognised
PUA UR/PUUR	Private Unaided Unrecognised
RtE	Right to Education
RWAs	Resident Welfare Associations
SC/ST	Scheduled Caste/Scheduled Tribe
SDGs	Sustainable Development Goals
SDMC	South Delhi Municipal Corporation
SEC	Secondary Education Commission
SS	Senior Secondary
SSC	Secondary School Certificate
TE	Teacher Education
TET	Teacher Eligibility Test
TfI	Teach for India
UDHR	Universal Declaration of Human Rights
UEE	Universal Elementary Education
UNCRC	United Nations Convention on the Rights of the Child
UNESCO	United Nations Educational, Scientific and Cultural Organization
UP	Uttar Pradesh
USP	Unique Selling Proposition

Introduction
Education in India between the state and market – concepts framing the new discourse: quality, efficiency, accountability

Rahul Mukhopadhyay and Padma M. Sarangapani

The changes in the Indian school education landscape since the 1990s have witnessed the massive expansion of and enrolment into the government school system. Simultaneously, there has been an expansion of the private school sector, especially driven by low-fee private schools. The overall growth of the private has manifested in a more differentiated typology of private providers and a stratification of these providers that mirrors the existing inequalities in the Indian society. These transitions have also been accompanied by an increased attention to the idea of 'quality' of education by policy makers, educationists and researchers, mainly focusing on the broader differentiation of the 'public' (government schools) and 'private' (private or non-state) providers of education in the country. In the ensuing debates a number of key conceptual categories have been invoked to sharpen this idea of 'quality' of education and frame a new discursive regime of educational ideas around specific understandings of these concepts and the idea of 'quality'.

Though the idea of 'quality' of education in relation to learning outcomes finds a place in Indian policy documents as early as 1986 (Sarangapani, 2010), the explicit operationalisation of 'quality' as measurable learning outcomes has come to occupy the centre stage of policy and public concern with the publication of the *Annual Status of Education Survey* and the corresponding *Annual Status of Education Reports* (ASER), which started in 2005. This year-on-year large-scale learning assessment survey conducted by Pratham, a non-government organisation working on educational issues, has over the years reported and emphasised how achievements of children undergoing school education in India are abysmally below grade-specific learning levels. The findings from this oft-quoted report have subsequently been reinforced by other studies that have also indicated how, at a broad level, only close to 50 per cent of students in primary and upper primary grades can successfully perform reading and arithmetic tasks as expected of them.[1] The set of measurable indicators common across most of these studies includes students' achievement level, physical infrastructure, teacher absenteeism, pupil-teacher ratio, enrolment, student absenteeism and dropout. Broadly, these studies treat student academic learning scores as the 'outcomes'/indicators of quality, and they gather information on other variables for their hypothesised relationship to quality. As some educationists have argued, these studies, in their conceptual underpinnings, align with the economist's predilection for 'efficiency' as evident both in the 'school effectiveness' research tradition and the World Bank's understanding of quality as acquisition of foundational skills in literacy, numeracy and reasoning in the most cost-effective manner (Kumar and Sarangapani, 2004; Sarangapani, 2010).

The concept of 'efficiency' underlying the 'outcomes as quality' idea has received further prominence with this approach to quality being used to compare provisioning and outcomes of public versus private schools in a number of studies. These studies claim that private schools, even low-fee private unrecognised schools, provide better inputs in terms of both basic infrastructure facilities such as toilets and desks and teaching-learning processes such as teachers' presence and time-on-task (Goyal, 2009; Kingdon and Teal, 2007; Muralidharan and Kremer, 2006; Tooley and Dixon, 2006). Going one step further, research has examined differences in student achievements across public and private schools and the findings from this research has reinforced the notion that private schools outperform public schools. Using regression analysis, these studies have stressed the private school advantage, in terms of both raw scores uncorrected for other possible causes (Wadhwa, 2009) and analyses that have made corrections for possible alternative explanatory variables (see, e.g. Goyal and Pandey, 2009; Muralidharan and Kremer, 2006; Tooley et al., 2010). Following similar conceptual and methodological assumptions, a few studies have indicated that there is a small private school advantage in terms of student outcomes even after controlling for selection bias – the tendency of better-off and more informed families to enrol their children in private schools (Desai et al., 2009; French and Kingdon, 2010). Overall, the influence of the 'outcomes as quality' idea has intensified significantly and is quite evident in the emphasis that the current government has been giving to annual census-based achievement surveys of all children in the elementary level in government and aided schools.[2]

A second concept that has been influential in shaping the new discursive regime of quality is that of 'accountability', which comes to the foreground of educational discourse in the previous decade through a different group of studies. One strand from this group has emphasised the strong interlinkages between the education system, especially teachers, and the political system in different states of India (Beteille, 2009; Bhattacharya, 2001; Kingdon and Muzammil, 2003). For example, in their work on teachers' unions in the state of Uttar Pradesh, through an analysis of constitutional provisions and ongoing political processes, Kingdon and Muzammil (2003) showed how teachers have a substantial presence in formal elected forums at the state level. In addition, teacher unions, which were initially formed to protect the service interests of teachers, were seen to have morphed into associations patronised by different political parties. Thus, through such mechanisms, teachers have been shown to be agents actively involved in lobbying for the protection and improvement of only their employment benefits and warding off all attempts to ensure local-level accountability. Another strand of surveys and studies through which the concept of 'accountability' has received prominence are those that have focused on how teachers are 'unaccountable' at the level of school processes themselves. Large-scale surveys, including revisit studies, have noted the high rates of teacher absenteeism in government schools across states, ranging from around 18 per cent to more than 40 per cent with an all-India average of 25 per cent (Kremer et al., 2005; Muralidharan et al., 2016). Thus, the discursive framing of 'accountability', in reference to the aforementioned set of studies, has come to be one that stresses the need of policy solutions to address the problem of 'unaccountable' government-school teachers who have been responsible for the poor quality of learning in the public schools, especially when compared to the private schools.

Both concepts of 'efficiency' and 'accountability' underline the importance of 'value-for-money' in the delivery of public services such as education. Inputs to school education pertaining to the teacher, such as their salaries, their presence in schools and their active engagement in the classroom and the effective (real and notional) costs of these inputs, form the main thrust of this argument. Within this argument, even the marginal private school advantage that emerges from more rigorously designed regression studies is rationalised as being better, as this advantage is said to be achieved by the private schools at lesser costs per student (Jain and Dholakia, 2009; Kingdon, 2009). This argument understandably resonates with a state that does not show strong political will to invest adequately in the social sector, including education and health. Overall, the idea of 'outcomes as quality' and the concepts of efficiency and accountability have formed the basis of a new discursive regime, which is most significantly visible in policy discourses that have veered towards the efficacy of the private (or the market) over the state in the provisioning of – and gradually even the financing of – school education.

This centrality of the efficiency of the 'private' over 'public' (government) is evident in the policy solutions emerging from the discursive regime of ideas of 'outcomes as quality', 'efficiency' and 'accountability' that we have just examined. A set of studies around low-fee private schools in India and other developing countries seems to suggest that these schools would be a desirable alternative to the existing government elementary school system which had failed to deliver 'quality' education (Rangaraju, Tooley, and Dixon, 2012; Tooley and Dixon, 2006; Tooley, Dixon, and Gomathi, 2007).[3] A similar faith in the 'private' is evident from Plan documents of the Indian State and policy initiatives that have started to not only acknowledge but also endorse the increased role of the private and, in particular, public–private partnerships (PPPs) to help an 'ailing' government school system to transform itself (Srivastava, 2010; Srivastava, Noronha, and Fennell, 2013). However, more than such alternatives, the burden of the new discursive regime and the policy solutions arising from it has fallen disproportionately on the government school teachers.

At one level, policy solutions have been framed with the assumption that the regular teacher cadre has been 'unaccountable' and unable to deliver on learning outcomes. For example, the large-scale adoption of a para-teacher cadre by several Indian states over the previous two decades has pivoted around these ideas – the argument being that such a system is more 'efficient', 'accountable' and 'cost-effective' as compared to the existing cadre of teachers. The para-teacher cadre has primarily been recruited on short-term contractual arrangements and the members are often from the local community, with lower educational qualifications and much lower salaries than those of the regular teachers. The benefits of this 'private' contractual nature of teachers' employment have been emphasised in studies that show the lower absence rates of para teachers and comparable or better student learning outcomes under para teachers with respect to regular teachers (Atherton and Kingdon, 2010; Goyal and Pandey, 2009; Kingdon and Sipahimalani-Rao, 2010).

At another level, similar assumptions of efficacy drawn from the 'private' management of organisations (including schools), as well as the need of a 'healthy tension' in the service conditions of teachers to ensure accountability, underpin another solution from the same discursive regime, that of incentive-based pay structures for teachers (Muralidharan, 2012; Pritchett and Murgai, 2006; Muralidharan and Sundararaman, 2011). The other form in which government teachers have been targeted is in the policy proposals for and even adoption of technology solutions that seek to provide greater control over teachers' work (Duflo, Hanna, and Ryan, 2012; Muralidharan, Niehaus, and Sukhtankar, 2016). Even the recent Economic Survey proposes that 'an option to address teacher absenteeism that can be explored is biometric attendance of all teachers in primary schools for each scheduled class/lecture/session' and that any such pilot project 'should be accompanied with an evaluation of learning outcomes' (GoI, 2016: 163). In its overall intent, proposals of a student tracking system, already launched in some states, seem to be aligned to the same idea of 'control' over teachers' work by focusing on student achievements, while simultaneously claiming a more transparent administration of schemes and the system at the school level.[4]

Another set of policy arguments, that for school vouchers, derives from the same discursive regime. Although school vouchers have not, as yet, been implemented widely across the country, footprints of both private-sponsored and government-sponsored vouchers schemes are already visible in Delhi, Uttarakhand and Andhra Pradesh (Muralidharan and Sundararaman, 2015; Shah and Miranda, 2013). Proponents of school vouchers endorse it as a form of demand-side financing where the parents can exercise their 'choice' with respect to the schools they want to send their children to, which, in turn, would generate 'competition' among schools to ensure the desired 'quality' of education. The larger argument is in favour of provisioning of education by the private sector, with the government only playing the role of a financier and regulator for such an open play of market forces to determine school choices and educational quality. The role of economic competition and the managerial efficiency of the private sector, thus, become the driving logic of such a policy move. The proponents of this solution see an explicit endorsement of their position in the 25 per cent provision under the Right to Education Act, 2009, which provides for inclusion of children from marginalised communities in private unaided schools, albeit with reservations about the limited ambit of both 'choice' and 'competition' in its current avatar.

It is not as if these conceptual categories and the assumptions around which the new discursive regime has marshalled itself have gone unchallenged. Theoretical and empirical works from many educationists have launched incisive criticisms against the arguments that we have summarised above. In the next section, we provide an outline of the critique that proposes a distinctively different understanding of the conceptual categories that have formed the keystone of the new discursive regime.

Developing a critique of the new discursive regime

The conceptual categories that form the backbone of the new discursive regime are not new to education. However, the ways in which they are being reconfigured by the new discursive regime have been noted to be problematic, primarily in terms of the 'thin' managerial conceptions that underlie the understanding of these categories and their little or no reference to fundamental aims and purposes of education, the context of a segregated and stratified school institutional system that characterises the Indian landscape, or the weak institutional structures and outdated frameworks of educational governance that are expected to regulate the relationship between the state and the market in education. Here, we discuss this critique of the new discursive regime with reference to some of its key conceptual categories to lay the ground for our arguments, which align with this critique but substantially deepen it in terms of both its conceptual and empirical engagement.

Foremost among the conceptual categories, as we saw earlier, is that of 'quality' of education. Existing notions of 'quality of education', whether it be the ASER Reports or studies that have underlined that the quality of low-fee private schools is better than that of the government schools, have tended to focus on the immediate institutional aspects of education delivery. However, as educationists have argued, 'quality of education' is impossible to conceptualise without making normative judgements about the worthwhileness of any system of education. In the conceptualisation of such educationists, 'quality of education' is a 'master concept' that necessarily has a multidimensional nature (Kumar and Sarangapani, 2004; Sarangapani, this volume; Winch, 1996, 2010). As Winch (2010: 36) elaborates, rejecting the idea of examining the quality of educational systems through inputs and outputs, 'input – output talk is not helpful to understand it (quality), but traditional categories such as aims, standards, performance, curriculum, pedagogy and assessment are.' Emerging research has also problematised the hitherto easy mapping of good quality onto private schools and bad quality onto government schools. As one study shows, there is a complex interplay between household choices and the institutional environment of a local school system. This, in turn, leads to a mapping of issues of quality and equity among schools in this school system that need not follow the easy equivalence of good quality with private and poor quality with government schools (Hill, Samson, and Dasgupta, 2011). Another study underlines the overall poor quality of both government and private unrecognised schools, in terms of school infrastructure and academic performances of children in rural areas and that the 'shift from cost-free education in government schools to cost-paid private schools is making no difference to learning outcomes and quality of education' (Kaur, 2017: 63). Besides interrogating questionable conceptions of quality of education, yet another strand of work has challenged the conceptual and methodological impulses that have guided studies and reports emphasising the good-private and poor-government difference in the school system (Mehendale, 2014; Sarangapani and Winch, 2010; Vellanki, 2015). A primary argument made in these works is that the government–private binary fails to examine closely institutional processes (of a more variegated school environment with large differences in institutional parameters) and social processes (of participants accessing these different schools) that comprise the empirical reality in the highly differentiated school system in India.

Another idea of the new discursive regime, that of 'efficiency', has gained prominence through the comparison between the purported 'inefficiencies' plaguing the existing public service delivery of education by the state apparatus and the 'efficiencies' shown by the private sector in terms of delivery of products and services to consumers in a market regime. Interestingly, the state itself has used such a logic to make a case for increased involvement of private actors, especially PPPs in education, in recent plan documents (Srivastava, 2010). Evidently, these arguments adopt the binaries of government – 'inefficient bureaucracy' – and market – 'efficient corporate'– in terms of their explanatory capabilities of how efficiency in education is produced only in the latter. Further, there is no effort in these arguments to outline the nature of 'efficiency' in education or what could constitute or produce such efficiencies and how. As a result, inputs in education could be substituted by anything, from blackboards to televisions, and from trained teachers to unqualified novices, so long as the provisioning of these inputs are found to be better in one regime (market – corporate) as compared to the other (government – bureaucracy). Educationists working on budget schools (Nambissan, 2013) and in the area of teacher education (Jain and Saxena, 2010; Ramachandran, 2009) have countered the claims of these arguments in terms of the very nature of education that such a paradigm of efficiency would then seek to endorse – that of a consumer product that could well be produced with minimum resources or even resources made to be desirable by the prevailing market regime.

Similarly, the endorsement of school vouchers in the new discursive regime, deriving from a notion of market efficiency promoted by mechanisms of 'exit' and 'choice', has been critiqued to be premised on an inadequate understanding of how mechanisms of exit and choice can and do operate in the contexts of disadvantaged communities (Härmä, 2011; Srivastava, 2007). More importantly, some of these studies have underlined the negative consequences for equity that could possibly result from school vouchers in a context of a stratified schooling system that almost mirrors larger social inequalities. In addition, referring to a key study on school vouchers by Muralidharan and Sundararaman (2015) in the Indian context, a recent study has challenged the efficiency arguments for private schools, in terms of relative advantage of student outcomes, on which endorsement of school vouchers have depended (Karopady, 2014). As the study shows with reference to the voucher programme operationalised, 'even after 5 years of exposure, the children who shifted to private schools from government schools when given a choice under a scholarship programme are not able to perform any better than their government school counterparts' (Karopady, 2014: 52). A more recent study has also posited a strong critique about some of the interpretational limitations of the study by Muralidharan and Kramer (Tooley, 2016).

Another key category of the new discursive regime – accountability – has come under scrutiny in reference to its explicit connotations of 'control' and 'management' of teachers' work. Such a conceptualisation has been observed to align with New Public Management theories and the understanding of teachers' work as that of an 'executive technician' rather than that of a professional (Winch, 2014). What is displaced in such a conceptualisation is, first, an understanding of the complex career histories, multiple identities and intricate network of formal and informal relationships that constitute the figure of the school teacher and her work in the government school system (Majumdar, 2011; Majumdar and Mooij, 2011; Sriprakash, 2012). Second, an individual conception of accountability at the level of the teacher remains inattentive to systemic issues that contribute to individual unaccountability – issues such as a poor teacher education system, inadequate mechanisms and support systems for in-service training and mentoring and a programmatic work environment at the lower levels of the education system with a multitude of schemes, programmes and documentary regime (often ad hoc) that detract from key teaching-learning tasks. Teacher educators have also critiqued the dominant notion of accountability as one that devalues the very nature of the teaching profession with its narrow focus on managerial control and little autonomy for the teacher in terms of her practice. As Batra (2013) notes, 'the emerging "corporatised" understanding of quality, viewed in terms of learning guarantee, teacher accountability and the scientific management of education, is antithetical to the understanding of quality seen as being integral to the concept and process of education' (p. 223). The existing understanding of accountability is also increasingly tied to learning outcomes and emphasises only *achievement accountability* over *process accountability*. As in other countries in the wake of large-scale testing, studies in India have also observed how such outcomes-based accountability often leads to 'fabrication' and orients teacher practices *only* towards students' outcomes in the large-scale assessment tests (cf. Mukhopadhyay and Sriprakash, 2011).

In this book, we deepen and extend the critique of the new discursive regime. We engage and articulate key concepts that should inform our understanding of a quality school education system – an understanding that enables us to be both descriptive and normative while assessing educational aims, processes and outcomes. We also extend the scope of existing empirical work around the changing nature of the government and private school system in India to the complex array of private providers emerging in the school arena and the understudied nature of this spectrum and complexity. The latter is important because the emergence of the new discursive regime is inextricably intertwined with the changing nature of the public and the private in school education over the previous two decades.

Significant changes in school education system in the last two decades

The early decades of Independence witnessed a continuous deferral of achievement targets for universal elementary education. However, this scenario seemed to alter quite remarkably with the decade of the 1990s, and several changes came to define this altered scenario that can be characterised in terms of an altered political economy paradigm of education and the discursive framework accompanying this shift. One, however, needs to contextualise this shift within the changing nature of the Indian state, its developmental agenda and class dynamics that have accompanied these changes. The policy priorities in school education, more often than not, have mirrored these shifts.

With education shifted to the Concurrent List in the 1970s, from being a state subject earlier, the federal relations underwent a substantial change and the central government started assuming a greater role for educational change interventions and to drive overall policy agendas. The decade of the 1980s saw the beginnings of large-scale centrally driven programmes in elementary education, a mode of state intervention that would thereafter become the preferred approach to educational change. The financial crisis of the early 1990s and the consequent structural adjustment programme that India embarked upon provided a rationale for aid for primary education from the World Bank for the first time. This ensured the beginnings of the District Primary Education Programme, which brought in project planning, management modules and project structures that were parallel to the then-existing education department processes and structures. Over the decade of the 1990s, India became a signatory to different international conventions – the World Conference on Education for All in Jomtien in 1990, the United Nations Convention on the Rights of the Child in 1989 (adopted by India in 1992) and the World Education Forum in Dakar in 2000. All of these treaties reinforced the agenda of universalisation of elementary education and provided the foundation for the large-scale, international-donor-funded, centrally sponsored scheme – the Sarva Shiksha Abhiyan. This became the principal vehicle through which the Indian state would pursue the objective of universalisation of elementary education, from around 2001 until the present times. Understandably, the neo-liberal turn of the larger polity in the aftermath of the structural adjustment programmes of the early 1990s provided a suitable political climate for these transitions (Kumar, 2006; Ramachandran and Sharma, 2009).

Indeed, the underwriting of the agenda of universalisation by the Sarva Shiksha Abhiyan has yielded an unprecedented expansion in physical infrastructure for elementary education (Govinda and Bandyopadhyay, 2011). However, our focus here is not this expansion in physical infrastructure, but the simultaneous changes in the role of the state and the mainly private non-state actors, regarding provisioning, financing and regulation of elementary education. These changes, understandably, have not always been through explicit policy endorsement. Rather, as we explore in this book, the nature of these changes has been both in terms of the redefined boundaries of the state and non-state actors *in practice* and through discursive regimes that have accompanied, and continue to accompany, such reconfigurations.

The larger changes in the political and economic landscape over this period went hand in hand with a visible change in the ordering of school preferences that was seen to prevail in the earlier decades. The aspirations of the middle classes found new expressions in a climate of industrial reforms and economic policies that started in the mid-1980s and were accentuated by structural reforms in the Indian economy in the early 1990s. With their professional and social interests intertwined with the emerging forms of corporate capital that came to dominate both the formal and informal economy, the new middle classes started exiting the government and government-aided provisioning of vernacular education in favour of a burgeoning range of private unaided schools. These schools now range from those offering international baccalaureate school education programmes at astronomically high fees for the elite to a spectrum of schools with a graded fee structure that cater to the highly segmented new middle classes, down to low-fee paying unrecognised schools catering to those from the lower rungs of the stratified social order aspiring to reach the middle classes. What unites them, however, is the tag of 'English-medium' education, which, especially in the post-liberalisation years, has come to signify the 'cultural capital' that would provide access to hitherto restricted social mobility for large sections of the society and to private employment in the face of shrinking and sparse government employment opportunities.

A growing literature has documented the gradual increase in the role of the 'private' in school education in the last two decades. For example, the Indian Human Development Survey (IHDS) of 2005 observed that enrolment in the elementary age group in private unaided schools increased from around 10 per cent in rural areas in 1994 to around 21 per cent in rural areas and 51 per cent in urban areas in 2005 (Desai et al., 2010). Recent reports indicate a continuation of these trends, with official District Information System for Education (DISE) data showing a growth in private school enrolments at the elementary level from 51 million in 2007 to 78 million in 2013 and a corresponding decline in government school enrolment from 133.7 million to 121 million over the same period (ASER, 2015).[5] Also, the nature of private providers has become increasingly varied, with business models in the form of low-fee schools for rural and urban poor, school chains for middle-class urban populations run as conglomerates or franchisees and niche elite schools catering to the upper classes, adding to a segregated access to schooling options already existing in the country.[6] Finally, besides playing an increasingly prominent role in provisioning of education vis-à-vis the state, the 'private' has expanded and consolidated its presence in elementary education as the provider of a diverse range of education services. Such services range from curricular materials and multimedia-supported solutions for classroom teaching-learning processes to in-service teacher training and teacher professional development modules. An implicit acceptance of a diminished role of the state in managing, financing and regulating elementary education and a call for a greater need of private support in these areas have also led to the emergence of public–private partnerships with a diversity of contractual relationships and agreements inking such partnership agreements. From building and managing schools to providing different types of education services, these PPPs have also come to occupy a significant role in redefining the expanded and diversified nature of the 'private' in recent years.[7]

Understandably, such changes have had consequences for the government schools at multiple levels. Already under-resourced and with severe capacity constraints, the government elementary schools have over the last decade become the recourse for only the extremely marginalised sections of the population. The expanded role of the state through its programmatic interventions on 'Education for All' has, on the one hand, increased the access to schools among socially disadvantaged groups hitherto without access to mainstream educational options. On the other hand, economic changes have veered towards a faith in market processes where even the lower-middle classes as well as the poor with some ability to pay have increasingly opted for private English medium education with its promises of socioeconomic mobility. These simultaneous transitions and the discursive frameworks underlying these transitions – that of the efficiency of the private and the market vis-à-vis the state – have further emaciated the government schools, which are now also regarded by large sections of the population as *schools of the last resort*. Albert O. Hirschman's framework of 'voice' and 'exit' has been used by several educationists to analyse these changes, with overall trends reflecting an 'exit' from government schools and a lack of 'voice' among the marginalised poor in government schools to effect substantive changes to the dysfunctional government elementary schools. One should also note that some of these larger socioeconomic transitions also play out in the lives of government school teachers who have increasingly started to identify themselves with the aspirations of the middle classes. This has led to an increasing social distance between the teachers and the social groups currently accessing government schools and the reinforcement of deficit assumptions about students based on their socioeconomic backgrounds, to the extent that a stereotyping of the 'culture' of government schools as being marked by distance, apathy, dysfunction and neglect has acquired widespread and uncritical circulation (see, for e.g. Vasavi, 2015).

Layout of the volume and chapters

The chapters in this collection have come about through a five-year collaboration between the authors to examine afresh the emerging landscape of schools in India and re-examine aspects of government versus private school provisioning and the claims regarding their differential efficacy. The research project took the view that there is value in returning to examine the empirical landscape of schools and their quality through a re-engagement with the core concepts analytically and historically. This approach was selected so that we are able to determine the scope of our empirical studies, select methodology, design tools and develop the analytical framework from conceptual and contextual grounding. In particular, we were concerned that (i) the everyday understandings of concepts such as quality or accountability are neither adequate nor self-evident and (ii) the recategorisation of schools into the government–private binary reflects new politico-economic compulsions operating in the policy discourse space and must be examined for its ontological validity in the Indian context – historically and empirically – rather than accepting them uncritically to conduct analyses and engage with policy based on these categories. Awareness of the historical development and shifts in categories, such as the 'government' and 'private' – which is being used today as a binary – also increases our awareness of the contexts and functions of categorisation in different historical periods and the shifting place of the state and the non-state (including the market) in Indian education. Lastly, by allowing the framework to extend to the landscape of schooling as a whole, rather than limiting it to education of the poor, and by examining not only 'elementary school' but also preschool and secondary school, we also allow the phenomenon to be understood at a societal level – in relation to the ecosystem of schools occupying economic niches in a market, the segregated nature of the Indian society and the Indian state – as the background against which to examine the specific question of the trajectory of schooling for the poor.

The book is divided into two sections. The first part is devoted to conceptual and historical studies of 'quality', 'the market' and 'the state' in relation to education and the evolution of the categories of private and public. The second part of the book presents two empirical exploratory studies carried out in the cities of Hyderabad and Delhi and four case studies of school managements and teachers and parents, which draw on the conceptual work laid out in Part I of the book.

Part I: conceptual papers

The six chapters in this section develop a set of core concepts and contextualise them to the Indian educational landscape, through conceptual, historical and policy study. These chapters aim at exploring the dimensions of a framework for understanding issues of the state and market in education in India that could guide the design of empirical studies, including the formulation of researchable questions, methodology and the design of tools, and interpretation. The concepts we examine are public and private, market and state, state regulation and accountability, aims of education, teachers and teacher work, and education quality, along with the shifts in and influences on policy and the changing nature of the state.

Manish Jain, drawing on political theory and feminist theory, and through a historical examination of the trajectory of the concepts of public and private in the Indian context, presents two arguments. First, that the meanings of these terms as relevant to understanding the organisation of an education system is not only economic in terms of financing of education but also importantly political – reflecting considerations in the formation of the public, the citizen and the nation. The second argument is that the meanings of the terms are neither singular nor static. Jain exposits the multiplicity of meanings, types and histories with reference to (a) the nature of the state, (b) distinct time-histories of colonial annexation, (c) levels of state, (d) changing understandings of the state's role and responsibility with regard to mass education, accessibility, neutrality and intervention in native affairs, culture and religion levels of education, (e) geographical differences, (f) levels of education and (g) emerging Indian 'publics' with the rise of the national movement and other axes of self-identities. He argues that we need to avoid looking at state–non-state and public–private as mutually exclusive binaries with strong boundaries and draws attention to the value of locating public and private schools and actors in relation to larger social processes, interests and forces. Through this chapter, Jain reminds us of the value of examining both the social and political significance of the diversity of schooling and the complexity of the economic arrangements in relation to state funding and attendant regulation. Jain also draws our attention to the long history of the coexistence of not only public and privately funded education but also commercial interests in education, serving both public and private aims, in the Indian context.

Christopher Winch's chapter opens up the discussion of the education market and of education as yet another good traded in the market, with reference to the Indian context. While in developed countries, what is found is a government-sponsored quasi-market, in India, even though education activity is not meant to be for profit, we find considerations in operation that suggest that we may be looking at a genuine educational market. Winch examines both the implications of a multitiered educational market for the production of educational goods, both private and public, and criteria for assessing the relative quality of education within such a complex and hybrid system. His conceptual analysis factors in considerations of practical circumstances to be found in India as evidenced in the empirical studies such as those that form the second part of this book. Important issues that he draws our attention to include the nature of the educational good that is on sale or bought: when parents pay for education, they are buying not only 'the opportunity to education' but also equally the outcome of 'becoming educated'. Both the process and the outcome have private, positional and public good elements and these are considerations for the purchaser of the good. The quality of the good may be a function of the price paid. The nature of the good may itself be differentiated and contested as parents, managements and government may have different views on what the 'good' is. Religious and caste-based communities could also have a strong influence on the educational good on offer. Winch argues that the need to retain the idea of the interests of the collective in relation to the education good brings to the fore the role of the state as regulator. However, he also points out that there are problems with such a proposition when the state is unable to guarantee its authority against powerful local interests.

The chapter by Archana Mehendale is an exercise in analysing 'aims of education'. Mehendale argues that with the public school system experiencing flux because of the changing role of the state and increasing expansion of private schools, exploring the normative framework of aims that underlie different policies can enable us to understand the relationship between the proclaimed aims of the state and the diverse curricular and pedagogic settings. It would also enable us to understand if the policy framework differentiates between various providers of schooling in terms of their roles or capacities to fulfil the public aims of education. She examines aims in international policies and covenants, to which India is a signatory, and those at the Indian national and sub-national (state) levels and their relative coherences. The chapter draws attention to important questions such as who is considered to be the subject of these aims – individual child, families, community or government; who is expected to ensure that the aims of education are fulfilled – the government, the market or the community; and by what means and methods are the aims expected to be realised. National aims tend to emphasise social aims such as citizenship for participatory democracy, social justice, peace, protection of the environment, predisposition towards social change and respect of human dignity and rights. Individual aims include the nurturing of qualities such as self-esteem, creativity, imagination, independence of thought and openness to learning. State curricular frameworks tend to emphasise aims that more closely endorse the individual and private benefits of education, particularly the acquisition of skills and knowledge that are valuable in gainful employment and becoming productive. Mehendale notes the marked absence of curricular aims in these official frameworks; she also notes that there could be defacto operation of implicit and intrinsic aims that do not make their way to official proclamations. Given the essential relationship between education aims and quality of education, this analysis of stated aims of the state provides us with a normative lens to both examine the diversity of aims that manifest in different institutional spaces run by state and non-state actors and assess whether what is on offer is worthwhile education; indeed, this itself could be one starting point for the assessment of quality.

In India, the state as a primary guarantor of education has the obligation to provide, fund and regulate. However, in the differentiated and stratified school system that has evolved over the years and exists even today, it is only 'regulation' that is understood to be the commonly performed function of the state across all categories of schools. This is a maligned and discredited activity usually drawing attention only for the distortions it produces between the formal and the actual and the differential standards it applies across types of education providers. Yet, even the most market-oriented neo-liberal framework of school provisioning cannot be operationalised without some view of how accountabilities other than those that are 'naturally' brought about in the market between the seller and the buyer can be instituted and made to function. Archana Mehendale and Rahul Mukhopadhyay's chapter on regulation examines theories and approaches of regulation in relation to the state, the market and the community and public versus private interests, with reference to the arena of school education in India, focusing on how regulation negotiates the changing nature of the public and the private in this arena. They draw attention to the complex and layered nature of regulatory frameworks that, in reality, contribute to defacto deregulation; this has particular implications in terms of the ways in which resolution of tensions between two contending set of actors – government and citizens on the one hand and market and consumers on the other hand – are resolved by regulatory frameworks in a stratified school system.

Padma M. Sarangapani, Rahul Mukhopadhyay, Parul, and Manish Jain's chapter looks at how the new discursive regime centred on efficiency and accountability in education has led to the reconceptualisation of teaching and the teacher. The chapter examines how ideas similar to that of New Public Management have entered the public and private schools in various ways and the structures through which these ideas find expression in schools. Two contrasting approaches to the work of a teacher are elaborated, one being that of the teacher as a 'technician' emerging from the new discursive regime and the other foregrounding 'professional identity and engagement' and emerging from a more contextually rooted understanding of the social, historical and institutional biographies of teachers and their work. Through these two distinct formulations, the chapter problematises some of the prevailing critical observations about teachers and their work and endorses teacher beliefs and their pedagogic efforts as central to both teaching and any policy efforts directed at educational improvement.

Padma M. Sarangapani's chapter examines and develops an understanding of 'quality' as relevant to education discussions. 'Quality' is mostly used as if there is agreement on what it refers to, and it is typically reduced to either 'inputs' or 'outcomes' of education. The term has been used in public education discourse since the 1950s to refer to the worthwhileness of education and the cost efficiency of its delivery, with an implicit recognition that differences in the organisation and resourcing of education could lead to it serving different purposes or aims and achieving differential outcomes. However, a more specific use of the term in Indian policy since the 1980s has tended to converge on measureable inputs, outcomes or both, to manage and improve 'efficiency' and to manage and improve 'equity'. Sarangapani's note takes 'education worthwhileness' as the starting point and builds a framework to understand the concept of quality, drawing primarily on the work of Naik (1975) and Winch (1996). What emerges is an understanding of quality as a 'systemic concept' with five dimensions: aims of education; provisioning and the curriculum; pedagogy; standards and outcomes; and, accountability. Assessing quality of education as well as understanding the production and management of education needs to address this scope of the concept. This brings focus on aims of education and the understanding that the variation between individual schools or management forms on the quality dimensions may be both in degree (i.e. more or less of something) and type (i.e. different forms/natures/characteristics). It also raises the question of the relevant unit of analysis of quality: schools or education systems.

Part II: empirical studies

The second part of the book presents six empirical studies. The first two chapters are based on surveys conducted in the cities of Hyderabad and Delhi between 2010 and 2012 (Sarangapani et al., 2013). This is followed by four qualitative case studies from these two cities, focusing on school ethos, private school managements, government school teachers and parental choice. The survey of schools in the two cities aimed to explore the nature of diversification of schools, of the education market of schools and of education quality. The survey was designed to enable us to engage with questions that arise in the context of a market functioning in education, drawing on the conceptual chapters presented in Part I. Education quality was investigated using the conception of quality discussed in Chapter 6 of this collection. Some of the questions that guided the design of the survey include the following:

1. How inclusive are the schools and how diverse are the clientele of schools, including private schools, given the segmented and stratified character of the Indian society?
2. What are the types of private schools and how do they differ from each other? How are they managed and how do they become financially viable?
3. What are the qualities of these schools on the dimensions of their aims, their provisioning, their curriculum, their pedagogy, the standards they strive to meet, and their outcomes, and the forms of accountability that are operational within and to which they submit?
4. Where are the poorest of the poor educated? What is the quality of the schools they attend?

The instruments included tools that were designed to support a process of observation of a range of sites in the school and interviews with the headteacher (HT) and a few teachers, and through which 'quality' could be understood and insights gained into the schools' clientele, teachers and management. Researchers were expected to arrive at the school in the morning before school began and observe it through the day until the end, spending on an average one day per school. The instruments and tools used are detailed as follows:

A   A school fact sheet was used to capture basic information of the school, including its affiliation, medium of instruction, timing, student strength, teachers, building type and the observations of infrastructure and facilities available and their maintenance.

B An instrument was used to observe morning assembly and capture its nature and content and the disciplinary practices surrounding it.
C School documents, including school diary, admission form, annual calendar, report cards and timetable, were used to note the explicit and stated practices and ideology of the school, beginning with its stated aims, identity and affiliations, rules and disciplinary mechanisms, attendance and uniform, the curriculum, subjects taught and time available for these. The nature of textbooks and other materials used was also noted. The record of student performance maintained by the school was studied and the patterns therein noted. (No separate test of student achievement was administered in this survey.)
D A detailed interview with the HT was the key instrument used to probe and understand a range of aspects of the school: school facilities and their maintenance, the management, the facts regarding the school's recognition, reasons for starting the school, the school's history, nature of the school clientele, the teachers, their selection and their management, standards, evaluation and accountability – in short, all the quality dimensions.
E An observation format was used to observe teachers' practice in classrooms – two per school, one in the primary school (preferably class IV) and one in the middle/high school. The physical organisation of space and displays, the content of teaching with a focus on the values and orientation of the teacher, pedagogic practices and nature of pupil interaction and involvement and disciplinary techniques employed were observed. The teachers were also interviewed to understand their own objectives and aims for teaching and their account of the pedagogic difficulties they dealt with.

The tools were designed as extensive lists of parameters to be noted and commented upon (over 700 parameters) and covered factual data, observations, accounts and inferences. However, it was not intended that these tools be used as survey questionnaires that would be administered individually to respondents or used as observation schedules. The tools and the list of parameters therein were intended to be used as guides by the field research team, predominantly comprising experienced students of education. This method was chosen because of the nature of the data that we sought to obtain from the survey and the nature of the schools to be observed. Rich qualitative and structured data were analysed together through a process of categorisation and recoding, and rendered amenable to basic quantitative measures of percentages. Our funding support could not extend to achievement tests, and the absence of these is a limitation of our exploration of quality of schools. Nevertheless, the rich data has yielded a range of insights on other quality dimensions as well as on the diversity of both government and private schools. The methodology constitutes an original contribution to the use of mixed methods and qualitative analysis in exploratory studies.

The chapter on Hyderabad by Padma M. Sarangapani and that on Delhi by Manish Jain are based on this survey. These chapters bring out the nature and extent of diversity in schools, variation in the clientele in relation to the dimensions of education quality and the pedagogic regimes that operate in the schools. The chapters provide insights on how schools are managed and how they achieve financial viability by positioning themselves in different niches of the education market and by managing their teachers. The Hyderabad study, having gained access to the full range of schools operating in the Mandal, provides new data based on which the landscape of different types of educational institutions has been mapped. This gives a detailed sense of the stratification and homogeneity that one may expect to find given the stratified nature of the Indian society. Further, it provides insights into how schools function 'in relation to each other' as an ecosystem – where the niches are defined by several factors, including costs and affordability, different motivations of providers and differential aims that appeal to community and specific interest groups and complementarity of functions within the homogenising effect of textbooks and examinations. The strong relevance of charitable institutions, particularly religious charities, in meeting the education needs of the poorest of the poor is a key finding from the study, along with the emergence of 'citizenship' as a dominant aim. The Hyderabad study also establishes the importance of English medium of instruction as a valued private and positional good. In addition, both Sarangapani and Jain develop and use the concept of 'pedagogic formation' to identify several distinctive pedagogic forms – bringing out the complex nature of pedagogy as more than a 'teacher characteristic' and suggesting how socioeconomic class feeds into and is determined by different pedagogic forms. This challenges stereotypic characterisations of school cultures: government schools as apathetic and dysfunctional and private schools as industrious and dedicated.

The four chapters by Sakshi Kapoor, Poonam Sharma, Eleanor Gurney and Niharika Sharma and Padma M. Sarangapani, respectively, that follow provide us with a greater in-depth qualitative sense of institutions and actors. These studies draw on the conceptual framing presented in Part I in developing the lines of investigation and analyses presented in these chapters. Sakshi Kapoor looks at school managements in 10 schools of Hyderabad, drawn from the same set of schools that were part of the larger survey in Hyderabad. Poonam Sharma studies home-school relationships in a few private schools in the urban periphery of Delhi. Eleanor Gurney explores parental choice in a Delhi slum, and Niharika Sharma and Padma M. Sarangapani explore the practices and beliefs of a few government school teachers working in schools located in low-income and slum areas in Delhi. These studies present detailed descriptions and new insights from the world of private schools and government schools, and three key actors – the managements, the parents and the teachers.

In her chapter on the production and management of quality, Sakshi Kapoor uses data from her qualitative study of 10 schools in Hyderabad to substantiate her thesis that the school's practices – which ensue from and constitute the school's 'ethos' – better explain as well as account for the school's quality rather than the management categories – government, aided and private – to which it belongs. The concept of ethos is generally used in relation to subjective, less measurable features of the atmosphere of schools, such as the relationship between people and the values and principles underlying policy and practice; or it may refer to the core values of the school, which are deep and fundamental in its life and work. To explain how a certain type of curriculum comes to be produced and managed in a school, the author identifies six types of school ethos attributable to (i) strong school leadership, (ii) managerialism, (iii) affiliation to a centralised curriculum board, (iv) the school being run as a small-scale family business, (v) complacency of staff and (vi) strong communitarian ideology.

Poonam Sharma looks closely at the provider–user relationship in the context of budget schools in Delhi's fringe village and towns and notes the role of the school 'owner' in establishing and managing the image and 'brand' of the school to ensure and retain the schools' clientele and teacher base. Parents are important as the source of finances for the institution as well as for other uses that they may have for the school. In enabling managements to further their own interests, the teacher emerges as a valuable worker who needs to be not only retained at low cost, with minimal attrition, but also 'managed', so that her exposure to and influence on parents is controlled and mediated by the school owner. The chapter explores the deficit discourses and positioning of 'school as a modern parenting expert' through which parents' voices are managed and muted. Simultaneously, traditional cultural notions of the school principal are found to shape the management of teachers by the school and the school's relationship with the home.

The chapter by Eleanor Gurney draws upon fieldwork on issues of school choice among low-income communities in Delhi. She problematises the notion of school choice emerging from the new discursive regime through an exploration of parental understanding of ideas of school quality. Gurney's study indicates how such conceptions of school quality arise from embedded social contexts and how they intertwine with non-quality-related factors in the making of schooling decisions among parents in low-income communities. The findings from the study show that there are no 'optimal' definitions of school quality that can be gauged from approaches that seek to assess quality through parental choices, as such definitions are often moderated in the context of more structural constraints within which schooling decisions are made.

Niharika Sharma and Padma M. Sarangapani's chapter looks at the constitution of practice among government school teachers. These teachers are observed to labour and teach their ward with an earnestness that suggests that they believe their work matters and can make a difference. This documentation of the work of six government school teachers goes 'against the grain' and by challenging the popular perception of government teachers as apathetic and disinterested because the system does not hold them to account. Sharma and Sarangapani's study suggests that accountability is important and that we need to take the wider view of multiple axes of accountability rather than the narrow view. In the case of these Delhi teachers, the formation of dedication in professional practice drew from the teachers' professional ethic and accountability towards the students they teach, rather than from an institutional accountability mechanism.

Conclusion

The landscape of school education in India has been witnessing significant transitions over the last two decades. These changes, primarily recorded in public attention as an unprecedented expansion of the supply of education across different socioeconomic sections of a still-stratified society, have been accompanied by other changes that have escaped similar attention. Primary among them has been a reconfiguration of the relation between the state and the market in terms of provisioning, financing and regulation of school education. Though much of this reconfiguration is of a visible nature, in terms of expansion of the range of schools catered to by non-state actors and types of education services in which the private has slowly moved into, there is also much that has been happening insidiously. This has mainly assumed the form of a 'withdrawal of the state' within a more neo-liberal conjuncture, of both larger political and economic changes and those specific to education. These transitions have seen concurrent changes in the discourse around school education, with a new discursive regime being shaped around arguments for a greater presence of the market and non-state actors in the realm of school education. However, as with any discursive regime, there has been a strong counter-current that has seen educationists argue strongly against the assumptions, ideas and policy thrusts that have come to characterise the new discursive regime. The fundamental inconsistencies of this new discursive regime with both broader philosophical aims of school education and notions of equity in a country such as India have been posited. This book seeks to add to this critique by contextualising its arguments within a political and historical understanding of the key conceptual categories that frame current debates around the new discursive regime and by engaging squarely with these conceptual categories, through nuanced and new theoretical and empirical approaches, in terms of their foundational implications for school education in the Indian context. The crossroads at which we stand, in terms of the different discursive trends we outline, will undoubtedly shape the education system that the future generations of Indians will come to inherit – for good or bad.

Notes

1 For a summary overview of the various reports and their findings on student learning outcomes, see Dundar et al. (2014).
2 See, for example, 'Learning Outcomes'; GoI; *MHRD*, available at http://mhrd.gov.in/sites/upload_files/mhrd/files/learning.pdf
3 These low-fee private schools are mostly unrecognised schools that have of late proliferated in a poorly regulated environment, primarily in response to parental demands of 'English-medium' education.
4 See, for example, 'Student Tracking System from July', *The Hindu*, June 25, 2016; available at www.thehindu.com/todays-paper/tp-national/tp-karnataka/Student-Tracking-System-from-July/article14400607.ece; 'HRD Ministry to launch student tracking system', *The Indian Express*, May 25, 2016, available at http://indianexpress.com/article/india/india-news-india/hrd-ministry-student-tracking-system-shala-asmita-yojana-smriti-irani-2817574/
5 ASER (2017) indicates that though private school enrolment increased from 18.7 per cent in 2006 to 30.8 per cent in 2014, there has been a marginal decrease to 30.5 per cent in 2016.
6 For a detailed overview of the scale and diversity of schooling options and the nature of segregated access to schooling of different social groups in India, see Juneja (2011).

7 For more details of how recent Plan documents have encouraged a larger role of the private in elementary education and the emerging scenario of PPPs in school education, see Srivastava, Noronha, and Fennell (2013).

References

Annual Status of Education Report (ASER). (2015). *Annual Status of Education Report (Rural) 2014*. New Delhi, India: ASER Centre/Pratham.

———. (2017). *Annual Status of Education Report (Rural) 2016 (Provisional)*. New Delhi, India: ASER Centre/Pratham.

Atherton, P., and Kingdon, G. (2010). 'The Relative Effectiveness and Costs of Contract and Regular Teachers in India', Centre for the Study of African Economies (CSAE) Working Paper Series, 2010–2015, University of Oxford.

Batra, P. (2013). 'Positioning Teachers in the Emerging Education Landscape of Contemporary India', in *India Infrastructure Report 2012: Private Sector in Education* (pp. 219–231). New Delhi, India: Routledge.

Beteille, T. (2009). 'Absenteeism, Transfers and Patronage: The Political Economy of Teacher Labor Markets in India', Unpublished Ph.D. Dissertation, Stanford University.

Bhattacharya, D. (2001). '"Civic Community" and Its Margins: School Teachers in Rural West Bengal', *Economic and Political Weekly*, 36(8): 673–683.

Desai, S., Dubey, A., Vanneman, R., and Banerji, R. (2009). 'Private Schooling in India: A New Educational Landscape', *India Policy Forum*, 5(1): 1–38, National Council of Applied Economic Research.

Desai, S. D., Joshi, A., Sen, B. J., Sharif, M., and Vanneman, A. R. (2010). *Human Development in India: Challenges for Society in Transition*. New Delhi, India: Oxford University Press.

Duflo, E., Hanna, R., and Ryan, S. P. (2012). 'Incentives Work: Getting Teachers to Come to School', *The American Economic Review*, 102(4): 1241–1278.

Dundar, H., Béteille, T., Riboud, M., and Deolalikar, A. (2014). *Student Learning in South Asia: Challenges, Opportunities, and Policy Priorities*. Washington, DC: The World Bank.

French, R., and Kingdon, G. (2010). 'The Relative Effectiveness of Private and Government Schools in Rural India: Evidence from ASER Data', DoQSS Working Paper No. 10–03, June 2010. London: University of London Institute of Education.

Government of India (GoI). (2016). *Economic Survey 2016–2017*. New Delhi, India: Ministry of Finance.

Govinda, R., and Bandyopadhyay, M. (2011). 'Access to Elementary Education in India: Analytical Overview', in R. Govinda (Ed.), *Who Goes to School? Exploring Exclusion in Indian Education* (pp. 1–86). New Delhi, India: Oxford University Press.

Goyal, S. (2009). 'Inside the House of Learning: The Relative Performance of Public and Private Schools in Orissa', *Education Economics*, 17(3): 315–327.

Goyal, S., and Pandey, P. (2009). 'How Do Government and Private Schools Differ? Findings from Two Large Indian States', South Asia Human Development Sector Report 30, World Bank, Washington, DC.

Härmä, J. (2011). 'Low Cost Private Schooling in India: Is It Pro Poor and Equitable?' *International Journal of Educational Development*, 31(4): 350–356.

Hill, E., Samson, M., and Dasgupta, S. (2011). 'Expanding the School Market in India: Parental Choice and the Reproduction of Social Inequality', *Economic & Political Weekly*, 46(35): 99–105.

Jain, M., and Saxena, S. (2010). 'Politics of Low Cost Schooling and Low Teacher Salaries', *Economic & Political Weekly*, 45(18): 79–80.

Jain, P. S., and Dholakia, R. H. (2009). 'Feasibility of Implementation of Right to Education Act', *Economic &Political Weekly*, 44(25): 38–43.

Juneja, N. (2011). 'Access to What? Diversity and Participation', in R. Govinda (Ed.), *Who Goes to School? Exploring Exclusion in Indian Education* (pp. 205–247). New Delhi, India: Oxford University Press.

Karopady, D. D. (2014). 'Does School Choice Help Rural Children from Disadvantaged Sections?' *Economic & Political Weekly*, 49(51): 46–53.

Kaur, S. (2017). 'Quality of Rural Education at Elementary Level: Evidence from Punjab', *Economic & Political Weekly*, 52(5): 58–63.

Kingdon, G. G. (2009). 'School-Sector Effects on Student Achievement in India', in R. Chakrabarti and P. E. Peterson (Eds.), *School Choice International: Exploring Public-Private Partnerships* (pp. 111–139). Cambridge, Massachusetts: MIT Press.

Kingdon, G. G., and Muzammil, M. (2003). *The Political Economy of Education in India: Teacher Politics in Uttar Pradesh*. New Delhi, India: Oxford University Press.

Kingdon, G. G., and Sipahimalani-Rao, V. (2010). 'Para-Teachers in India: Status and Impact', *Economic & Political Weekly*, 45(12): 59–67.

Kingdon, G. G., and Teal, F. (2007). 'Does Performance Related Pay for Teachers Improve Student Performance? Some Evidence from India', *Economics of Education Review*, 26(4): 473–486.

Kremer, M., Chaudhury, N., Rogers, F. H., Muralidharan, K., and Hammer, J. (2005). 'Teacher Absence in India: A Snapshot', *Journal of the European Economic Association*, 3(2–3): 658–667.

Kumar, R. (2006). 'Introduction: Equality, Quality and Quantity – Mapping the Challenges Before Elementary Education in India', in R. Kumar (Ed.), *The Crisis of Elementary Education in India* (pp. 13–56). New Delhi, India: Sage.

Kumar, K., and Sarangapani, P. M. (2004). 'History of the Quality Debate', *Contemporary Education Dialogue*, 2(1): 30–52.

Majumdar, M. (2011). 'Politicians, Civil Servants or Professionals? Teachers' Voices on Their Work and Worth', *Contemporary Education Dialogue*, 8(1): 33–65.

Majumdar, M., and Mooij, J. E. (2011). *Education and Inequality in India: A Classroom View*. London: Routledge.

———. (2014). 'The Question of "Quality" in Education: Does the RTE Act Provide an Answer?' *Journal of International Cooperation in Education*, 16(2): 87–103.

Mukhopadhyay, R., and Sriprakash, A. (2011). 'Global Frameworks, Local Contingencies: Policy Translations and Education Development in India', *Compare*, 41(3): 311–326.

Muralidharan, K. (2012). 'Long-Term Effects of Teacher Performance Pay: Experimental Evidence from India', *Society for Research on Educational Effectiveness*.

Muralidharan, K., Das, J., Holla, A., and Mohpal, A. (2016). 'The Fiscal Cost of Weak Governance: Evidence from Teacher Absence in India', Policy Research Working Paper 7579, World Bank Group.

Muralidharan, K., and Kremer, M. (2006). 'Public and Private Schools in Rural India', in *Harvard University, Department of Economics*. Cambridge, MA: Harvard University Press.

Muralidharan, K., Niehaus, P., and Sukhtankar, S. (2016). 'Building State Capacity: Evidence from Biometric Smartcards in India', *The American Economic Review*, 106(10): 2895–2929.

Muralidharan, K., and Sundararaman, V. (2011). 'Teacher Opinions on Performance Pay: Evidence from India', *Economics of Education Review*, 30(3): 394–403.

———. (2015). 'The Aggregate Effect of School Choice: Evidence from a Two-Stage Experiment in India', *The Quarterly Journal of Economics*, 130(3): 1011–1066.

Naik, J. P. (1975). *Equality, Quality and Quantity: The Elusive Triangle of Indian Education*. Bombay, India: Allied Publishers.

Nambissan, G. (2013). 'Low-Cost Private Schools for the Poor in India: Some Reflections', in *India Infrastructure Report 2012: Private Sector in Education* (pp. 84–93). New Delhi, India: Routledge.

Pritchett, L., and Murgai, R. (2006). 'Teacher Compensation: Can Decentralisation to Local Bodies Take India from the Perfect Storm Through Troubled Waters to Clear Sailing?' *India Policy Forum, Global Economy and Development Programmes, The Brookings Institution*, 3(1): 123–177.

Ramachandran, V. (2009). 'Right to Education Act: A Comment', *Economic & Political Weekly*, 44(28): 155–157.

Ramachandran, V., and Sharma, R. (2009). 'Introduction', in R. Sharma and V. Ramachandran (Eds.), *The Elementary Education System in India: Exploring Institutional Structures, Processes and Dynamics* (pp. 1–32). New Delhi, India: Routledge.

Rangaraju, B., Tooley, J., and Dixon, P. (2012). *The Private School Revolution in Bihar: Findings from a Survey in Patna Urban*. New Delhi, India: India Institute.

Sarangapani, P. M. (2010). 'Quality Concerns: National and Extra-National Dimensions', *Contemporary Education Dialogue*, 7(1): 41–57.

Sarangapani, P. M., Jain, M., Mukhopadhyay, R., and Winch, C. (2013). 'Baseline Survey of the School Scenario in Some States in the Context of RTE: Study of Educational Quality, School Management, and Teachers

(Andhra Pradesh, Delhi and West Bengal)', Unpublished report submitted to the Sarva Siksha Abhiyan, Ministry of Human Resources Development, New Delhi, India.

Sarangapani, P. M., and Winch, C. (2010). 'Tooley, Dixon and Gomathi on Private Education in Hyderabad: A Reply', *Oxford Review of Education*, 36(4): 499–515.

Shah, P. J., and Miranda, L. (2013). 'Private Initiative in India's Education Miracle', in *India Infrastructure Report 2012: Private Sector in Education* (pp. 74–83). New Delhi, India: Routledge.

Sriprakash, A. (2012). *Pedagogies for Development: The Politics and Practice of Child-Centred Education in India*. New York: Springer.

Srivastava, P. (2007). 'Neither Voice Nor Loyalty: School Choice and the Low-Fee Private Sector in India', Occasional Paper, 134.

———. (2010). 'Public-Private Partnerships or Privatisation? Questioning the State's Role in Education in India', *Development in Practice*, 20(4): 540–553.

Srivastava, P., Noronha, C., and Fennell, S. (2013). 'Private Sector Study: Sarva Shiksha Abhiyan', Report submitted to DFID, India.

Tooley, J. (2016). 'Extending Access to Low-Cost Private Schools Through Vouchers: An Alternative Interpretation of a Two-Stage "School Choice" Experiment in India', *Oxford Review of Education*, 42(5): 579–593.

Tooley, J., and Dixon, P. (2006). '"De Facto" Privatisation of Education and the Poor: Implications of a Study from Sub-Saharan Africa and India', *Compare*, 36(4): 443–462.

Tooley, J., Dixon, P., and Gomathi, S. V. (2007). 'Private Schools and the Millennium Development Goal of Universal Primary Education: A Census and Comparative Survey in Hyderabad, India', *Oxford Review of Education*, 33(5): 539–560.

Tooley, J., Dixon, P., Shamsan, Y., and Schagen, I. (2010). 'The Relative Quality and Cost-Effectiveness of Private and Public Schools for Low-Income Families: A Case Study in a Developing Country', *School Effectiveness and School Improvement*, 21(2): 117–144.

Vasavi, A. R. (2015). 'Culture and Life of Government Elementary Schools', *Economic & Political Weekly*, 50(33): 36–50.

Vellanki, V. (2015). 'Government vs Private Schools in ASER 2014', *Economic & Political Weekly*, 50(7): 24–26.

Wadhwa, W. (2009). 'Are Private Schools Really Performing Better Than Government Schools', Annual Status of Education Report (Rural), New Delhi, India.

Winch, C. (1996). *Quality and Education*. Oxford: Wiley-Blackwell.

———. (2010). 'Search for Educational Quality: The Dialectic of Inputs and Outputs', *Contemporary Education Dialogue*, 7(1): 19–40.

———. (2014). 'Theory and Teacher Education – Anglo-German Perspectives', in D. Kuhlee, J. van Büer, and C. Winch (Eds.), *Changing Governance in Initial Teacher Education (ITE): Perspectives on England and Germany*. Wiesbaden: Springer-VS.

Part I
Conceptual papers

1 Public, private and education in India
A historical overview

Manish Jain

Most often, contemporary discussions about 'public' and 'private' in the context of education are carried out with a narrow 'economistic' frame. With this frame, the focus is on the distinct source of funding, ownership and management of 'public' and 'private' educational institutions. Further, in such discussions, 'state' and 'non-state' are treated as homogenous and synonymous with 'public' and 'private', respectively. These deliberations assume that these categories have a singular and unchanging meaning, are mutually exclusive binaries with strong boundaries and have no internal plurality. In this process, we seem to forget that there are two other registers of political theory and feminism where the conceptual binary of public and private has been debated for long. While there may have been ideas in each society about what is private and public, this distinction gained greater weight with liberalism as an ideology that tried to simultaneously limit the spheres of state intervention and lay out the ground for emergence of a public and democracy. Given the colonial history of India, it is important to be historically aware about the history of emergence and usage of conceptual categories like public and private, to take note of the import and trajectories of these concepts, their appropriation and reconstruction in our own society.

This chapter undertakes a historical interrogation of the meanings, varieties and interactions of the public, the private and education in India from the colonial period to the period before the 1970s. In the first section of this chapter, I will briefly refer to how political theory and feminism have engaged with the conceptual binary of public and private. The second section examines the deployment of the categories of public and private in colonial India. The third section tries to locate public and private schools and actors in relation to larger social processes and forces and to attend to their internal dynamics that have larger ramifications. The fourth section provides a brief overview of the state (public) and non-state (private) actors in education in colonial and post-independence India with reference to formation of the state, community identity along religious and caste lines and gender relations and their interplay.

The meaning(s) of public and private

The ideas of public and private that inform Western political theory are results of a particular historical juncture in Europe and are intricately connected with the emergence of the 'modern'. These ideas of public and private that emerged with and are tied to the history of liberalism were different from the meanings and practices associated with these conceptual categories in ancient Greece and Rome. In classical Greece, the public or *polis* was seen as purely political and 'separated from both production and reproduction' that centred on the household and was treated as a private affair (Hall, 2001: 219). To Victorian men and women, the word public denoted 'the world of business and commerce, the market, and the world of politics'. In contrast, private constituted around home and family and provided solace from anxieties of the market (ibid.). This distinction between the public and the private was revised from the late eighteenth century. Adam Smith conceptualised the market as private because it operated through freely made contracts in contrast to the public elements of life that were under the control or regulation of the state (ibid.). This reformulation was in response to the development of the market and wage labour in an era of industrial capitalism. This placement of the market in the private and association of the public with regulation undertaken by the state is one dominant strand in the distinctions drawn between the public and the private in the context of education. Freedom, a key tenet of liberalism, is a concept closely related to privacy and private. In the liberal exposition, freedom as an area of non-interference from other individuals and social pressure exerted by one's community, the majority community and the state allows an individual 'a sphere of thought and action that should be free from "public" interference' (Arblaster, 1987: 43–44). Thus, in the classical liberal formulations, both family and individual beliefs were classified as the private sphere and were to be outside the domain of state regulation. The boundaries of the private to counter the interference of religious and political institutions outlined in this conceptualisation were further extended by placing the market in the domain of the private by the advocates of *laissez-faire* (Mahajan, 2003: 12–16).

In this liberal individualistic conception, the self-contained and self-sustaining man needs 'a private area of withdrawal from society,

Public, private and education in India 33

not merely for rest and refreshment, but as the essential condition of self-realization' (Arblaster, 1987: 44). Unlike the classical Greek view, where a person conceptualised as a social being found fulfilment through participation in the collective life of the *polis*, in the liberal view, humans are not social animals (ibid.). John Stuart Mill in his classic, *On Liberty*, gave three reasons to oppose state interference: (a) individuals can better do few things directly, (b) allowing individuals to use their own invention and initiative has positive consequences and (c) adding to the power of the government is 'the great evil' (Arblaster, 1987: 45). This focus on uniqueness of the individual – the private being – who is free and equal is also closely associated with the idea of autonomy, whereby an individual using his capacities to reason becomes a self-determining and self-governing person who critically evaluates all received knowledge and beliefs and pursues distinct interests and engagements without violating the rights of others (Mahajan, 2003: 13–15).

If on the one hand, the political philosophy of liberalism has always been sceptical of the over-regulating powers of the state, on the other, it has been simultaneously concerned about carving a role for individuals and initiatives beyond the state to form self-led and self-governing communities that enrich democratic association among citizens. These concerns have led to highly enriching debates and conceptualisations about private and public and the contested terrain of civil society has been one such site. Inspired by Adam Smith, the market is also conceptualised as a civil society that could counter the state and allow opportunities for private initiatives and creativity. Historically, individual philanthropic and collective initiatives by the members of the community to better the lives of its members have been part of the republican conceptions of a citizen's role in forging and strengthening the community. Establishment of trusts by individuals and corporate bodies to support other individual and community initiatives financially has taken a distinct form in recent times in the form of corporate social responsibility, which is expected to supplement the efforts of the state.

In the discussions on the private in the context of education, private educational institutions draw on all of the above virtues associated with the private individual and the arguments against non-interference by the public. While we may note here the slippages to pass of and/ or equalise an institution with an individual, it would be pertinent to also look at the silences involved in the liberal conceptualisation of the individual and the private. Arblaster points out that this usage of individual that lays much greater emphasis on the differences than on what may be common among them, allows for 'the vital historical and ethical role of exceptional individuals' and in the process, the individual really means the 'exceptional individual' (Arblaster, 1987: 46–48). Frevert (2003) has drawn our attention to the class origins of the public. She has argued that 'the public was, at least in Europe, constituted by the attitudes, norms and interests of the middle classes' (Mahajan, 2003: 25).

Hall (2001: 220) has explained that in the classical liberal theory of Locke and Hobbes, rationality came to represent the domain of public and passion or desire was relegated to the world of private. For both Hobbes and Locke, it was not an adult individual but the male-headed family that formed the basis of political philosophy, because the male head represented interests of family in the wider society. Locke's argument that by giving consent to marriage, women had forfeited their civil rights to their male protectors was very identical to the distinction drawn between male and female characteristics by Rousseau. To Rousseau, reproductive functions characterised women as opposed to a limitless potential of men for rationality and abstract thinking (Hall, 2001; Martin, 1986). Designated as physical and sensual, women were seen as deficient in rationality and incapable of rational thought by Rousseau who saw patriarchy as natural (Hall, 2001: 220). Feminist critiques[1] pointed out that a separation of the family classified as private from the public scrutiny amounted to continuation of the patriarchal privileges. Instead, they have demanded that questions of violence, unfair treatment and inequality within the family be opened to public examination on grounds of justice and democratisation (Mahajan, 2003: 12). In contrast to the representation of family as a site of relief from the public world of competition for men, several feminists have identified it as a key site of oppression and work for women. Black feminists have seen family as a site to resist racial oppression and many East European women have found family to be a bulwark against totalitarian states (Lister, 2000: 25).

Feminist scholars (Martin, 1986; Lister, 2000) have drawn our attention to the parallel dichotomies between reason and nature, intellect and emotion and universal and particularistic that operate along with and underpin the public–private dichotomy. They have critiqued the artificial nature of the public–private divide and pointed out how it is premised on gendered constructions of division of work and responsibilities, areas of concern, citizenship virtues/vices and capabilities. Through this interrogation, feminists have pointed to the political nature of the 'private', how the state plays a significant role in regulating and defining the private and how public is formed in the private domain as well.

In contrast to the guiding principles of individual freedom and autonomy in the context of the private, the guiding norms of the public are 'equality, collective deliberation and accountability' (Mahajan, 2003: 13). The public comes to signify both openness and inclusiveness. The institutions are (supposedly) equally accessible to all and no distinctions are made between citizens on the basis of their ascriptive identities. Individuals access these spaces and institutions to collectively deliberate on and participate in matters of public concern, on issues and anxieties that have a bearing on the collective life. As 'reasoning subjects', the citizens have the freedom and capacities to question the fellow citizens and powers that be for their positions and decisions, to publicly articulate and defend an alternative conceptualisation of the issues involved and the action to be taken and to express their demands (Mahajan, 2003: 19–20). The idea of a rationally driven consensus emerging from this democratic process underpins this modern sense of the public. The processes of democratisation in the society shape the public sphere and public institutions and the latter themselves partake in enabling and promoting such processes. Bhattacharya (2005: 139–140) in an excellent formulation points out the need to conceptualise the public sphere also with reference to communities, who in their effort to reconstitute themselves as public are '*forced* to come together – overcoming their insularity and exclusivity and recognizing the need to connect' and yet these 'bounded communities' do not dissolve 'into an amorphous public' (emphasis added).

In the light of this ongoing discussion, we may like to ask whether these ideas of openness, equality, inclusiveness, democratic participation, use of reasoned dialogue to arrive at shared consensus about publicly defendable purposes and accountability of the rulers to the ordinary citizens have significant bearing only on the conceptualisation of a public education institution. Or are private institutions also amenable to these principles in a democracy as they too admit public, the citizens, in their institution? Further, in what ways do 'bounded communities' shed their exclusiveness when they enter the domain of public and establish educational institutions, and in what ways does this exclusiveness not get dissolved, is a question worth asking when we think about private education institutions and their public nature.

Public and private in colonial India

There are at least five ways in which the idea of public was articulated in colonial India. During the colonial period, a new set of institutions and vocabulary was introduced that simultaneously drew upon and reworked the prior existing classifications of status, rights, powers and social relations. Various modes of colonial modalities, from law to census to survey, attempted to overcome the fuzziness, ambiguities and flexibilities of interpretations of the past and replaced them within enumerated, 'fixed, determinate, publicly recognized categories and public codes' of rights (Cohn, 1996; Kaviraj, 1992; Bhattacharya, 2005: 132–133). In addition, this state claimed to represent a dispassionate and impersonal public power. It promised to be impartial and neutral in its dealings in the conflicts among different castes, religious groups and 'races' through its insistence on institutional procedures and policy of maintaining distance from all the colonised groups. It was to rationally decide and distribute on behalf of these sections and to protect the vulnerable groups from the tyranny of the dominant groups. The colonial state claimed that Indians lacked any sense of public as a collective and could not conceive in terms of a public purpose, which is beyond their immediate sectional interests. The colonial rule was presented as performing a historic pedagogic role in creating a public where none existed.

But the institution of colonial regime with its attendant ideologies of civilising mission and difference between the coloniser and the colonised also introduced other meanings of the public. The colonial experience created a new dynamic that led to the demand for and birth of the national public that conceived itself in opposition to the colonial power. This third idea of public in the colonial context challenged the claim of the colonial state to represent the interests and will of the colonial public and aimed at taking control over one's own destiny.

The fourth usage and meaning of public relates to different religious, caste and linguistic communities that sought a new self-identity in the context of enumerated boundaries and competition to garner a greater share in colonial employment, education and representative politics. These communities attempted to reconstitute themselves as public through a variety of means that involved forging extra-local networks and associations (Kumar, 2000: 84; Rudolph and Rudolph, 1972b: 19–20). Other means employed for such a consolidation included publication of community newspapers, origin myths and histories; public marking of identity signs; bringing issues of community practices and reform before the members of the community as well as the audiences outside; and using the rhetoric of 'public good' and 'national progress' to make claims over public resources and shape public opinion (Bhattacharya, 2005: 140–142; Kumar, 2000: 84). Education was one such site where boundaries, identities and publicness of the community were reconstituted and mobilised. Schools, colleges, hostels and scholarships for the young members of the community were instituted with professed aims of protecting community interests, achieving social mobility and status improvement and promoting cultural norms. The colonial period also witnessed a reconfiguration of the linguistic publics with 'reflections on civilizational heritage and shared pasts' (Bhattacharya, 2005: 142) and both education and schools were sites of these politics and enactments of decisions that were taken elsewhere.

The fifth deployment of the public, as discussed by Partha Chatterjee, was the sphere of the colonial state, the material world and the outer domain in contradistinction from the private classified as the realm of culture and the inner and spiritual domain of the nation, where interference of the coloniser was opposed and challenged. Though Chatterjee's distinctions provide a conceptual apparatus to think through the differential strategies employed by the colonised in their negotiations with colonialism, this neat binary separation overlooked how the colonial interventions in the outer public domain of law, health and education were shaping the inner private domain of family, body, behaviour and clothing. According to Bhattacharya, the public sphere in India is 'as much a sphere of national refashioning as the private domain' (Bhargava, Reifeld, and Stiftung, 2005: 37). Further, the space of private was a site of individuation, of scripting 'individual volition and desire' on the one hand, and of both rebellion and conforming on the other (Bhattacharya, 2005: 151). The languages of tradition and reason and those of public good and community interest mixed with each other in the public discourse (Bhattacharya, 2005: 154).

This foregoing discussion leads to some other lines of inquiry about public and private education. We can attain a far richer understanding of the private educational institutions (both nationalist and other community-public founded) when we examine them with reference to these histories, contests and quests. We need to trace the articulation of reason in the establishment, justification and functioning of the public and private education with attention to the language of tradition and that of appropriation of tradition 'through the framework of modern reason' to appreciate their histories since the colonial period. Unlike America, where there were differences 'between private and public founding and support', in India, 'public financing of private institutions began early' and point to the 'permeable boundaries between public and private' (Rudolph and Rudolph, 1972b: 14).

Initiatives and support of various individual philanthropists and local notables in establishing and running schools in different parts of India calls for recognising the ethic of service that drew on a multiplicity of traditions rooted in religion, sense of duty, anxieties related to cultural corruption by missionary schools (Kishwar, 2008) and a sense of participation in constructing the future national community and state (Srivastava, 1998). Kumar (2000: 21) points out that most founders of these private educational institutions were produced by colonial education. Here, the limits and futility of a neat binary of the products of colonial-public education and of private schools founded by the Indian public become very obvious.

Although the private enterprises were established with a view to resist colonial dominance, to introduce new ways of socialisation of the young that would generate love and respect for the nation, culture, traditions and religion of the community/nation and to develop character among the young, by not paying enough attention to the pedagogies of learning, they failed in achieving their professed goal (Ellis, 2009: 365). Later, a majority of these institutions became dependent on the public funds in the form of grant-in-aid from the post-colonial state. Then, in such a situation, whether the lines that defined boundaries of their distinction from the state and public have blurred is a moot question to ask.

Locating public and private schools and actors

Establishment, institutionalisation, consolidation and change of the post-colonial state and their educational policies have a complex history. This has significant bearings on the issue under discussion. As argued before, the meaning of the terms 'state/public' and 'non-state/private' are neither singular nor static, and hence, we should not look at state/non-state and public/private as mutually exclusive binaries with strong boundaries. In this section, I will argue that this multiplicity of meanings, types and histories needs to be understood with reference to (a) nature of state, (b) distinct time-histories of colonial annexation, (c) levels of state, (d) changing understandings of the state's role and responsibility with regard to mass education, accessibility, neutrality and intervention in native affairs, culture and religion levels of education, (e) geographical differences, (f) levels of education and (g) emerging Indian 'publics' with the rise of the national movement and other axis of self-identities. We should try to locate public and private schools and actors in relation to larger social processes and forces such as land revenue systems, urbanisation and industrialisation, demographic differences, social class formation, consolidation of social dominance and challenges, social reform movements and formation of new political subjects. Then, we can better appreciate how colonial and post-colonial educational policies and emergence, functioning, growth and decline of public and private education were a response to these processes and forces and shaped them in turn.

Deciphering the state and its involvement

There was more than one state during the period under discussion. The meaning of state in the contexts of the colonial state, that is, British India, the princely states and the post-independent Indian state differs considerably. The East India Company (EIC) became the ruler of India after the battle of Plassey in 1757. But this did not mark the annexation of entire colonial India. There was a difference of almost a century between the colonisation of Bengal (1757) and that of Punjab (1849). Further, there were significant inter-regional, intra-regional and urban–rural differences in terms of educational provision and enrolment.

Discussion about the role of the colonial state's involvement in education needs to take note of the levels of the colonial state: central, provincial and local as well. Chaudhary (2010: 187–188) has explained the shifts in responsibility of education from the central government to provincial to municipal to Indian hands. She points out that while in the mid-nineteenth century, the central government had absolute fiscal authority, from the 1870s, the provision of education was first decentralised to provincial governments. This was followed by further decentralisation to lower levels of government such as rural district and urban municipal boards in the 1880s. This decentralisation moved along with a division of responsibility across levels of education. The local boards were largely responsible for primary education, whereas provincial governments controlled and supervised the secondary and collegiate education. After introduction of the system of diarchy in 1919 that introduced provincial legislatures with elected Indian members, education became a transferred subject under their control. With certain kinds of revenue such as land revenue under their control, expenditure on education increased. A similar pattern of increasing fiscal independence and greater educational investments was witnessed with the introduction of provincial autonomy in 1935.

During the colonial period, there were significant differences and changes in the understanding of the state's role and responsibility with regard to mass education and accessibility. Earlier articulations of state responsibility towards the education of Indians were centred on the downward filtration theory. The Governor General of

Bombay Presidency, Mountstuart Elphinstone, in his minute on education, dated 13 December 1823, had feared that if English education first took roots among 'the lowest castes', whom he characterised as 'the best pupils', it 'would never spread further' (cited in India Board Report of the Board of Education, 1851: 14–15, para 23). The Wood Despatch (Halifax, 1854) rejected the idea of downward filtration and separate schools for lower castes as it opened education to all castes (Rao, 2009: 64). But mass education never became a priority in actual practice despite high rhetoric of the colonial state. Chaudhary (2010: 182) notes that India had a larger number of secondary and post-secondary students than several industrialised countries did, even though its primary school enrolments were among the lowest in the world. The social background of these students adds another dimension to the provision of education in the colonial period, as it cannot be understood with reference to public–private and levels alone. Different yearly reports of the Director of Public Instruction across various provinces in colonial India and Seal (1968: 61, 87) show that while the enrolment and percentage share of caste Hindus, especially Brahmans and writer castes, swelled manifold with an increase in the level of education, there was concomitant decline of backward and lower-caste Hindus.

Provincial differences

Chaudhary (2010: 182) points out that 'at every level, enrolment rates in the coastal provinces of Bengal, Bombay and Madras exceeded those in the interior provinces of Bihar and Orissa, Central Provinces and United Provinces'. She further notes, 'by 1931, almost 40 per cent of the children in the coastal provinces were enrolled in some school, compared to 20 per cent of the children in the interior provinces'. Bombay and Madras had higher primary school enrolment than that of Bengal presidency. Bengal had the largest number of private aided and unaided schools. Bihar and Orissa too had development of private schools (Chaudhary, 2010: 195). Bombay, Central Provinces, Punjab and United provinces focused on public schools. Madras was in the middle of these extremes, where share of public schools increased from less than 20 per cent of total schools in the 1890s to 40 per cent by the 1930s.

With the highest provincial spending per capita in each decade, Bombay left behind other provinces, whereas Bihar and Orissa spent the least (Chaudhary, 2010: 189). This led to a robust public education system in Bombay presidency. In contrast, the unique location of

Calcutta as the capital of the Indian empire with its attendant large state bureaucracy fuelled higher private demand for schooling, which was met by private revenues that 'compensated for the low levels of public spending' in Bengal (ibid.). As Bihar and Orissa lacked similar opportunities for the educated workforce and were commercially less developed, their private spending remained low like their public spending (Chaudhary, 2010: 189, 201). Introduction of financial decentralisation from the late nineteenth century strengthened the differences in public expenditures. These variations were also related to the regional differences in land revenues that accounted for about 60 per cent of provincial revenues (Chaudhary, 2010: 194). The land revenues in turn were directly related to the kind of land settlement (Zamindari or Ryotwari) that had been introduced by the British in different parts of colonial India. The amount of this land revenue had consequences for even rural district boards, as their income through additional surcharges was strongly related to land revenues (Chaudhary, 2010: 191–194). Chaudhary (2010: 195) concludes that there were more public schools in provinces with access to larger public revenues and that a greater share of and reliance on private funding might have led to 'a more unequal school system' (Chaudhary, 2010: 181).

Basu (1974: 203) presents a different possibility by arguing that a large number of English schools in the Dacca division of Bengal during 1905–1914 'were unaided, with low fees and easy admission' that made 'English education more widely diffused than elsewhere in India'. She draws our attention to a set of other factors that explain this peculiar condition (1974: 204). Central and East Bengal had an 'enormous density of population' and 'concentration of the *bhadralok* castes', most of whom were rent collectors. They were forced by economic pressures to look for non-agricultural occupations, which swelled the demand for English education.

Various kinds of groups operated in the private sector across different provinces. While Christian missionaries led the way in private school development in the early years, private schools managed by Indians far out-numbered mission schools by 1882. Chaudhary (2010: 195–197) reports that Indians managed 97 per cent of primary schools and 63 per cent of secondary schools in 1881–1882. Indians had a larger share among secondary schools in Bengal, Bombay and Madras, whereas in Punjab, a majority of the private English schools in the 1880s were mission schools (Chaudhary, 2010: 197; Naik and Nurullah, 1951: 260, cited in Chaudhary, 2010). In 1917, out of all the mission institutions, 88 per cent were primary schools and there were about 4 per cent English schools, 3 per cent high schools, 1.3 per cent middle vernacular schools and only 0.40 per cent colleges. This shows that missionary involvement was highest at the primary level. Also, 66 per cent of all students in missionary institutions were studying at the primary level, about 20 per cent in high schools, 10 per cent in English schools and only 2 per cent each in colleges and middle vernacular schools (Sharp, 1918).

Public versus private schools: social inequality and ethics

Among Indians, one can discern at least five kinds of trends in relation to the establishment of private schools. Upper castes and landed elites in Bengal, with their strong preference for English medium secondary schools for their children, established such schools and opposed any official effort to extend mass primary education until the early twentieth century (Chaudhary, 2010: 200). Nationalist leaders such as Tilak advocated giving general education to those who had a 'natural inclination' for it, whereas peasant's children were to receive 'the education befitting their rank and station in life' (Rao, 2008: 4–6). In contrast, Phule and other anti-caste reformers who wanted to form social institutions based on reason and equality argued for a thorough education for lower castes that would teach them to distinguish between right and wrong (O'Hanlon, 1985: 118–120).

Second, establishment of private schools was also a response to increasing education and economic mobility among the untouchable communities. Constable (2000) in his excellent historically rich study of controversies around caste and education shows that while earlier Hindu upper castes sought admission in missionary schools, with the entry of lower castes, their own attitude about these schools changed. They began to demand separate new schools, private class under new private management and funding with availability of Brahmin teachers.

The third trend was of endowment and patronage by wealthy landlords and local kings to reform movements such as the Arya Samaj that established many private schools, especially in Punjab (Chaudhary, 2010: 197). The fourth trend was the emergence of untouchable and tribal communities as new political subjects who questioned caste inequalities and took initiatives to open schools for themselves in the wake of upper-caste opposition and ambivalence of the colonial state (Constable, 2000; Rao, 2009). The fifth trend was of involvement, encouragement and support by the missionaries in the efforts of Indians to promote education among depressed classes and tribals, which also created a politically conscious and mobile group within them (Constable, 2000; Rao, 2009; Bara, 2015).

Policies and contestations around caste and educational inequality provide a different set of parameters to examine public and private education institutions. Though cases of social exclusion, discrimination and segregation vis-à-vis the lower castes in the public schools were recorded by different colonial reports (Report of the Indian Education Commission, 1883: 514–515; Richey, 1923: 206), colonial officials had an ambivalent attitude towards enforcing access of untouchables to schools (Rao, 2009; Constable, 2000). Several anti-caste reformers argued that being maintained by public funds including education cess, to which depressed classes made a significant contribution, public schools could not stop children from these communities from attending these schools. In Madras presidency, in the 1930s, the government made the enrolment of depressed classes a mandatory condition for recognition of elementary schools, and in their absence, the school was considered to be inaccessible (Satyanarayana, 2002: 70). Rudolph and Rudolph (1972c: 88) note that in the context of private institutions managed by Brahmans, Christians, Lingayats and Muslims, the social composition 'reflects the community of the controlling group, except in the case of small or underprivileged communities whose size or social backwardness may limit the supply of available teachers and students'. Further, they contrast this with public institutions, which reflected social composition of the territorially defined community of the school district though socially and economically advanced castes and communities had stronger representation. This discussion suggests that if equality is an aspect of quality in education, then the presence or absence of intra-institutional segregation in public and private schools with reference to meals, hostels, caste, religion, class and efforts of integration needs to be studied carefully.

A variety of other ethical issues, which are often not discussed in the context of private institutions, emerges from studies by Kishwar (2008) and different essays in Rudolph and Rudolph (1972a). Pointing to corruption and mismanagement among private schools in the colonial period, Kishwar (2008) reports that many aided schools existed on paper and the number of schools declined from 2,539 in the year 1868 to 2,084 in 1869–1870. To control this situation, the government decided to give grants to only those schools which were open to inspection but not much was achieved (Kishwar, 2008: 207). Rudolph and Rudolph (1972c: 83) suggest that privately managed institutions are more vulnerable to politicisation since government institutions are under closer supervision and scrutiny by administrators and professional educators. They point to strong ties between such institutions and the local community, as the former needed support, suffered from inability to raise funds themselves and, 'very often', had 'a bad and even unscrupulous management'. They point to other costs that need to be taken note of in discussions about private educational institutions. These include the cost of 'the laxity of private schools in conforming to minimum standards', 'the potential use of public authority and resources for private goods (individual and collective)' and 'the problematic nature of the relationship of private education to universalistic values' (Rudolph and Rudolph, 1972c: 86).

Public and private in colonial and post-independence India

This section provides a brief overview of the public and private actors in education in colonial and post-independence India. As colonial India was not a monolithic period, we begin with looking at public and private during different phases of colonial rule.

Public and private in colonial India

1600–1813

In the early period of the presence of the EIC in India (1600–1765), Christian missionaries established some charity schools in the late seventeenth and early eighteenth centuries. Though these schools received support from the EIC in the form of grants, lotteries, collection of funds by the officers of the EIC and higher interest rate on deposits made by schools, they were 'maintained by subscriptions and donations' (Naik and Nurullah, 1974/2004: 33–35). These schools do not qualify as examples of state support of non-state efforts because the colonial state had not been established before 1757, and they did not represent a policy for education of Indians.

The period from 1765–1813, considered the prime of Orientalist policy and influence in the sphere of education, was marked by efforts of the EIC to continue the policy of previous Hindu and Muslim rulers to support higher learning in classical languages and establish such institutions with a view to secure loyalty for the new regime as well as to bring *improvement* through its policy of engraftment. Public education was not on the agenda and the private educational institutions were almost entirely indigenous.

1813–1854

In this period, private enterprise, dominated by missionaries, also included EIC officials, some European and almost negligible Indian non-official initiatives with regard to 'modern' schools. Each of these agencies had different perceptions about the educational needs of Indians and had distinct, and at times, contradictory motivations that guided their effort.

The Charter Act of 1813 made a financial provision of Rs. 100,000 for the education of Indians, which was increased to an annual grant of Rs. 1,000,000 from 1833 onwards. This money was used by EIC to run its own institutions and very little was offered as grant-in-aid to mission schools, thus paving the way for secular schools that rivalled mission schools (ibid.: 119–120). After the Charter Act, a larger number of missionaries were permitted to enter and operate in India. During 1813–1833, missionaries opened a large number of schools in the vernacular medium and after 1833, they shifted the focus on English as the medium of instruction (ibid.: 116–117). Several Protestant institutions and the students in them were 'almost equal to official enterprise' (ibid.: 119). Missionaries worked among lower classes and caste groups of India and used their language as the medium of instruction and took the lead in the field of education for women at a time when officials were hesitant to enter it (ibid.: 114–115). They popularised English schools, which were later also demanded by Indians such as Raja Rammohan Roy.

Some British officials such as J.E.D. Bethune in their individual capacity and non-British officials such as David Hare also established educational institutions that represent the individual non-Indian private effort. With encouragement from Mountstuart Elphinstone, then Governor of Bombay, the Bombay Native Education Society (later renamed as School Book and School Society) was established. Limited grant-in-aid helped it to open schools in Bombay between 1822 and 1840, which were later inherited by the Board of Education formed in 1840 (Naik and Nurullah, 1974/2004: 80–81). Similarly, Judge Sir Edward Hyde East impressed upon the Bengali elite in 1816 to form an association to open a school for their children and his influence allowed the school, which was a private endeavour with private funds, to receive private funds as well as appeal for government funds at a later date in 1823 (Rudolph and Rudolph, 1972a: 14–15). Moral and financial support by these officials was aimed at encouraging a 'private Indian enterprise' that could 'provide the bulk of the educational institutions' (Naik and Nurullah, 1974/2004: 126). Unlike Adam, Munro and Elphinstone, Lieutenant-Governor Thomason of the North-Western Provinces received support for his proposals to use indigenous schools to educate the people. He supplemented the funds collected through a levy on land-revenue for schools with equal grant-in-aid from the government to maintain *halkabandi* schools[2] (Naik and Nurullah, 1974/2004: 108–109).

1854–1902

Compulsory education was introduced in England by different acts in the 1870s, but the colonial state maintained a studied silence on this issue as it did not identify itself with the colonised. Irrespective of its high rhetoric on the significance of education for the development of the people of India, it repeatedly used paucity of funds as the reason to invite private enterprise and justify the grant-in-aid system. These policies along with the practical transfer of education since 1884 to local bodies with little resources at their disposal resulted in serious damage to the cause of mass education.

In this period, though both missionaries and initiatives by Indians and Indian agencies to establish educational institutions were classified as private, a distinction was drawn between the two, where 'local' and 'people' meant Indians (Report of the Indian Education Commission, 1883: 452–454). Indians were encouraged by the colonial state to 'combine with the agency of the government',[3] for 'educational means' of the country to be 'co-extensive with educational wants' (Naik and Nurullah, 1974/2004: 170). Private involvement was justified for three reasons. Financial justifications involved addition from private agencies 'to contributions from the State',[4] to 'relieve and assist the public funds', and as a cost-saving mechanism (Naik and Nurullah, 1974/2004: 170). Other reasons were self-reliance and sensitivity to local needs and aspirations (Report of the Indian Education Commission, 1883: 452–454) and the encouragement of civic spirit, engagement and participation. In this period, the educational efforts of the British officials in their individual capacity disappeared totally.

On the one hand, the system of grant-in-aid established by the Wood Despatch of 1854 resulted in a large number of private schools, many of which became colleges by the end of the nineteenth century (Rudolph and Rudolph, 1972a: 15). On the other hand, it also witnessed the death of indigenous schools with the adoption of a system of 'payment by result' for indigenous schools along with their neglect (Naik and Nurullah, 1974/2004: 157, 213–214, 223). Aid to private schools was inadequate and aided schools were not rigorously controlled by the department of education except in matters of general inspection, examination and how grant was spent (ibid.: 178). These developments indicate that indigenous educational institutions did not die a natural death and another system was consciously implanted in its place.

The policy of religious neutrality announced by the crown in the wake of the revolt of 1857 resulted in an unsympathetic attitude towards missionary activities until 1882, and a policy of direct competition by the education department threatened the existence of missionary schools. By 1881–1882, the Indian private enterprise with 54,662 primary and 1,341 secondary schools surpassed the 1,842 and 757 schools run by non-Indian managers (Naik and Nurullah, 1974/2004: 172). Missionary enterprise was given a subordinate position in the development of education in India and they restricted their operation to selected educational institutions and maintained a high degree of efficiency there (ibid.: 158–166).

Contemporary coupling of efficiency with private enterprise has one source in this historical legacy of missionary involvement in education. The other historical legacy of missionary enterprise of working with and for the education of the marginalised sections of the Indian society is a key argument in the contemporary discourse on school choice, vouchers and public funds for private schools. Missionaries had also called for the withdrawal of government intervention from education, arguing that it resulted in higher costs while they could provide it at a lower cost – an argument echoing loudly in contemporary discussions.

As discussed before, there were significant provincial differences in the promotion of public and private schools. This implies that the growth of private enterprise cannot be attributed to either its inherent superiority or a result of the necessary weakness of the public system. In Madras, government schools (1,263 in 1881–1882) were opened only in absence of private schools (13,223 aided and 2,828 unaided indigenous) and the payment-by-result system was introduced in 1868. For primary education, the education department in Bombay 'relied almost exclusively on its own schools'. It neglected indigenous schools (only 73 schools received aid though 3,954 indigenous schools existed in 1881–1882).

In Punjab, private schools were encouraged after the Wood Despatch as government schools were to be opened only where 'no effective schools under missionary superintendence or in which the ground might not have been otherwise preoccupied' and whenever a private body 'established' schools, these government schools were to be withdrawn. If a private body 'was able and willing to administer the institution owned and managed by Government', then they were to be handed over to such private agency (Punjab Records, March 1855, cited in Mehta, 1929/1971: 50, 54–55). With the provision of grant-in-aid available to only those schools complying with government rules, indigenous schools and purely vernacular schools were eliminated from such aid since 1869 in Punjab (Kishwar, 2008: 208). Following the reform measures introduced in Punjab in 1859–1860,

'Government was to provide chiefly for Higher School and Middle School education while the people themselves were to find money for elementary schools' (Mehta, 1929/1971: 46). During 1860–1861 to 1871–1872, expenditure from educational cess ranged from one-third to one-half of educational expenditure from imperial revenues (Mehta, 1929/1971: 47).[5] Although local committees for public instruction were formed in different districts of Punjab from 1864–1865, they did not show much interest in the work and progress of elementary schools (Mehta, 1929/1971: 45).

We have already discussed how Indian private entrepreneurship expressed through initiatives of caste, sect, religious and linguistic communities had established educational institutions. If ideas of social reform, patriotic sentiments and cultural preservation were one set of inspirations that guided the agency and entrepreneurship shown by Indians in establishing schools in colonial India, then motivations of maintaining the social dominance or promoting social mobility of their own caste or religious group, creating a cohesive group and self-identity, disseminating cultural norms and defining collective goals formed another set of reasons that influenced their efforts (Rudolph and Rudolph, 1972a: 19–21; Kumar, 1990: 7–8; Kumar, 2000: 84). This resulted in rapid growth of the Indian private enterprise, which took benefit of the grant-in-aid system.

The interaction between public and private and their response to each other was also shaped by their perception of the purpose and content of education. Both merchants and artisans in Benaras felt that the subjects taught in the government schools that had no place for selections from religious texts or respect for traditional skills thus neither paid attention to the development of morality nor were relevant to their vocational future (Kumar, 2000: 80–83). The disrespect towards the country, its history and culture in the public education led to concerns to teach these in the new educational institutions established by Indians. Hereby, the private enterprises were imbued with a different or additional public purpose, distinct from those defined in the school curriculum. But the problems involved in carrying it out in the already packed school curriculum or at home meant that, increasingly, the private came to lose its distinctness vis-à-vis the public and soon lost that purpose as well (ibid.: 91).

1902–1921

In this period, a greater role for the state in the field of education with respect to finances, regulation and supervision and standard of instruction and institutions was envisaged. During this period, huge central grants were made for education along with an active role by the state in provision of education that resulted in unprecedented expansion of recognised institutions. Though better collection of revenue and the boom in world finance provided greater resources to the government, their allocation was also dependent on political will of the rulers. This increase allowed the improvement of government schools to become models for private enterprise. Thus, the ideal and the desirable were associated with the public, while the private was to follow it as an example.

Under Curzon, the state considered opening and maintaining 'a few institutions of every type as *models* to private enterprise' one of its duties (Naik and Nurullah, 1974/2004: 239–243, emphasis in original). A set of three influences and concerns led to a strengthened system of inspection and supervision of private schools. Two of these reasons pertained to greater regulation of private schools and concern with improvement of quality of education in England. The third reason was the perception of colonial officials that private schools were a breeding ground for sedition among Indians (ibid.: 241, 258). Several conditions[6] were laid down by the Government Resolution of 1904 for grants-in-aid, scholarship to students and ranking as 'recognised' schools for all private secondary schools, both aided and unaided (ibid.: 258–259). To encourage private schools to seek recognition and achieve prescribed higher standards, the grant-in-aid to private schools was increased. Automatic transfer of students from unrecognised to recognised schools was stopped with a view to bring the unrecognised schools under control of the education department (ibid.: 260). The system of payment by result was discarded all over India (ibid.: 264).

In the colonial context, 'public' referred to both the colonial state and the colonised. Thus, the schools established by the colonial state were public. But one strain of private enterprise motivated by nationalist feelings and aspirations also claimed to represent the colonised national public. In the colonial context, the enactment and implementation of newer state policies for greater regulation of private schools was seen as an attempt to scuttle the development of nationalist feelings and of the private Indian enterprise. This history suggests that Indian and British response to public and private was also influenced by political factors and contexts.

Increased private contribution in the form of endowments, donations and subscriptions was a result of an awakening among Indians, the recognition of education as central to the task of national regeneration and the innovative efforts made by community leaders and reformers including women to raise funds for schools established by them (Kumar, 2000). The foundation of this private enterprise was also based on the entry of a large number of women who used their personal circumstances and what was considered as traditional womanly virtues of patience, selflessness and cheerful devotion to enter the public arena and promote women's education. In this process, these women developed a different personal and public persona (Kishwar, 2008: 221). At the same time, the entry and role of women in the public sphere was not free of their caste locations. Rege (2006: 48–49) gives instances of how while claiming to speak on behalf of all women, upper-caste women suggested differential education and opportunities for women from different communities and caste groups. Thus, the private initiatives in education in colonial India worked along the inter-related axes of caste, class and gender. Their efforts to 'invent' and preserve indigenous traditions and culture through education also defined boundaries of self and other and were part of other processes to frame 'public' and 'counter publics'.

1921–1947

With the introduction of diarchy under the Government of India Act 1919, education as a transferred subject came under the control of Indian ministers. The central government stopped taking interest in and providing grants for education. A report of the Hartog Committee noted that in this period, education was seen as 'an indispensable agency' for nation building. Educationally backward communities, such as Muslims, depressed classes and 'tribal aborigines' took interest in 'the need and possibilities of education for their children' and demanded 'education as a right'.[7] During 1935 and 1947, the growth of primary education 'on a voluntary basis' reached 'a saturation point in most areas' (Naik and Nurullah, 1974/2004: 375). J. P. Naik believed that in this situation, compulsion of education became a necessity for further expansion.

A resolution proposed to be moved by Rao Bahadur Kale in the Legislative Council, Bombay in 1921[8] provides evidence of a set of opinions that wanted withdrawal of the government 'from the management of schools imparting secondary education'. It recommended that government high schools should be abolished 'in places where other facilities for secondary education already' existed and private enterprise should be 'encouraged . . . by increasing the proportion of grant-in-aid from one third to one half' and by 'removing the restriction on the number of boys attending a private school'. Even though this resolution was disallowed, it gives an indication that some private schools wanted elimination of competition from the government schools to become the only institutions available for education at the secondary level. They also desired for greater public funding for *encouragement* of the private enterprise. The meaning of the third recommendation may be better appreciated if we remind ourselves that 'enterprising individuals and associations' opened a large number of new secondary schools during 1921–1937 'in mofussil towns and bigger villages', which resulted in a massive increase in the enrolment of students from rural and semi-urban areas (Naik and Nurullah, 1974/2004: 336–337). In this context, the third aspect of the resolution may have meant removing restrictions on the number of students that a private school could admit. Combined with the proposal to abolish government schools, this provided better possibilities of growth for the private enterprise with support from public funds. Such attempts also warn us that idealism, social reform and improvement were not the sole motives that guided the private effort in colonial India.

Discussion about public and private in colonial India would not be complete without reference to those unaided private schools that were modelled on the grammar schools of England meant for the elite of society. On the one hand, in their attempt to imitate the English public schools, they accepted the latter's superiority and tried to achieve authenticity by being as approximate to the ideal as possible by 'adopting and adapting ideas of culture, morality, the cult of manliness, and the magical and immutable qualities of heredity . . . towards its own circuits of power' (Srivastava, 1998: 6). On the other hand, they became spaces that would serve the cause of producing national citizens for the would-be free India by training the young in the ethos and modes of participation in the civil society and the state. These schools posed themselves as custodians of liberal values, modernity and rationality in India. Their products were to bear the stamp of character, a shorthand term for a host of virtues such as responsibility, self-reliance, self-initiative, self-discipline, flexibility, co-operation, sacrifice, service, an ability to control worldly passions and morality. These attributes and their development by public schools became a justification of their ability to lead and represent the nation on account of superior understanding and intellectual advancement in contrast to the backward fellow brethren and to work for those who were weak, poor and ignorant. To attain independence, the anti-colonial struggle in India used the language of inclusion to enlist every member of the national community as an equal citizen against the colonial power. With independence, these same members were asked to improve the 'self' and become 'modern' so that the status of the 'citizen' of the new sovereign nation could be legitimately conferred on them (Srivastava, 1998). The responsibility of constructing the new nation and exhorting and nurturing the masses to help them overcome their shortcomings to enter the post-colonial civil society was self-assumed by the educated middle class. Within this group, the bodies bearing marks of elite private schools came to signify the post-colonial ideal citizen and their locations of class/caste dominance were masked through a reconstitution of these differences by the presence or absence of certain traits that marked the *other lacking* them as *backward* instead of being defined as exploited and marginalised.

Independent India

With the change of political goals from independence to competitive politics for power, there was a shift in motives from an ideal-based motivation to efforts to garner 'material rewards, power, and prestige' and gave a 'narrow and partisan meaning to founding and managing education' (Rudolph and Rudolph, 1972b: 20). 'The ability to affect affiliation was of considerable interest to those seeking local influence' (Rudolph and Rudolph, 1972b: 18).

Public and private in the age of national reconstruction

Speeches of the political leaders, senior judges, officers of the army and academicians – many of whom served on the governing boards of private schools – give us an idea of the characteristics associated with the private and public school and their role in independent India.[9] Doon school was appreciated as 'good' for being 'run efficiently', 'good methods of education', 'making boys to do work', 'amount of science taught' (DSW, No. 286); 'for the proper trainings of its youth', 'its corporate life' that led to 'the development of the total personality of the child', and the students' involvement in village service and efforts to eliminate illiteracy (DSW, No. 353). To remove the 'psychological gulf' between 'the English-educated and the other people of this country', the public schools were also called upon to use Hindi as the language of instruction, along with the recognition of 'important difficulties in that being done' (ibid.). One was to look to such schools 'for future leaders in different spheres of work' (DSW, No. 422). Such a school developed 'the corporate sense' and encouraged them to not use their abilities for their 'own honour and glory, but for the public good'.[10] Responding to the critique of public schools mentioned by the principal in his speech, speakers bemoaned the existence of unrest in schools and colleges and traced it to 'excessively large numbers admitted into schools and colleges, to the very inadequate and indifferent staff' and 'absence of extracurricular activities'. 'Great achievements' were attributed to 'the capacity of people' to 'think for themselves' and 'not submit to the crowd' (DSW, No. 521). In addition, Doon school received appreciation for orderliness and friendliness, 'equal emphasis on academic work as well as physical attainments, in the development of learning as well as character'. Further, the students were exhorted to have 'no room for narrow self-interest' (DSW, No. 555).

The Secondary Education Commission (SEC) in its report noted that it had received 'extreme views' on the need for such public schools. One set of these opinions dubbed these schools as 'an anachronism' in a modern democracy that made no 'material contribution to the educational progress of the country', produced 'narrow-minded snob[s]', served the rich, perpetuated class feeling, and hence, it was inappropriate to the democratic set-up (Government of India, 1953: 53). Others such as Sir John Sargent, who were familiar with the students of such institutes, argued that the product of a private school, despite its limited intellectual range, narrow sympathies and arrogant assumptions, had 'a capacity to set up, and abide by, standards of conduct and a readiness to accept responsibility', which are qualities necessary for 'any real public servant' (cited in Government of India, 1953: 53).

SEC concluded that the alleged shortcomings of the private schools could be overcome if they reformed themselves. Moreover, with proper organisation and training on the right lines, they could 'develop correct attitudes and behaviour' and make their students 'useful citizens'. It further maintained that given the 'special facilities' that these schools could offer, they had 'greater opportunities' than a 'majority of secondary schools' to develop 'certain essential traits of character – including the qualities of leadership'. Moreover, until other schools could provide such facilities, 'it would be *unwise* to reject their special contribution in this direction'. Some of the 'principles and methods' practiced in these schools could serve as models to be followed 'in *all* schools' (ibid., emphasis added). These schools needed to give due stress on 'the dignity of labour and a social sense' and had a 'limited but definite place' in the educational system (ibid.: 53–54). In his founder's day address at Doon school, Dr Mudaliar, who was the Chairman of the Secondary Education Commission and the Vice Chancellor of Madras University, asked these schools to provide such training that made students 'always shine not by any adventitious aids but by their own mental and moral gifts' (Doon School Weekly, No. 619, Saturday, 1 November 1958).

In the above addresses, the private schools were justified in terms of initiative, range of activities, developing an integrated and balanced personality with the ability to take decisions beyond narrow self-interest and courage to stand apart in the crowd. They were seen to be training students to be citizens of the new nation with no caste, religious or linguistic affiliation. Students of the private schools were applauded for working for public good and serving in villages unlike the other young who wasted their energies in different expressions of discontent. The learners and learning in these private institutions were perceived as being superior to others.

It is important to note that the class position of students studying in such elite private schools, designated as 'public schools', and the advantages that it bestowed on them did emerge as a concern, but a correction in their training was suggested as a solution to overcome their narrow and snobbish attitude. In this discourse, the class advantage, vertical divisions of resources and unequal power relations were masked by shifting the focus to 'mental and moral gifts' and 'character', which allowed them to 'always shine' on the national scene as public-spirited, responsible citizens and leaders among the pool of illiterate and ignorant population. English also became a code to discuss and critique privilege and their distance from the masses, but it was a privilege that could not be dispensed with.

In this conceptualisation, these schools were private on account of their accessibility and the agency that established them, but they were public with reference to the educational aims, pedagogic processes, institutional ethos and purposes served in the nascent democracy.

Public and private in Kothari Commission

The report of the Education Commission (EC) 1964–1966, popularly known as the Kothari Commission, noted that private educational institutions at different levels of schooling constituted about one-third (33 per cent) of total institutions but dominated pre-primary (70.9 per cent) and secondary schools (69.2 per cent) (NCERT, 1970: 447, para 10.03). The class basis of the system of private and public schooling (NCERT, 1970: 449, para 10.05 (3)) and its role in entrenching and perpetuating the class divide and class-based access to quality education was strongly criticised by the EC.[11] The EC favoured the abolition of this divide and the establishment of a common school system that was to function as a neighbourhood school for children of all communities and social backgrounds. Since 'most schools show an average performance' and were 'isolated from [their communities]' (NCERT, 1970: 450, para 10.07), this common school system had to be 'maintained at an adequate level of quality and efficiency', failing which the parents could 'ordinarily feel' the need to send their children 'to the institutions outside the system, such as independent or unrecognized schools' (NCERT, 1970: 448, para 10.05).

Here, a differentiation emerges between the private and the public. Public comes to subsume the recognised and aided schools since 'most of their expenditure comes from government grants and fees' (NCERT, 1970: 452, para 10.09) and they were to be part of the common school system (NCERT, 1970: 448, para 10.05). The report of the Education Commission also notes that while many grant-in-aid codes provide aid only if the institutions are conducted by non-profit-making bodies, in certain areas, proprietary schools were 'still recognized and aided' (NCERT, 1970: 457, para 10.16). Schools maintained by the government, local authorities and private managements receiving aid needed to have more 'freedom' (NCERT, 1970: 452, para 10.08), improve their 'performance', achieve and maintain 'an adequate level of quality and efficiency', which are features identified with the private.

The Kothari Commission classified private schools into three groups: recognised and aided institutions, recognised but unaided or independent institutions and unrecognised institutions (NCERT, 1970: 452, para 10.09). Recognised and aided institutions had merits of close ties with the local community, a fair degree of freedom though disappearing with increasing controls by education departments and loyalty of teachers. These schools suffered from 'precarious financial position' due to uncertainty of government grants and inability to raise funds themselves and 'very often' had 'a bad and even unscrupulous management' (ibid.). Management of such schools, to borrow a phrase from J.P. Naik, could aptly be described as 'new zamindars'.[12] A small group of these schools were efficient and a larger number were 'weak and undesirable ones' established by 'a number of voluntary organizations which are dominated by sectarian considerations' and 'run, not for purposes of education or social service, but for exploitation and patronage and are like commercial undertakings' (NCERT, 1970: 452–453, para 10.10).

This analysis was the recognition of grant-in-aid as a mechanism to allow private institutions 'within reach of public authority and its definition of public interest' and to provide conditions for use of 'public resources for private ends' by private interests. This system was making way for 'institutionalized means' to strengthen 'private community organizations' even when the institution may be secular and open for admission to all without any compulsion to participate in or honour 'the rituals and symbolism of the sect or community that manages the school' (Rudolph and Rudolph, 1972a: 23–24). These institutions established by private entrepreneurs 'for profit and power' offered both the best and the worst education and were being used to build political organisations and achieve the influence and support necessary to influence policy and win elections. They reflected both the political influence achieved and the use of such institutions as a means to gain and consolidate it (ibid.: 84).

How does attention to this political embeddedness of the aided schools in the 1960s allow us to understand the laxity in the enforcement of the minimum legal conditions to establish such institutions and receive grant-in-aid? These achievements of the private institutions are not as much a reflection and effect of weakness of administration but provide an insight in the operation of power and contestation. They point to the shared and overlapping space of private and public in the post-colonial Indian democracy where the processes through which different social forces try to defend their interests and counter others have 'become *autonomous* from the institutions and norms that are supposed to inform their participation' (Bhargava, Reifeld, and Stiftung, 2005: 40). This recognition allows us to appreciate that the self-aggrandising motives of politicians can bring schools into localities where due to poverty and apathy of the local population they would not have been established otherwise (Gould, 1972: 95). This attention to the political networks of the founders of private schools also sheds light on their influence as a pressure group, an aspect that remains deeply neglected in contemporary accounts of private schools. Rudolph and Rudolph (1972c: 87) noted that when individuals and groups operating private schools come to occupy positions of public authority as ministers, then they are reluctant to act against private schools. And any moves by the government to bring greater control and monitoring to remove the abuses in which these schools are engaged results in opposition to such moves.

The 'local' in the discussion of closer local ties of the private schools refers to two kinds of locality. The first one is the shared caste or religious affiliation of the management, parents and teachers that allows for greater possibilities of use of these attachments by founders and parents to seek admission in the institution and of co-operation and mobilisation of these memberships to resolve situations of conflict. Second, it refers to networks of founders and managements that influence choice of school as a desired destination, use of local influence and resources to receive land grants from the government to establish schools at specific locales and the ability to stop the release of adverse government orders. Jeffery, Jeffery, and Jeffrey (2006) in their study of a network of private schools in the Bijnor district of Uttar Pradesh have pointed to use of 'visible and semi-public "events"' to reaffirm social dominance and to test and develop loyalties 'between parents and management, pupils and teachers, or the local administration and the management'.

The EC explained that independent and unrecognised educational institutions had the right to exist under different constitutional provisions.[13] The independent schools charged high fees, paid higher salaries to teachers, were English medium and enjoyed high prestige. This prestige was, in the opinion of the EC, 'partly because of their standards and traditions, but mainly because the children of the most powerful groups in society attend them' and such schools 'created an important problem in social integration by segregating the richer classes from the rest of the community' (NCERT, 1970: 485, para 10.79). In contrast to the discussion about these schools in the speeches at Doon school and the Secondary Education Commission, where efficiency and tradition were characterised as the defining features of such institutions, class emerged as a key figure and the basis of critique in the EC. The EC was not concerned about reforming these schools by training students to be more service-oriented towards the disadvantaged but in ushering in a new system of common school with abolition of tuition fees up to standard 10. It expected that this system would deter the parents from sending their children to private schools and would lead most of the fee-charging private schools to seek grant-in-aid and be part of the common school system (NCERT, 1970: 454, para 10.13; 457–458, para 10.18). At the same time, in its report, the benchmark of quality and efficiency continued to be measured with reference to private schools. A new set of criteria to define minimum and optimum levels of a 'good' school and classification of schools was also proposed (NCERT, 1970: 462–463, para 10.30 (3)).[14]

The second set of private schools, the unrecognised institutions, is 'a very heterogeneous group about which little is known' and included preschools in urban areas that did not seek recognition; coaching classes that caused more harm than good; private institutions striving for recognition but failing due to bad standards; institutions giving religious instruction contrary to the Constitution;[15] and those restricted to certain castes or communities (NCERT, 1970: 486, para 10.80). Some of these did 'useful work', while others made 'a negative contribution to education and society' (ibid.). Under the provisions of the Constitution, their emergence could not be stopped and the education department had no control over them as they did not seek recognition. This situation, the EC concluded, had led to 'the first steps to introduce legislation for the compulsory registration of all educational institutions' and to the terming of the operation of an unregistered institution an 'offence'. Using the Education Act, 1944 of England, it suggested various criteria on which the government could remove institutions from the register.

Government of India (1968) makes a single reference to private schools, which were categorised under 'special schools' as 'public schools' in the section on Equalisation of Educational Opportunity. The policy stated, 'public schools should be required to admit students on the basis of merit and also to provide a *prescribed* proportion of free-studentships to prevent segregation of social classes'. Here, 'private' was identified with the rich and the heterogeneity of private schools remained unrecognised. The problem of class segregation was resolved by a modest and suggestive 'should' of merit-based admission and free seats. While the provision of free seats in private schools had to wait for more than three decades for its insertion in the state policy under the Right to Education (2009), it continues to be contested.

Concluding remarks

What does this long discussion portend for the contemporary debate on public and private? Does it call for giving up the categories of public and private with reference to their ownership and management? Would such a move not amount to losing the opportunity to critically examine the claims of the market that private entrepreneurship driven by the possibility of profit can bring in greater cost and work efficiency in managing educational institutions, achieve better learning outcomes and yet serve the marginalised communities?

This chapter argues that by bringing politics and history also to the discussion of public and private, we can better appreciate the limits of the economistic frame, which posits them as homogenous binary categories and ignores their considerable internal diversity and histories. These schools exist and are experienced in certain geo-socio-historic contexts and spaces. The meanings, purposes and practices of public and private educational institutions are not frozen in time and can be better appreciated if we pay attention to the contestations and operations of power, of both the state and the society. For this purpose, the public and private schools and actors need to be located with reference to the shifts in state policies at the national, provincial and local levels. This simultaneous attention to different levels of the state can help to look at their inter-linkages, divergences, provincial differences, negotiations with and operation of the state in relation to local networks of patronage and diverse ideas of publics and state–citizen relationship. Attention to the provincial-localised gendered histories of caste and community formation, relationships and mobility, changes in occupational structure, attempts to cement social dominance and/or challenge it by denying/achieving access to education by opening new schools may help us to capture the participation of an institution in the structures of inequality. Through this historic examination, we have argued for locating the development of public and private schools in the larger socio-political processes of urbanisation and industrialisation, reconstitution of communities, forging of identities and development of new political subjectivities and aspirations. We may ask, how are public and private schools situated vis-à-vis the pedagogic role of the post-colonial state in the creation of a public?

With this frame, we can examine the multiple ways in which the category of public is mobilised. In the context of public schools, it represents the unmarked citizens of the nation who come together, interact and learn. It hides the class–caste character and the location of the bodies that enter this space. At the same time, the hierarchical differentiation among the public schools in terms of budgetary provisions, infrastructure, basis of selection, their socio-geographic locations, the bodies that desire and inhabit them and the declared aims forewarn us from collapsing the public in one unifying category. The ongoing debate about the recognition of marginalisation and privilege and framing policies that simultaneously address equality, difference and dignity tells us that public schools need to be examined against these yardsticks in terms of both principles and practices to understand what educated public gets produced in these institutions.

In the context of private schools, the idea of public is deployed in multiple ways with consequences for defining the concomitant idea of public good. Producing the above-mentioned unmarked citizen in fashioning the national self is only one of these ideas. As explained before, linguistic, religious and caste-bounded communities too claim and forge 'publicness' to promote community interests, achieve social mobility, improve status and uphold cultural norms. This public draws on the communitarian notion and locates the citizen not only as an isolated individual but also as a member of a group whose sustenance is necessary for his own cultural survival. The definition of this culture, 'invention of tradition' of the community and insistence on observing it in the public life of the institution to extend/multiply its practices to the private spaces can also place the burden of cultural reproduction on women and deny individuals the autonomy to choose. How do insularity, exclusivity, reproduction and insistence on conformity play out along with ideas of equality, openness, connection, autonomy and reasonableness in private schools is an inquiry worth pursuing to understand both the aims and publicness of private institutions. This diverse, at times contradictory, usage of the 'public' in the private school context and inter-mixing of the languages of public good and community interest in the discourse of/on private schools underlines that the motives of profitability and market logics of efficiency in monetary terms are insufficient to capture and explain the variety of reasons that guide the emergence and operation of the private. This historical examination of the private stresses the need to disaggregate the private and to recognise that the private exhibits a range of characteristics. It serves different aims of education and the logic of profit and community boundedness may both inform and obfuscate these aims.

Modernity, progress, development and cultivation of a citizenry trained in the use of reasoned dialogue for the purposes of democratic participation is only one register within which the rationale(s) for the establishment of public and private institutions are articulated. How does this language deploy, appropriate and circumvent tradition within and through the framework of modern reason and even (re)frame the modern in this process is a question worth pursuing in our quest to understand the public and the private. Within the liberal frame of democracy, education is more than a preparation to attain skills for future employment and contribute to national growth. Developing capacities for making informed and autonomous judgement to enter in reasoned dialogue with other citizens about the purposes of the national collective life requires spaces, opportunities and pedagogies that promote and respect individuation. Do public and private educational institutions script and/or circumscribe individual choice, desire and articulation of one's ideas, and to what extent? In what ways is this related to ideas of their own institutional and educational purposes and imaginations about the future trajectories of the young bodies that enter these spaces? And how does this individuation or its absence combined with institutional goals unproblematically partake of the discourse of development and progress and make the private–public distinction meaningless as both begin to see and reason like the state? If we collapse this complexity to the public–private binary, then we lose opportunities to understand why quality of education manifests itself in diverse ways in these institutions.

Public, private and education in India 61

The economistic frame presents a very neat picture of the establishment of a private educational institution. This founding is preceded by a survey of the educational market and demand–supply. It is the result of an individual's entrepreneurial spirit to invest, to undertake risk, to seek profit, to manage it efficiently with hard work and achieve success with continuous efforts to better one's self. In this perspective, the ability to satisfy the consumer with a good product and responsive service explains the demand and reputation of the private school. This picture ignores that the emergence of private schools is not just an economic process but is simultaneously also a political process. It is oblivious to the everyday messiness of politics and the particular trajectories of state formation and democracy in India that provide the context for establishment and operation of private schools. It cannot capture how the private involves networking with politicians, bureaucracy, influential local patrons, drawing upon community links and projection of its own sensitivity to the needs of the community. Attention to politics and history allows us to look at both discursive and material constructs of what private schools and the community consider suitable to the needs of the community. Examination of the motivations of founders and managements of different private schools and developing thick descriptions of the school processes, events and their network for both political and educational purposes can be useful to understand their quality, performance of service, assertion of dominance, formation of political clout and 'local' loyalty. Thereby, we can develop a disaggregated and complex picture of the ways in which the private schools continue to operate within or shed the bounded communities from which they originate.

Acknowledgement

I am grateful to Manisha Goel for making calculations about mission schools from Sharp (1918).

Notes

1 This brief summary of feminist critiques on the public–private distinction does not do justice to the rich debates and differences among feminist scholars on account of (a) multiple theoretical perspectives (e.g. liberal, socialist, radical, post-colonial) within the broad feminist stance, (b) geographical (Western–non-Western, Arab feminism) and locational differences (e.g. Black and dalit feminism) and (c) different connotations of the terms in everyday language usage and political philosophy.
2 A *halka* refers to a circle or group of villages. A school was established at a central location, which was not more than two miles from any village

of the circle. Voluntary consent of the landowners to pay tax was a necessary condition to establish such a school. This description is based on the *Despatch of 1859* quoted in (Naik and Nurullah, 1974/2004: 109).

3 'Dispatch of the Court of Directors of the East India Company to the Governour General of India in Council', No. 49, dated 19 July 1854, in Richey (1922: 378).

4 Wood Despatch of 1854 cited in Naik and Nurullah (1974/2004: 139).

5 Educational cess was collected only from zamindars. The Supreme Government proposed for collection of fees from boys of commercial and non-agricultural classes who attended village schools maintained by the cess collected from zamindars. In 1860–1861, fees were levied in government schools of all grades except Female Schools and Normal Schools (Mehta, 1929/1971: 49). In 1859–1860, government aid was Rs. 19,669 for 20 institutions. By 1883–1884, it amounted to Rs. 208,792 to 195 institutions. The expenditure from other sources during 1860–1861 and 1883–1884 was Rs. 25,323 and Rs. 233,249, respectively, which was higher than the aid provided by the government.

6 These included sound education; actual need of school; financial stability; proper constitution of managing body; teaching of proper subjects; provisions for teaching, health and discipline of students; suitability of teachers with regard to character, number and qualification; and a fee that does not result in competition that harms education.

7 *Report of the Hartog Committee*, 31, cited in Naik and Nurullah, 1974/2004: 325.

8 *Secondary Education; Encouragement to Private Enterprise and Abolition of Government Schools (Resolution by Rao Bahadur R.R. Kale)*, 1921, Educational Department Legislative Council Index 1921–1935, Accession No. LC 71-F, Archives of Maharashtra.

9 For this analysis, addresses of the first Indian Governor General C.R. Rajagopalachari, the first president of independent India Sh. Rajendra Prasad, the then Governor of Punjab Sh. Chandulal Trivedi, philosopher and the second president Dr. Radhakrishnan and Chief of Army Staff General S.M. Shriganesh, given at *Doon School* in the first decade of Indian independence 1947–1957, are examined as a representative sample. These addresses were respectively printed in the following issues of *Doon School Weekly* (DSW): No. 286, Saturday, 30 October 1948; No. 353, Saturday, 28 October 1950; No. 422, Saturday, 8 November 1952; No. 521, Saturday, 29 October 1955; and No. 555, Saturday, 3 November 1956. These are referred as *DSW*, with their issue number.

10 This address was given before 1955 and is printed in one of the issues of DSW, but I have lost its reference.

11 Common schooling was required because 'able children from every stratum of society' were not receiving 'good education' and it was 'available only to a small minority, which is usually selected not on the basis of talent but on the basis of its capacity to pay fees' (NCERT, 1970: 18, para 1.37).

12 J.P. Naik argued that the Congress Party had created 'Zamindari in Education'. The managers of colleges were the new zamindars who used profits from institutions to benefit themselves and used educational institutions as a mean of economic and political power. See 'The Role and Problems of Private Enterprise in Education', in I.S.S.-Feres *Consultation*

of *Principals of Christian Colleges*, Tambaram, 1967, The Christian College and National Development, cited in Gould (1972: 94).

13 These provisions include Article 30, which allows minorities to 'establish and administer educational institutions of their choice' and disallows any discrimination against them in receiving grant-in-aid, Articles 28 (10) and 28 (2), which give freedom to establish private educational institutions to provide religious instruction and clauses (c) and (g) of Article 19 that give rights to form associations and carry out any profession, occupation, trade or business and included the right to establish educational institutions for these purposes. These provisions are discussed in the EC report (NCERT, 1970: 485, para 10.77).

14 The factors for classification include relations with the local community; qualifications of staff and its continuity; in-service training; special programmes, enriched curriculum, new methods of evaluation developed by the school; attention to gifted or retarded students; school discipline; wastage and stagnation; results of public examinations; scholarships achieved; after-school careers of students; and co-curricular activities.

15 In contemporary times also this concern about instruction in certain private educational institutions being contrary to constitutional values and vision is raised repeatedly in scholarly studies and Government Committee reports. See, Sarkar, Tanika (1996). 'Educating the Children of the Hindu Rashtra: Notes on RSS Schools', in P. Bidwai, H. Mukhia and A. Vanaik (Eds.), *Religion, Religiosity and Communalism*. New Delhi: Manohar Publishers; Sundar, Nandini (2004). 'Teaching to Hate: RSS' Pedagogical Programme', *Economic and Political Weekly*, 39(16), April 17: 1605–1612; and Report of the Committee of the Central Advisory Board of Education (2005), popularly known as Zoya Hasan Committee Report, titled *Regulatory Mechanisms for Textbooks and Parallel Textbooks Taught in Schools Outside the Government System: A Report*. New Delhi: Ministry of Human Resource Development, Government of India.

References

Arblaster, A. (1987). *The Rise and Decline of Western Liberalism*. Oxford: Basil Blackwell.

Bara, J. (2015). 'Western Education and Rise of New Identity-Mundas and Oraons of Chotanagpur, 1839–1939', *Economic and Political Weekly*, 32(15): 7–8.

Basu, A. (1974). *The Growth of Education and Political Development in India, 1898–1920*. Oxford: Oxford University Press.

Bhargava, R., Reifeld, H., and Stiftung, K. A. (2005). *Civil Society, Public Sphere, and Citizenship : Dialogues and Perceptions*. New Delhi, India: Sage.

Bhattacharya, N. (2005). 'Notes Towards a Concept of the Colonial Public', in R. Bhargava, H. Reifeld, and Konrad-Adenauer-Stiftung (Eds.), *Civil Society, Public Sphere, and Citizenship : Dialogues and Perceptions* (pp. 130–156). New Delhi, India: Sage.

Chaudhary, L. (2010). 'Land Revenues, Schools and Literacy', *The Indian Economic & Social History Review*, 47(2): 179–204.

Cohn, B. S. (1996). *Colonialism and Its Forms of Knowledge : The British in India*. Princeton: Princeton University Press.

Constable, P. (2000). 'Sitting on the School Verandah: The Ideology and Practice of "Untouchable" Educational Protest in Late Nineteenth-Century Western India', *The Indian Economic & Social History Review*, 37(4): 383–422.

Doon School Weekly (different years). Dehradun: Doon School.

Ellis, C. (2009). 'Education for All: Reassessing the Historiography of Education in Colonial India', *History Compass*, 7(2): 363–375.

Frevert, U. (2003). 'The Middle Classes as Public and Private: Culture, Gender and Modernization in 19th Century Europe', in G. Mahajan and H. Reifeld (Eds.), *The Public and the Private: Issues of Democratic Citizenship* (pp. 74–87). New Delhi, India: Sage.

Gould, H. (1972). 'Educational Structures and Political Processes in Faizabad District, Uttar Pradesh', in S. H. Rudolph and L. I. Rudolph (Eds.), *Education and Politics in India: Studies in Organization, Society, and Policy* (pp. 94–120). New Delhi, India: Oxford University Press.

Government of India. (1953). *Report of the Secondary Education Commission*. New Delhi, India: Ministry of Education, Government of India.

Government of India. (1968). *National Policy on Education*. New Delhi: Ministry of Education.

Government of India. (2009). *The Right of Children to Free and Compulsory Education Act*. New Delhi: Ministry of Law and Justice, Legislative Department.

Halifax, C. W. (1854). Despatch from the Court of Directors of the East India Company to the Governor-General of India in Council.

Hall, C. (2001). 'Private Persons Versus Public Someones: Class, Gender and Politics in England, 1780–1850', in M. Evans (Ed.), *Feminism: Critical Concepts in Literary and Cultural Studies, Vol. 1* (pp. 217–235). Oxon: Routledge.

India Board Report of the Board of Education from January 1, 1850 to April 30, 1851 (1851). Bombay: Bombay Education Society's Press.

Jeffery, R., Jeffery, P., and Jeffrey, C. (2006). 'Parhā'ī Ka Māhaul? An Educational Environment in Bijnor, Uttar Pradesh', in G. Neve and F. H. Donner (Eds.), *The Meaning of the Local: Politics of Place in Urban India* (pp. 116–140). London: Routledge.

Kaviraj, S. (1992). 'The Imaginary Institution of India', in P. Kaarsholm (Ed.), *Modernisation of Culture and the Development of Political Discourse in the Third World*. Occasional Paper no. 5 (pp. 41–63). Roskilde: International Development Studies. Roskilde University.

Kishwar, M. P. (2008). 'The Daughters of Aryavarta: Women in the Arya Samaj Movement, Punjab', in S. Sarkar and T. Sarkar (Eds.), *Women and Social Reform in Modern India: A Reader* (pp. 201–229). New Delhi, India: Permanent Black.

Kumar, K. (1990). 'Hindu Revivalism and Education in North-Central India', *Social Scientist*, 18(10): 4–26.

———. (2000). *Lessons from Schools: The History of Education in Benaras*. New Delhi, India: Sage.

Lister, R. (2000). 'Gender and the Analysis of Social Policy', in G. Lewis, S. Gewirtz and J. Clarke (Eds.), *Rethinking Social Policy* (pp. 22–36). London: The Open University and Sage.

Mahajan, G. (2003). 'Introduction, the Public and the Private: Two Modes of Enhancing Democratization', in G. Mahajan and H. Reifeld (Eds.), *The Public and the Private: Issues of Democratic Citizenship* (pp. 9–33). New Delhi, India: Sage.

Martin, J. R. (1986). 'Redefining the Educated Person: Rethinking the Significance of Gender', *Educational Researcher*, 15(6): 6–10.

Mehta, H. R. (1929/1971). 'A History of the Growth and Development of Western Education in the Punjab 1846–1884', Punjab Govt. Record Office, Monograph No. 5. Patiala: Languages Department, Punjab.

Naik, J. P., and Nurullah, S. (1974/2004). *A Student's History of Education in India 1800–1973*. New Delhi, India: Palgrave Macmillan.

NCERT. (1970). *Education and National Development: Report of the Education Commission 1964–1966* (Kothari Commission). New Delhi, India: NCERT.

O'Hanlon, R. (1985). *Caste, Conflict and Ideology; Mahatma Jotirao Phule and Low Caste Protest in Nineteenth-Century Western India*. Cambridge: Cambridge University Press.

Rao, A. (2009). 'Caste Radicalism and the Making of a New Political Subject', in idem, *The Caste Question: Dalits and the Politics of Modern India* (pp. 39–80). Ranikhet: Permanent Black.

Rao, P. V. (2008). 'Educating Women and Non-Brahmins as "Loss of Nationality": Bal Gangadhar Tilak and the Nationalist Agenda in Maharashtra', Occasional Paper No. 50 (pp. 1–42). New Delhi, India: Centre for Women's Development Studies.

Rao, Y. C. (2009). 'Educational Development as a New Horizon for Reservations: Neo-Social Movement of Andhra', in Y. C. Rao (Ed.), *Dividing Dalits: Writings on Sub-Categorisation of Scheduled Castes*. New Delhi, India: Rawat Publications.

Rege, S. (2006). 'Debating the Consumption of Dalit "Autobiographies": The Significance of Dalit 'Testimonios', in idem, *Writing Caste/Writing Gender: Narrating Dalit Women's Testimonios* (pp. 9–91). New Delhi, India: Zubaan.

Report of the Committee of the Central Advisory Board of Education. (2005). *Regulatory Mechanisms for Textbooks and Parallel Textbooks Taught in Schools Outside the Government System: A Report*. New Delhi: Ministry of Human Resource Development, Government of India.

Report of the Indian Education Commission. (1883). Calcutta: Superintendent of Government Printing.

Richey, J. A. (1922). *Selections from Educational Records, Part II, 1840–1859*. Calcutta: Superintendent Government Printing.

———. (1923). *Progress of Education in India 1917–1922, Eighth Quinquennial Review, Vol. I*. Calcutta: Superintendent Government Printing.

Rudolph, S. H., and Rudolph, L. I. (Eds.) (1972a). *Education and Politics in India: Studies in Organization, Society, and Policy*. New Delhi, India: Oxford University Press.

———. (Eds.) (1972b). 'Historical Legacies: The Genetic Imprint in Education', in idem, *Education and Politics in India: Studies in Organization, Society, and Policy* (pp. 13–24). New Delhi, India: Oxford University Press.

———. (Eds.) (1972c). 'Introduction to Part II', in idem, *Education and Politics in India: Studies in Organization, Society, and Policy* (pp. 83–93). New Delhi, India: Oxford University Press.

Sarkar, T. (1996). 'Educating the Children of the Hindu Rashtra: Notes on RSS Schools', in P. Bidwai, H. Mukhia, and A. Vanaik (Eds.), *Religion, Religiosity and Communalism* (pp. 237–248). New Delhi: Manohar Publishers.

Satyanarayana, A. (2002). 'Growth of Education Among the Dalit-Bahujan Communities in Modern Andhra, 1890–1947', in B. Sabyasachi (Ed.), *Education and the Disprivileged: Nineteenth and Twentieth Century India* (pp. 50–83). Hyderabad: Orient Longman.

Sharp, H. (1918). *Progress of Education in India 1912–1917, Seventh Quinquennial Review, Vol. II*. Calcutta: Superintendent Government Printing.

Srivastava, S. (1998). *Constructing Post-Colonial India: National Character and the Doon School*. London: Routledge.

2 Markets, state and quality in education
Reflections on genuine educational markets

Christopher Winch

Background

This volume covers an area of educational activity in India in which market forces play a significant role in the allocation of educational resources and in the production of educational goods.[1] This chapter discusses the key characteristics of genuine educational markets as opposed to the government-sponsored quasi-markets to be found in many developed countries; the implications of a multitiered educational market for the production of educational goods, both private and public, and criteria for assessing the relative quality of education within such a complex and hybrid system. This requires both conceptual clarification and consideration of practical circumstances.

Conceptual clarification: markets, quality and education

A market is a place (real or virtual) where commodities are exchanged, usually through the medium of money. The principal actors are sellers of commodities and potential and actual buyers of those same commodities. In the ideal market of neoclassical economic theory, the prices of all offers are instantaneously known to all buyers and sellers. The implicit assumption is that buyers will also be aware of the quality of the goods on offer. Although these assumptions make it easy to model the behaviour of markets, they are a poor reflection of the situation in real markets. In order to take account of this, we need to relax the assumptions of neoclassical economics considerably. In a world of less than perfect information, offer and bid prices are not known instantaneously by all participants in the market, but filter through by word of mouth or other finitely fast means of communication (O'Neill, 1999). Furthermore, the offer price is not just dependent on the *kind* of thing that is being sold, but also on its *quality*. However, it is often the case that the quality of an offer is not straightforward to assess. This is particularly true of education.

Is education a commodity?

The first issue that needs to be dealt with is an ambiguity in the term 'education'. It can mean the *process* by which one becomes educated, which could be schooling, tutoring, self-learning or whatever, which is something that plausibly could be sold in a market (see Tooley, 1998) or it could mean the *outcome* of an educational process, such as an educated person or educated population. Both senses of the term are clearly connected: one undergoes a process of education to become educated. Someone is educated as the result of taking part in some kind of educational process. Someone who buys participation in an educational process usually (but not necessarily) has in mind the outcome of an educated person or persons. So, although it is quite plausible to say that an educational process such as a child's schooling may be sold as a commodity, it is less plausible to maintain that the only thing that need concern either buyer or seller is the *quality of the process* as if this is totally disconnected from the quality of the educational outcome. By and large this is now accepted by participants in debates about markets and education (although this has not always been the case) and much of the debate about whether educational processes should be offered as commodities focuses on the potential of those processes to produce acceptable outcomes.

There is a separate question about whether the outcomes or goods produced by education should also be treated as commodities. Generally speaking, this has not been a focus of debates about the marketisation of education. However, we should note one important consequence of the conclusion of the previous paragraph. A private individual who buys an educational process for a child wishes to realise a benefit, typically either for the child or himself or herself or both, rather than the public at large, unlike the state which seeks to satisfy public aims of education. In a market, therefore, where the educational process is treated as a commodity, that commodity is the process whose intended outcome is the *private good* of education rather than any public good element. Being educated is a quality of an individual, arguably itself of marketable value.

Economists use technical definitions of public goods. A common approach is to say that, in contrast to private goods, they are *non-rivalrous* (enjoyment by one individual does not preclude enjoyment by another) and *non-excludable* (enjoyment is available to all potential beneficiaries irrespective of whether or not they pay for the good) (Varian, 2006). If education is taken to be a private good, then its possession by one individual excludes its possession by another; likewise its enjoyment by one person would exclude its enjoyment by another. The issue for education is complicated by the fact, already noted, that there are two aspects to education, as process and as outcome.

Taking outcomes first, it is not difficult to see that a successful educational outcome is to the personal benefit of the educatee. But it is less clear that *in every case* others are excluded from enjoying its benefits. Likewise, possession by one need not prevent acquisition by another. If X becomes literate, this is of potential benefit to all who interact with him. Likewise, X's literacy does not preclude Y becoming literate. There is, however, one important *caveat*. The outcome of an educational process may be access to a unique position which, by its nature, is exclusive and which Y cannot enjoy if X does. Such outcomes could be access to desirable employment, social positions or financial reward. *Positional* educational outcome goods do, therefore, seem to have a strong private good element to them. Needless to say, this aspect of education as an outcome does not go unnoticed by purchasers and may be one of the strongest factors influencing purchase of education (as a process).[2] But we can, at any rate, conclude that there is a strong public good element to many educational outcomes.

What of education as a process? When financed through taxation, it is free at the point of use, and in most circumstances, the provision is uniform for all beneficiaries.[3] It is both non-rivalrous and non-excludable except in circumstances where there are positional effects which may arise from the scarcity of some resources such as teachers and school buildings, but also school intakes with differing levels of social and cultural capital. Government-run, taxpayer-financed education does, therefore, have a significant public goods element according to the conventional economic definition. What about privately financed education? This looks much more like a private good. There are strong positional effects through the conferment of status through attending a prestigious and exclusive institution and even through the mere fact of having purchased private education. Gurney in this volume provides an interesting insight into the way in which parents who send their children to low-fee-paying schools might consider this to provide positional benefits. But it is also the case that when parents purchase their child's education, they are (a) laying exclusive claim on a finite resource and (b) preventing another child from enjoying the same resource. The important point when considering action and motivation in educational markets is that the buying and selling of educational processes can be treated as a market in a particular kind of private good if we make the enormous proviso that any public goods or bads that may result from the operation of an educational market can be ignored.

It is, of course, true that private provision of education for the benefit of individuals may have public good effects through a kind of law of unintended consequence. If private educational goods are provided in sufficient quantity – for example, literacy – then everyone benefits, whether or not they have paid for the education of those who have become literate. But by the same token, the mass production of education as a private good may create public *bads* or disbenefits which the public must, willy-nilly, suffer. If, for example, differential access to private education creates a highly stratified society with large relative income differentials, then there is ample evidence that all kinds of social ills may result (Wilkinson, 2005; Wilkinson and Pickett, 2009). The operation of a market in education, therefore, entails that an educational *process* is being sold whose main (although not only) intended outcomes are private goods for the intended beneficiary (e.g. a child), whether or not they produce any public goods or *bads*. We can, however, safely conclude that the provision of education through a market mechanism is a matter of public as well as private interest, as the public is inevitably affected through such an institution. Governments, whatever their views of the private provision of education, cannot remain indifferent to the way in which education is provided in their jurisdictions, since it affects the long-term interests of the public and hence gives a *prima facie* ground for regulating it. And politics, as Hume reminds us, concerns attention to our long-term interests, making them the short-term interests of those who have political responsibility (Hume, 1978: Bk III, Pt 2, p. 537). It is, therefore, not surprising that the legal and regulatory framework set in place by the Indian government does not just concern the operation of government-funded schools but seeks to regulate the operation of educational markets financed by private purchases.[4]

Assessing educational quality – a fraught issue for the government

To talk about the quality of education is to talk about what is meant by a good education. A good education is one that leads to desirable outcomes via desirable (or at least ethically acceptable) processes. What one means by a good education is an especially challenging question for a state (and the government that actually has to deal with the issue) because of the plurality of values and range of interests that need to be taken into account. Compromise on the implementation of diverse and sometimes incompatible values is almost inevitable and is reflected in the aims chosen for the system (see Mehendale's chapter in this volume). Sometimes, the issue is deemed to be so controversial that governments prefer to leave aims implicit rather than set them out explicitly in a way that makes them subject to controversy. This is partly true of India. And, as we shall see below, the complexity of education as a good poses particular challenges for governments, particularly in a hybrid public–private system where the writ of the state does not always run very strongly.

In addition to the onerous responsibility of negotiating the implementation of values and the determination of aims, governments have responsibility for setting the framework for the provision of adequate resources, curricula and pedagogies that are capable of meeting the aims of the system. There is a constant dilemma between imposing too much control, which can lead to demoralisation and loss of autonomy at the local level, eventually leading to the undermining of the control systems through gaming strategies and evasion, and on the other hand, leaving a system that is too loosely coupled to develop in ways that are in harmony with stated aims. There are no easy answers to such complex questions of governance and the difficulty of dealing with them is greatly increased when state education has to coexist and compete with, as well as regulate, an extensive and vigorous private education sector.

The role of purchasers in determining educational quality

In a market, the purchasers of a commodity, if they are making a considered purchase,[5] have a view as to what makes up the qualities of that commodity. This is true as much for education as for any other commodity. However, in the case of education, there is a great deal of conceptual complexity that lies behind the idea of a 'good' education. First, the purchase of education is, if considered, intentional. The purchaser wishes for something through making the purchase. This is the educational *aim* to which the purchaser aspires.[6] The educational aim needs to be realised through appropriate resources, a curriculum (the prescribed content to yield the aims) and pedagogy (the teaching and learning methods through which the aims are to be realised). Success in the educational process can then usually be realised through some form of *assessment*.

It follows that, to understand the purchasing behaviour of actors in an educational market, we need to understand what their aims are in purchasing educational processes and also whether they are capable of making purchases that are *informed* as well as *considered*. By an informed purchase is meant one that is made according to an accurate assessment of the quality of what is to be purchased.[7] The quality, it must be remembered, depends on the aims, including the educational aims, of the purchaser.[8] This is a major preoccupation of this volume and the evidence collected sheds significant light on the rationale behind educational purchasing decisions in the area under study.

Process versus product

We have noted the binary nature of education as process and product. So, which is being purchased, process or product? This question is not so easy to answer as it might at first sight appear. The most obvious answer is that a purchaser (typically a parent or relative) purchases the opportunity for a child to take part in an educational process (schooling or tutoring) in order to realise an educational outcome (literacy, numeracy, etc. or access to a high-prestige institute of technology). How, then, does one assess the quality of what is to be purchased? One would assume that a rational buyer seeking to make an informed purchase would (a) assess the quality of the educational outcomes achieved in the past; (b) assess the means currently available in the school to realise such outcomes in the future and (c) assess the suitability of the user (the child) for the institution under consideration.

But it has to be noted that making an informed purchase using these criteria is far from straightforward. First, one has to assess whether the outcomes achieved in the past are really as impressive or as bad as they at first seem. This may well require specialist knowledge of what expectations are reasonable within a given school population and catchment area or an ability to assess the value added by a school. Second, one has to assess the suitability of the current resources available for realising good outcomes in the future. Once again, specialist knowledge is required to make an informed decision on this matter. Finally, one has to make an assessment of the extent to which this particular child is fitted to this particular school, taking into account the financial resources available to the purchaser. It is hardly surprising, therefore, that purchasers may use proxy criteria for making such complex purchasing decisions, and evidence presented in this book gives us some idea of what these might be.[9] Finally, we have to take account of the fact that the purchasing decision may be made partially on the basis of non-educational criteria, for example, the amount of social prestige that is thought to accrue to the purchasers by buying a private education for their child. This brings us straight to another important issue for educational markets, the purchaser–user dichotomy.

The purchaser–user split

The child does not purchase education, even though he or she is usually the primary beneficiary. This is not merely because the child does not command the financial resources necessary, but also because until a certain level of maturity is reached, it is not considered appropriate for a child to make such a decision because of limited knowledge, rationality and experience. Classical liberalism has long recognised this issue[10] and has affirmed the role of parents in making decisions in the interests of their children. We have already noted one of the problems that parents may have in making such choices in the market, namely, a form of information asymmetry where proxy indicators have to serve for the quality of the education offered. But there is another issue, related to but distinct from the *competence* of parents to make educational purchasing decisions. This is the issue of *motivation*. Hume, as already noted, drew attention to the human tendency to work to relatively short time horizons and, as a consequence, to discount in value benefits and disbenefits that are temporally far removed from the present when making decisions. Briefly, the benefits to a child of education (and also possibly to the parent) of an educational process are temporally distant, and educational expenditure, in terms of its opportunity cost, may appear like an unfavourable expense relative to one that brings an immediate benefit. Locke, Smith and Mill recognised this problem and proposed sanctions to avoid it: Locke that parental rights to order their children's affairs are not unconditional; Mill, to fine parents for neglect of their children's education; Smith to prevent entry into sections of the labour market if a certain educational level was not reached.

Interestingly enough, although the problem undoubtedly exists in cases where children are not given a schooling in order that they can earn money for the family immediately, there is plenty of evidence in this study that parents are prepared to make great sacrifices to pay for the education of their children, including and perhaps especially, parents earning low incomes. However, we cannot exclude the possibility that some parents see a short-term non-educational benefit arising from the purchase of education for their child, namely, the social cachet that goes together with the perception that one is educating one's children privately. This point needs to be borne in mind when we consider the operation of an educational market as in the study described here. Naturally, one would need good evidence that this was the case, which may be difficult but important to gather. We should bear in mind this feature of educational markets which may mean that their behaviour is different from that of markets where the purchaser and the beneficiary are (a) the same and (b) the benefit is always immediate or nearly immediate.

We should note one final issue relating to the purchaser–beneficiary split. Education is not a commodity in one very important sense. Education *as an outcome* cannot be *conferred* on a putative beneficiary, the intended beneficiary himself or herself has to make an effort to become educated. This is an important reason why it is dangerous to conceptualise the process side of education (e.g. schooling or tutoring) just as the provision of an educational *opportunity*. Arguably, it is also in the nature of an educational *request*. A parent who is told that their poorly performing child had been offered educational opportunities by the school but has declined to take them up would probably be unhappy, even if they believed that such opportunities had been offered. They would expect the school to recognise a *duty of care* such that the request that they make to the school that the child be educated is heeded and responded to, by the school requesting of the child that he participate in attempts to make him learn.[11] It is clear that this duty of care is usually recognised within the commercial market of educational provision and that it is reflected in the aims of the school.

Price and quality differentiation within an educational market

The third issue concerning real educational markets, which is of the utmost importance in understanding what is offered and provided, is that different prices determine different forms of education.[12] As a general rule, parents believe and are encouraged to believe that the higher the school fee, the higher the quality of the education bought (both in process and outcome sense). The fee buys a certain level of resource in terms of teacher quality, curriculum, environment and positional status. The higher the fee, the higher the expectation that these resources will be relatively better than those provided by lower-fee institutions.

In one sense, price differentiation leads to palpable differences in resource provision between different private schools. One may expect, therefore, as a default, that these differences in resource provision lead to direct differences in educational outcomes.[13] There is no unambiguous evidence to support this view. What about the interaction of the educational market with government-supplied schooling, which is free at the point of access? The cases of the cities of Hyderabad and Delhi (discussed in Chapters 7 and 8 of this book) are not unique, but the studies give an insight into the interplay of market forces in a multitiered educational market which at the same time interacts with government schooling and exists within the regulatory and legislative framework of the Indian Constitution and educational legislation. Given that so many in Hyderabad, Delhi and other parts of India are prepared to commit a large proportion of their household income to private education, economic rationality would suggest that the positive signals for the superiority of private (including LFP) education would be overwhelming. Even if the outcomes are more difficult to assess, at least the process variables should be palpably superior even for the relatively undiscerning purchaser. The studies in this volume do not, however, suggest that this is the case. Earlier work by, for example, Tooley et al. op. cit. in Hyderabad suggests that this is indeed the case, but this view is not corroborated in this study. One interesting feature of our findings is that government schools all have recreational space, while this was notably absent even in some high-fee private schools. One can assume that opportunities for physical exercise are not high priorities for either parents or the schools. This raises the issue of whose aims should have effect within a hybrid education system such as the Indian one and whether parents necessarily always have a good understanding of the long-term interests of their children.

When one comes to consider educational outcomes, no clear picture emerges. Data produced by Tooley et al. (2010) suggest a small advantage in some outcomes for LFP schools in Hyderabad. However, another study by Chudgar and Quin (2012) suggests otherwise, as does previously unpublished work funded by the World Bank. We can be reasonably sure, however, that the overwhelming majority of parents who purchase private education for their children will not have access to reliable information concerning relative outcomes, let alone information that would allow them to judge whether the value they were obtaining from private education was cost-effective expenditure when considered from an economic point of view. This has important consequences for the way in which we consider the actions of agents in an educational market.

Two issues are important. The first we have already mentioned, namely, the information asymmetries that exist between sellers and most buyers in educational markets, usually in favour of the former. To a large extent, this asymmetry grows stronger the less the social and cultural capital of the buyer. The second issue, however, brings us much nearer to the concerns of the next section, namely, the role of buyers in the market. There are two sub-issues in play in relation to the first issue: first, the purchaser–beneficiary split already referred to; second, the public goods element of what is purchased as a private good. Let us take the first issue. The buyer considers that he or she has good reason to purchase an education for his or her child. By definition it is a good reason *for the buyer*. This does not mean, although it may, that it is an act of self-love,[14] it may also be a self-interested decision in the sense that the buyer includes the welfare of the children within the definition of his or her self-interest.[15] However, the purchasing decision will be based on what he or she considers to be a good education, and he or she may not be a good judge of what is best in the long-term interests of his or her child (or children, since parents may decide to treat different children differently in regard to educational purchasing decisions).

The second issue concerns the fact that an educational purchase by a private citizen necessarily has an effect on other people in the society. This may be because education (in both the process and the outcome sense) can be a positional good. But it may also be because it is potentially a public good (or a public bad) which affects the interests of everyone else within the society.

The second point brings us straight to the issue of the second section.

Educational goods, the market, the state and regulation

In the previous section, we looked at the way in which economists tend to distinguish between public and private goods and noted that there is not a hard and fast distinction between the two and that, for example, educational goods in both process and outcome senses are hybrids with both private and public elements to them. A general point about public goods, though, is important. Without denying that non-excludability and non-rivalrousness are important attributes, to see them purely in this sense is to miss an important point about public goods – namely, that they are goods (rather than bads) which affect the collective (rather than just the individual). This suggests that we should conceive of a 'public interest' which is something more than the sum of all individual interests, but rather concerns the conditions that need to obtain within a polity for everyone to lead a worthwhile (or, if you prefer, a flourishing) life. The polity as a whole, thus, has a common interest in producing and preserving such goods, even if the short-term and even the long-term interests of some individuals may not be best preserved through maintaining them.[16]

This gives the state, in Hume's sense of a body whose short-term interest is the long-term interest of the population, a responsibility for such goods. The state may choose to provide them directly through government schooling, through intermediaries like the provision of grants to private entities or through the regulation of private providers of the service. It may choose to do all three, and the third form of intervention is the minimum needed if one chooses to have a substantial private sector operating as a market with some attempt made to protect the public interest.

The state as provider

In this case, the state provides the resources for educational provision with certain aims in mind. These aims may be stated explicitly (as some of them are in the RtE, see Chapter III of the Act) or may be inferred from the legal framework within which education is conducted (see the contribution by Mehendale in the current volume). They are taken to express the values that inform and underpin the society. Consequent on this, the state undertakes to provide a curriculum, suggest pedagogical methods (see the emphasis on child-centredness in various government documents) and even assessment (see the emphasis on continuous comprehensive evaluation – CCE). It is important that these decisions are reversible, particularly as they may be made by politicians whose knowledge of educational matters is limited and may also be made with short-term interests in mind.[17]

The situation is not that different when the state appoints or allows a proxy to provide education which it is funding or cedes space for other actors to provide it. The proxy may well be allowed to do certain things which the government[18] does not consider to be its business such as the provision of religious education, but, in other respects, the proxy is accountable for the provision just as the government school is.

The state as regulator

In a system with such a large non-governmental sector as exists in India, the role of government in regulating education provision that lies beyond its immediate day-to-day control is very important. To obtain legal status, schools must be recognised by the government and to do this, they need to satisfy minimum criteria across a range of indicators including physical provision, curriculum, staffing and other matters. These criteria are stated both within the RtE and also in specific state legislation. The government of India has also, through the Right to Education Act (RtE) of 2009, set out a preferred pedagogical approach, which supplements the indicative curriculum that has already existed for some time. In addition, there are regulations concerning the proportion of children from scheduled categories that must be admitted to privately run schools and there is a ban on for-profit education.

A state which has ambitions to regulate education across the government-aided and private sectors has a large job to do. It has undertaken this task because it recognises what we have called the public good nature of education and knows that in order to secure desirable public goods such as some equality in educational provision, elimination of discrimination, access and to ensure the rights of children to a good and safe education, some rules have to be set to make this happen.

As will become apparent in the discussion of the locations which the authors of this book describe, however, the ability of the state to enforce such regulations is limited. India is still characterised by for-profit education, often in an unregulated sector, although legally schools cannot earn profits and all excess income has to be reinvested in the education enterprise.[19] Even regulated schools do not always appear to conform to the regulations that allow them to be recognised. Such practices show the limitations of state power in India and the abilities of sectional and commercial interests to act in ways which, although technically illegal, are widely recognised as common and condoned practice. This makes the provision of education as a public good problematic as there is little evidence that the public good elements of education can be guaranteed solely through the operation of unrestrained market forces. And, if this is so, then the ability of the state to secure the goods of education, both private and public, is compromised to the extent that regulations developed to ensure that these goods are provided are ignored in practice.

Without claiming that so-called modern states in developed societies like Europe and North America are free from corruption and clientelism (and they clearly are not), it does seem that India faces particular problems in creating a modern education system according to its stated ideals arising from a relatively weak state which is unable to assert its authority against often powerful local interests.

A very good example of the problems in securing some of the basics of educational resourcing is the provision of recreational space and provision for exercise for children. Children who fail to get enough space to work in comfort, to have opportunities for informal exercise or who do not have the opportunity to play games and engage in other forms of physical recreation will have their current and future health compromised. Thus, not only is one of the process desiderata of education ignored, but one of the important private goods, the ability to lead a healthy life, is also compromised. A healthy population that does not make excessive demands on healthcare is also self-evidently a public good from which all in the society benefit. Government school building is governed by regulations that lay down the size of mandatory play areas for children. It is evident from the study described in Chapter 7 of this book that even minimal opportunities for exercise and physical recreation are not provided in many privately run schools and not just in the LFP sector, even though the provision of such spaces is a legal requirement under the RtE. It should be noted that many parents, including many who are relatively wealthy and well-educated, send their children to such schools, raising the question as to whether parents are always and only the most competent individuals to determine what a good education for their children should consist in.

Conclusion

To conclude, the Indian education system is illustrative of the operation of a mixed educational system which includes a very significant private sector that operates in a genuine educational market where price is a significant factor in determining quality. Although formally regulated, this sector appears often to act as if at least some regulations do not apply to it. This makes it unlike many other markets, even lightly regulated ones, where the regulations are observed.[20] This chapter has also drawn attention to some particular features of educational markets, which must be taken into account to understand those markets. These are:

1   Education has to be seen as outcome as well as process.
2   Education as both outcome and process has significant private, positional and public good elements.
3   Ideas of what constitutes a 'good' education (in both senses) are contested by different parties: government, schools and parents. There is little consensus within society on this issue.
4   There is a purchaser–beneficiary split so that those who pay for education have interests which may or may not be aligned with those of the educatee whose education they are financing.
5   There are strong informational asymmetries between purchase and provider in educational markets and these asymmetries depend to a considerable degree on the social and cultural capital of the purchasers.

All these factors make the understanding of a complex mixed system of education such as is to be found in contemporary India a highly challenging matter.

Notes

1. 'Educational goods' refers *both* to educational processes (e.g. schooling) and outcomes (e.g. educated people). As we shall see, there is also an ambiguity in the concept of an educational outcome.
2. It is important not to lose sight of the fact that government-provided education can also have strong positional effects.
3. An important and obvious reservation is that schools and classes contain students with variable amounts of the cultural and social capital necessary to benefit from educational processes.
4. It is important not to forget that some private education is funded by external agencies like the World Bank who provide funding for the purchase of, for example, educational vouchers as was relatively recently the case in Andhra Pradesh.
5. In what follows, we assume that education is not an 'impulse buy', considering its importance and the significant amount of private family resources that are devoted to it. A 'considered purchase' is not, however, necessarily an 'informed purchase'. See below.
6. The aim, in turn, is underpinned by *values*, which are ethical commitments non-negotiable for the purchaser. These, in turn, are underpinned by empirical or metaphysical beliefs about reality, for example, through religious beliefs or commitment to a class or caste system. Educational aims, by prioritising certain values at the same time, have the tendency to exclude aims which express other values; a point to which we will return.
7. This in turn assumes the availability of accurate and accessible information on potential purchases, something that cannot be taken for granted.
8. This odd formulation is preferred because we cannot assume that all educational purchases are made for solely educational reasons – a point to which we will return.
9. See also Tooley, Dixon, and Gomathi (2007).
10. See Locke [1690] (1924), Ch. 7, on the duties of parents; Smith (1981: V2, Bk V, pp. 785–786) and Mill [1859] (1974: p. 160) on the same.
11. Obviously there have to be ethical limits as to what measures a school can take to ensure that its request is heeded, but unless one assumes that children always and everywhere have an intrinsic motivation to learn what the school thinks is suitable for them to learn, the need to press that request will be potentially present.
12. Whether this means *different quality education* in either process or outcome sense cannot be automatically assumed. We can, however, assume that most parents take this to be the case.
13. And we need to bear in mind the continuing social and cultural capital effects which are the consequences of the 'club good' element of private education. Almost invariably children are taught together in a class and, in the case of LFP schools, in very large classes. However, the evidence

of these different outcomes, at least within some price bands of private schooling, is not so clear (Chudgar and Quin, 2012).
14 That is, the buyer considers the purchase of education for his or her child as primarily a benefit to him or her, for example, an accrual of social prestige.
15 Notoriously, Adam Smith elided the distinction between self-interest and self-love and provoked much subsequent confusion, cf. Smith [1776] (1981: Bk 1, pp. 26–27).
16 We can justify this through the invocation of something like Rousseau's idea of a 'general will'. All members of the polity benefit from being members of some polity rather than none. In doing so, they agree to abide by majority decisions and are accountable for complying with such decisions. We do not need to invoke the notion of a social contract (as Rousseau does) to secure the idea of a democratic binding will, see Rousseau [1762]. The notorious passage about 'forcing people to be free' can be seen as the idea of holding individuals to agreements for the common good freely entered into. See Rousseau [1762a] (1913: 15).
17 Despite Hume's view of the role of politicians, they do, particularly under short-term electoral pressures, make decisions without sufficient regard to their long-term consequences.
18 The state is the entity which sustains the political order of the society; the government is the current administrator of the business of the state. The government is directly responsible for education within the parameters set by the state.
19 It is also possible to circumvent restrictions on profit-making by splitting educational enterprises into sub-entities which can sell services to the explicitly educational component (i.e. the school) and thus make a profit for the enterprise as a whole.
20 We should note, however, that such regulations can often be 'gamed'. This is also true of various kinds of incentivisation structures that governments sometimes put in place to regulate the behaviour of schools, both in the private and the public sectors. England would be a good example of this.

References

Chudgar, A. and Quin, E. (2012). 'Relationship Between Private Schooling and Achievement: Results from Rural and Urban India', *Economics of Education Review*, 31: 376–390.

Hume, David. (1978). *A Treatise of Human Nature*. Oxford: Clarendon Press, first published 1739–1740.

Locke, J. (1924). *Second Treatise of Government*. London: Everyman, first published 1690.

Mill, John Stuart. (1974). *On Liberty*. London: Dent, first published 1859.

O'Neill, J. (1999). *The Market: Ethics, Knowledge and Politics*. London: Routledge.

Rousseau, J. J. (1913). *The Social Contract*. London: Dent, first published 1762.

Smith, A. (1981). *The Wealth of Nations*. Indianapolis: Liberty Fund, first published 1776.

Tooley, J. (1998). 'The "Neoliberal" Critique of State Intervention in Education: Reply to Winch', *Journal of Philosophy of Education*, 32(2): 267–281.

Tooley, J., Dixon, P., and Gomathi, S. V. (2007). 'Private Schools and the Millennium Development Goal of Universal Primary Education: A Census and Comparative Survey in Hyderabad, India', *Oxford Review of Education*, 33(5): 539–560.

Tooley, J., Dixon, P., Shamsan, Y., and Schagen, I. (2010). 'The Relative Quality and Cost-Effectiveness of Private and Public Schools for Low-Income Families: A Case Study in a Developing Country', *School Effectiveness and School Improvement*, 21(2): 117–144.

Varian, H. R. (2006). *Intermediate Microeconomics* (7th ed.). New York, London: Norton.

Wilkinson, R. (2005). *The Impact of Inequality: How to Make Sick Societies Healthier*. New York: The New Press, Routledge.

Wilkinson, R. and K. Pickett. (2009). *The Spirit Level*. London: Penguin.

3 Normative articulations of the aims of education
An exploratory analysis

Archana Mehendale

Background

The establishment of public education systems and the motivations for state investment in education has been a subject of scholarly interest for some time. In Western countries, the state-initiated free and compulsory education in the nineteenth century played an important role in the spread of mass education. In Europe and in the United States, this growth has been linked with the state–church alignment (Soysal and Strang, 1989), the onset of the Industrial Revolution (Weiner, 1991; Nardinelli, 1980), the need for having skills to read religious texts and law (Jernegan, 1919), the processes of state formation, which required an efficient working force as well as citizenry devoted to a certain culture and ideology of nationhood (Green, 1997; Curtis, 1983) and the assimilation and acculturation of immigrants (Liggio and Peden, 1978; Green, 1997). In non-Western countries, codification of free and compulsory education legislation has been linked to the state's urgency to curtail the rate of street crime and nuisance and for bringing in social reform of the poor communities (Sirisena, 1967). In the Indian context, there were demands for colonial education by the masses and calls for state support to education by the local elite. While the nationalist elite also looked at mass education as a pedagogic device to transform the citizens to meet the cultural demands of citizenship of the impending national state (Srivastava, 1998), there were significant differences and debates about the character of such education (Bhattacharya, 2003). Basu (1982) discusses the motivation of colonial governments in supporting education for the preservation, strengthening and consolidation of colonial interests. On the other hand, the opening of schools by caste and religious communities and philanthropists in colonial India can be viewed as the 'publicness' of private initiatives, as discussed by Jain in this volume.

The justification for state intervention in school education has also been examined on economic grounds with the human capital theory (Schultz, 1960; Becker, 1993) and on social and political grounds (see Sen, 1999; McMahon, 1999). Notwithstanding the various reasons that have justified state intervention in public education at different points of time, public school systems were established to serve public goals and to meet a set of objectives that served collective interests. The articulation and official expression of these goals along with the justification of their publicness is a matter that deserves further study along with an empirical verification of what constitutes public goals or aims of education.

Systems of public education were supported by legislative frameworks that differed significantly in the way they expressed directions or aims of education meant to be achieved through compulsory education. Kleinberger (1975) shows how governments can be located anywhere between 'totalitarian' and 'liberal', not in the sense of the political system they followed, but the extent to which they were rigid about specifying the aims of education that should be served through free and compulsory schooling. In totalitarian systems, all children had the duty to receive education of a particular kind, with its aims and content specified in law. Such systems, as Kleinberger points out, were 'designed to achieve uniform and binding aims of education' (p. 221) and as in the case of erstwhile Yugoslavia, every school was to be organised such that the entire internal life and processes contributed to the realisation of aims of education. On the other hand, approximations to the liberal system were found in England and France, where the parents had the discretion to choose the kind of education that their child should undergo and where it should be offered, including public schools, private schools and home-schooling. In other words, while governments imposed compulsory education, it was not necessarily accompanied with an articulation or a prescription about the aims of education that this was meant to serve.

In contemporary times, with the nature of public school systems in countries such as India experiencing a change due to the changing role of the state and an increasing expansion of private schools, it is useful to explore the aims of education as they are being articulated at the normative level, especially in policy and legislation. Such an inquiry will help us to understand the nature of such articulations and reflect on what is proclaimed as an aim and why, and the purpose it serves in the organisation of the curriculum and pedagogical methods. It is also important to understand whether the policy framework differentiates between the public and private providers of schooling in terms of their roles or capacities to fulfil the public aims of education.

This is an exploratory study of the normative articulations of aims of education expressed in policy documents and legislation at international, national and sub-national levels, with reference to the context of the Indian school education system. The key questions that this review seeks to answer are as follows: what are the officially recognised aims of education and how are they expressed in policy documents? Who is considered to be the subject of these aims – the individual child, families, the community or the government? Who is expected to ensure that the aims of education are fulfilled – government, private entities or the community, and what are the methods or means envisioned to enable the fulfilment of the aims of education?

Normative framework on aims of education

Aims of education, although articulated at a normative level, are essentially meant to be fulfilled through formal educational institutions, often leaving out the non-formal educational opportunities as well as informal educational and socialisation processes. Thus, a school is seen as the primary institution for realising the public aims of education and it effectively becomes a space where aims are interpreted, co-created and mediated through curricular activities, pedagogical methods and social interactions. Literature does not inform us about the possible distinctions between the aims of education and aims of schooling, thereby entrusting schools with the responsibility of serving the public aims of education. In addition to the public aims, schools may be expected to serve the private aims of education as upheld by the school management or the community it caters to (see Chapters 7 and 8 for a discussion on how private schools serve the private aims of education).

Normative frameworks on education as applicable to schools in India have been prescribed at international, national and sub-national levels. These frameworks have also evolved over decades and have drawn from multiple sources. This section reviews the content of these frameworks insofar as what they prescribe as the aims and methods of education, the subject of these aims and the kind of values they seek to further. The review also seeks to understand if there is any period suggested within which the aims are meant to be realised. Table 3.1 lists the various texts that explicate the aims of education. While this is not an exhaustive list, it includes key documents that are considered as significant policy measures in the present times. By taking two

Table 3.1 Normative frameworks on aims of education examined

International	National	Sub-national (two examples)
Universal Declaration on Human Rights, 1948	National Policy on Education, 1968	Karnataka State Curricular Framework
International Covenant on Economic, Social and Cultural Rights, 1966	National Policy on Education, 1986 and revised policy formulation in 1992	Punjab State Curricular Framework
United Nations Convention on Rights of the Child, 1989	National Curricular Framework, 2005	
UNESCO Reports on 'Learning to Be' (Faure report) and 'Learning: A Treasure Within' (Delors report)	The Right of Children to Free and Compulsory Education Act, 2009	
World Declaration on Education for All, 1990 (Jomtien Declaration)	*Some Inputs for the Draft Policy on National Education Policy, 2016**	
Dakar Framework of Action on Education, 2000		
Sustainable Development Goals, 2015		

Source: Author's own research

* This is not a policy document but lays down the broad framework that would guide the preparation of India's new education policy.

examples of sub-national texts, the analysis allows us to identify how state specificities are playing out in relation to the national and international frameworks.

At the international level

The normative frameworks formulated at the international level by the United Nations consist of a 'soft law', comprising political compacts and declarations that are non-binding, and a 'hard law', comprising treaties, conventions and covenants that are binding on the governments ratifying them. India has been a signatory to and has ratified all the soft laws and hard laws related to education. In addition to this international law, there are important reports and recommendations made by international committees that suggest broad policy directions. These reports often feed into the formulation of international law and practice.

If we look at the hard law, we find that the aims of education have not been extensively laid out in most of the treaties except in the UN Convention on Rights of the Child (UNCRC) (UN General Assembly, 1989), which stipulates the aims of education. These are drawn from and build upon the principles and values that are upheld by the United Nations Charter. The aims of education as enunciated in the UNCRC are (a) the development of the child's personality, talents and mental and physical abilities to their fullest potential; (b) the development of respect for human rights and fundamental freedoms, and for the principles enshrined in the Charter of the United Nations; (c) the development of respect for the child's parents, his or her cultural identity, language and values, the national values of the country in which the child is living, the country from which he or she may originate and for civilisations different from his or her own; (d) the preparation of the child for responsible life in a free society, in the spirit of understanding, peace, tolerance, equality of sexes and friendship among all peoples, ethnic, national and religious groups and persons of indigenous origin; and (e) the development of respect for the natural environment.

This has been supported by the General Comment 1 of the UN Committee on Rights of the Child (hereafter General Comment), which specifically deliberated on the aims of education and recommended:

> the overall objective of education is to maximize the child's ability and opportunity to participate fully and responsibly in a free society. It should be emphasized that the type of teaching that is focused primarily on accumulation of knowledge, prompting competition and leading to an excessive burden of work on children, may seriously hamper the harmonious development of the child to the fullest potential of his or her abilities and talents. Education should be child-friendly, inspiring and motivating the individual child. Schools should foster a humane atmosphere and allow children to develop according to their evolving capacities.
>
> (para 12)

Thus, we find that the UNCRC as well as the General Comment prescribe the aims of education that uphold universal values and aid in the individual development of the child. On the other hand, the 'hard law' related to education, which includes the International Covenant on Economic, Social and Cultural Rights (ICESCR) (UN General Assembly, 1966), does not expressly provide for aims of education but upholds state obligation to provide free and compulsory education, parental choice and liberty rights of educational institutions. However, General Comment 13 of the Committee on Economic, Social and Cultural Rights (CESCR, 1999) begins by taking an instrumental view of education that is meant to fulfil aims at the societal level, including empowering children, marginalised persons and women, safeguarding children from exploitative and hazardous labour and sexual exploitation, promoting human rights and democracy, protecting the environment and controlling population growth. It also recognises education as one of the best financial investments that states can make because its importance is not just practical, because 'a well-educated, enlightened and active mind, able to wander freely and widely, is one of the joys and rewards of human existence' (para 1). Further, it declares that 'education is both a human right in itself and an indispensable means of realizing other human rights' (para 1).

The Universal Declaration of Human Rights (UDHR) (UN General Assembly, 1948) has been the primary benchmark for human rights standards, although it is not a binding document. The UDHR clearly specifies that

> education shall be directed to the full development of the human personality and to the strengthening of respect for human rights and fundamental freedoms. It shall promote understanding, tolerance and friendship among all nations, racial or religious groups, and shall further the activities of the United Nations for the maintenance of peace
>
> (Article 26(2))

thereby upholding the universal values of the United Nations.

The World Declaration on Education for All (Jomtien Declaration), (UNESCO, 1990), has been a milestone in consolidating international commitment for universal education. The aims of education are laid out for both the individual and the global community. For an individual, the purpose of education is to gather

> both essential learning tools (such as literacy, oral expression, numeracy, and problem solving) and the basic learning content (such as knowledge, skills, values, and attitudes) required by human beings to be able to survive, to develop their full capacities, to live and work in dignity, to participate fully in development, to

improve the quality of their lives, to make informed decisions, and to continue learning.

(Article 1.1)

However, the larger aims of education are articulated as addressing the global problems of 'debt burdens, the threat of economic stagnation and decline, rapid population growth, widening economic disparities among and within nations, war, occupation, civil strife, violent crime, the preventable deaths of millions of children and widespread environmental degradation' (Preamble). The goals of education are meant to 'help ensure a safer, healthier, more prosperous and environmentally sound world, while simultaneously contributing to social, economic, and cultural progress, tolerance, and international co-operation' (Preamble). The Declaration acknowledges education as a necessary but not a sufficient condition for personal and social improvement of individuals. It recognises the role of sound basic education as being fundamental to the strengthening of higher levels of education, and building scientific and technological literacy and capacity and therefore essential in order to achieve self-reliance and development. Keeping with the charter to uphold universal values, the Declaration recognises that 'another and no less fundamental aim of educational development is the transmission and enrichment of common cultural and moral values' (Article 1.3). The Declaration also suggests the means to reach these educational goals, which include focusing on 'actual learning acquisition and outcome, rather than exclusively upon enrolment' (Article 4), and 'mobilising existing and new financial and human resources public, private and voluntary' (Article 9.1).

The Dakar Framework of Action (UNESCO, 2000) reiterated the Jomtien Declaration of 1990 and held that the human right to education is meant to meet

> basic learning needs in the best and fullest sense of the term, an education that includes learning to know, to do, to live together and to be. It is an education geared to tapping each individual's talents and potential, and developing learners' personalities, so that they can improve their lives and transform their societies.
>
> (para 3)

Furthermore, education programmes

> should promote understanding, tolerance and friendship among all nations, and all ethnic and religious groups; and they should

be sensitive to cultural and linguistic identities, and respectful of diversity and reinforce a culture of peace. Education should promote not only skills such as the prevention and peaceful resolution of conflict, but also social and ethical values.

(para 58)

While these aims of education are directed at an individual level, the framework clearly emanated from an instrumental view of education. There was a recognition that without 'education for all, national and internationally agreed targets for poverty reduction will be missed, and inequalities between countries and within societies will widen' (para 5). Education was seen to be the key to sustainable development and peace and stability within and among countries, and a means to facilitate the inclusion of societies and economies in the process of globalisation. Despite the prevailing rhetoric, the Dakar framework provided for minimalist goals limited to reaching measurable learning outcomes for all, especially in literacy, numeracy and essential life skills. In addition, the more recent Sustainable Development Goals (2015) articulate the target of ensuring that 'all girls and boys complete free, equitable and quality primary and secondary education *leading to relevant and effective learning outcomes*' (emphasis added) by 2030. Further, the instrumental view of education wherein 'all learners acquire the knowledge and skills needed to promote sustainable development, including, among others, through education for sustainable development and sustainable lifestyles, human rights, gender equality, promotion of a culture of peace and non-violence, global citizenship and appreciation of cultural diversity and of culture's contribution to sustainable development' is evident in the goals (Target 4.7 of SDGs).

Besides the target-driven political compacts, the UNESCO reports on Learning to Be (Faure et al., 1972), popularly called the Faure report, and Learning: A Treasure Within (International Commission on Education for the Twenty-first Century, Delors, J., and Unesco, 1996), popularly called the Delors report, are key documents that throw light on the aims of education and how it would be achieved. The Faure report was written by the International Commission on the Development of Education, which was set up in the midst of student turmoil and developing countries falling into the trap of emulating their colonisers. As per its Terms of Reference, it sought to define 'the new aims to be assigned to education as a result of the rapid changes in knowledge and in societies, the demands of development, the aspirations of the individual, and the overriding need for international understanding and peace' (p. 269) and to put forward 'suggestions regarding the intellectual, human and financial means needed to attain the objectives set' (p. 269). It supported the idea of education that helps promote both democracy and the use of science and technology. At a philosophical level, it stated that the aim of education is to enable man to be himself and to 'become himself' (p. xxxi). At the individual level the development of affective qualities, and the physical, intellectual, emotional and ethical integration of the individual into a complete man was considered to be the aim of education. The report talked about the political and civic aims that are essential in any democratically oriented society. At a systemic level, education was meant to contribute to bringing about the objective conditions of its own transformation and progress. Further, the Faure report commented on the close links between social objectives and the aims assigned to education. It highlighted two key questions: what is the substance of the aims, beyond the language in which these are formulated; and who defined these? It clarified that aims must necessarily be both specific and general and be dictated by history, traditions and customs, by social patterns, economic and political systems and circumstances, and arise out of specific situations. The report said that the choice of aims should be based on a broad consensus, without leaving it entirely to either the politicians' discretionary desires or scientists' knowledge but involving active participation of the learners, parents and communities.

Twenty-five years after the Faure report, the Delors report called education the necessary utopia, an indispensable asset to help attain the ideals of peace, freedom and social justice. The report reiterated the instrumental goals of education to lead to personal and social development, to foster a deeper and more harmonious form of human development and thereby to reduce poverty, exclusion, ignorance, oppression and war. It highlighted seven tensions in contemporary times, namely, those arising between the global and local, universal and individual, traditional and modernity, long term and short term, need for competition and concern for equality of opportunity, expansion of knowledge and capacity to assimilate, and lastly, spiritual and material. It thus suggested a four-pillar approach of learning – to know, to do, to be and to live together. It recognised education as a public good that should be available to all through combined public and private funding, according to different formulae that consider each country's traditions, stage of development, ways of life and income distribution. Further, it suggested that the improvement of education was a responsibility of policy makers, who should not leave it to market forces or some kind of self-regulation to correct things when they go wrong. Thus, it stressed on a strong role for the public authorities to propose clear policy choices, regardless of whether the education system is public, private or mixed, and establish the system's foundations by regulating the system through the necessary adjustments. In other words, the Delors report clearly expressed the role of the state in laying down the overall aims of education that would apply to all categories of education providers.

At the national level

The core normative framework on education at the national level consists of the National Policy on Education, 1986, with revised policy formulations of 1992 (NPE) (Ministry of Human Resources Development, Government of India, 1992), the Right of Children to Free and Compulsory Education Act, 2009 (RtE Act) (Ministry of Law and Justice, Government of India, 2009) and the National Curriculum Framework, 2005 (NCF) (National Council for Education Research and Training, Government of India, 2005). This section presents the aims of education as reflected in each of these texts.

Formulated and revised after considerable deliberations, the NPE reflects a role that the education system is expected to play and the aims it is expected to strive for. It recognises that the 'education system expresses the country's unique socio-cultural identity and is developed to meet the challenges of the time' (para 1.1), thus being a product of the time and aiming to meet contemporary requirements rather than being a futuristic document. It takes an instrumental view and looks at education as a means to growth and inclusion. It makes a strong commitment to human values and social justice. At an individual level, the NPE proposes that education is for all-round development, both material and spiritual. At a systemic level, it recognises that education should play an acculturating role and help in building national integration, scientific temper and independence of mind and spirit. It also considers the economic aims of education and states that education is to develop manpower that will ultimately guarantee national self-reliance and hence it is 'a unique investment in present and future' (para 2.4).

The aims of the education system, as NPE suggests, are to further the constitutional goals of secularism, socialism and democracy, build international co-operation and strive for peaceful coexistence through the promotion of equality and provision of equal opportunity to women, SC/ST and persons with disabilities. The NPE also attempts to balance the local and global by expecting education to bring 'fine synthesis between change-oriented technologies and continuity with

Normative articulations of aims of education

cultural tradition' (para 8.1). It declares that education should be made a 'forceful tool for cultivation of social and moral values' (para 8.4) and that it should foster universal and eternal values, oriented to the unity and integration of people while simultaneously helping to remove obscurantism, fanaticism, violence, superstitions and fatalism. Apart from the moral utility of the education system, the NPE also suggests that all children should be in schools and achieve essential levels of learning. However, it does not qualify what constitutes the essential levels of learning and if that would help prepare students to achieve the aims of education it outlines. In contrast, the National Policy on Education of 1968 (Department of Education, Government of India, 1968) specifically suggested that 'the education system must produce young men and women of character and ability committed to national service and development' (para 3) and that education will play a vital role in promoting national progress, common citizenship and culture, national integration and social cohesion. It had also stated that 'a radical reconstruction of education was required for the economic and cultural development of the country' (para 3). Such a strong vision of reconstruction is not evident in the 1992 policy. The proposal of the Ministry of Human Resources Development to revise the national education policy in India builds on the report prepared by the TSR Subramanian Committee (2015). The vision outlined in the inputs on draft National Policy on Education seeks to build a

> credible and high-performing education system capable of ensuring inclusive quality education and lifelong learning opportunities for all and producing students/graduates equipped with the knowledge, skills, attitudes and values that are required to lead a productive life, participate in the country's development process, respond to the requirements of the fast-changing, ever-globalising, knowledge-based economy and society.
> (Ministry of Human Resources Development, Government of India, 2016: 5)

Thus, the focus as well as aims of education are clearly tied to the preparation of citizens to meet new demands and contribute in the face of globalisation (Dewan and Mehendale, 2015).

As a legislation, the RtE Act is weak in expressly recognising aims of education – either at the systemic level or at an individual level. It is silent on what the state-guaranteed free and compulsory education is expected to yield and rightly so, because a legislation is binding and is meant to be precise, unlike a policy document where moral rhetoric and high abstraction are permissible. The values that schools are meant to work towards are provided under Chapter 5 of the RtE on curriculum and completion of elementary education, which states that the curriculum should adhere to the constitutional values and lead to all-round development of the child, building the child's knowledge, potentiality and talent and developing the child's physical and mental abilities to the fullest extent. However, the systemic goals of citizenship building or national integrity that are evident in the National Policy on Education 1992 are not reflected in the RtE Act.

The key text as far as articulation of aims of education is concerned is the NCF, 2005, which lays down a framework through which the curriculum should be structured to achieve the aims. While locating the education system in the context of globalisation, the NCF is cautious about the application of market-related concepts to schools and school quality which creates pressure to commodify schools. It also explains that

> the aims of education serve as broad guidelines to align educational processes to chosen ideals and accepted principles. The aims of education simultaneously reflect the current needs and aspirations of a society as well as its lasting values, and the immediate concerns of a community as well as broad human ideals. At any given time and place they can be called the contemporary and contextual articulations of broad and lasting human aspirations and values.
>
> (para 1.7, p. 10)

At a systemic level, the NCF stresses on the goal of inclusion of all children by 'reaffirming the value of each child and enabling all children to experience dignity and the confidence to learn' (p. 5). It declares building a culture of peace for revitalising the nation and for the enterprise of healing as an important aim of education. In addition, it proclaims education to be an instrument of social transformation and an egalitarian social order, a tool for strengthening our cultural heritage and national identity, creation of a citizenry conscious of their rights, duties and commitment to the constitutional principles, ensuring equality of outcome as well as building human capabilities so that education can empower marginalised learners to overcome disadvantages and enable them to develop their capabilities of becoming autonomous and equal citizens. The NCF elaborates that the purpose of education is to strengthen participatory democracy and the values enshrined in the Constitution. It further makes references to the larger goals of education being quality of schooling, social justice, peace, protection of the environment. It specifically refers to the commitment to 'democracy and the values of equality, justice, freedom, concern for others' well-being, secularism, and respect for human dignity and rights' (p. 10). In addition, the NCF says that 'education should aim towards building the ability to work and participate in economic processes and social change. This necessitates the integration of work with education' (p. 11).

At an individual level, the NCF stresses on the development of self-esteem and ethics, the need to cultivate children's creativity, respecting native wisdom and imagination, building on independence of thought, sensitivity to others' well-being and feelings, knowledge and understanding of the world, learning to learn and the willingness to unlearn and relearn.

The NCF acknowledges that the education system does not function in isolation from the society of which it is a part and therefore proposes the use of critical pedagogy in all dimensions of school education as well as in teacher education.

At the sub-national level

Specific articulations of aims of education at the sub-national level are not very common. As education is a concurrent subject, state governments have largely confined themselves to the nationally prescribed norms and attempted to modify or build on them rather than expressing specific state-oriented goals of education and means to attain them. The two state curricular frameworks that are reviewed are Punjab and Karnataka, both states having an increasing percentage of privatisation in school education. This exploratory exercise shows how the state curricular frameworks are located within the larger normative and policy frameworks on education, and yet how they bring in state-level specificities concerning what are considered to be the aims of education.

The Punjab Curriculum Framework 2013 (PCF) (State Council for Education Research and Training, Government of Punjab, 2013) identifies aims of education at the systemic level and at the individual level. At the systemic level, the aim is to 'bring each and every child in the formal education system to impart quality education irrespective of religion, caste, creed and gender' (p. iii). At an individual level, the PCF pinpoints specific values that the education system should produce:

> patriotic, secular, disciplined, kind hearted, intelligent, and economically independent citizens, who are physically strong,

mentally mature, morally superior and emotionally balanced, fearless, free from superstitions, able to preserve cultural legacy, keen observers with a critical perspective and love for aesthetics, multifaceted personalities with a belief in dignity of labour, and universal brotherhood.

(p. iii)

It further states that the education system should 'enable children to make sense of life and develop their potential to define and pursue a purpose and recognize the right of others to do the same' (p. 6) as well as help the development of self-esteem and ethics and cultivate children's creativity. In addition, the PCF recognises that education should enable the development of respect towards people regardless of their religious beliefs and the building of 'fundamental traits of character such as honesty, compassion, courage, persistence and responsibility' (pp. 10–11). It specifies that the means to fulfil these is through a value-based education. In fact, the PCF lays a strong emphasis on the development of values by stating that 'a person who is morally educated will be better equipped to move up in life and succeed more than a morally bankrupt person with excellent academic qualification. Character building, teaching values and ethics come in the formative years because a child is not born with this knowledge' (p. 11), implying that the essential function of the education system is to undertake the moral development project of children, as they are born without pre-existing moral bases. Apparently, it also places a higher premium on moral education than on acquisition of curricular competencies.

As far as other methods to achieve the aims are concerned, the PCF looks at primarily the curricular design as an important means to help reach the aims. It suggests that curriculum design must 'reflect the commitment of Universal Elementary Education (UEE), not only in representing cultural diversity, but also by ensuring that children from different social and economic backgrounds with variations in physical, psychological and intellectual characteristics are able to learn and achieve success in school' (p. 8). It urges adopting appropriate policies and schemes to address disadvantages in education due to gender, caste, language, culture, religion or disabilities.

The PCF embraces values including democracy and the constitutional values of equality of status and opportunity. However, while on the one hand, it states that 'education should function as an instrument of social transformation and an egalitarian social order' (p. 9), on the other hand, it also acknowledges that the 'continued exclusion of a vast number of children from education and the disparities caused through private and public school systems challenge the efforts towards achieving equality' (p. 9). Yet, it remains silent on the kind of transformation that may be required and the manner in which it would have to be undertaken to address the disparities caused by the nature of public and private provision.

The aims of education also reflect a need to ensure continued traditional legacy by including content about the rich cultural heritage and the glorious history of the state so that 'children feel proud and be motivated to preserve the cultural legacy' (p. 11).

Further, the PCF emphasises that the purpose of the education system is to undertake skill training from a very young age so that 'the youth has 2 or 3 skills of his interest in his hand and even earns when he leaves the school' (p. 17), and for this, it suggests programmes such as 'earning while learning' (p. 17) to be integrated in the school curriculum to ingrain the value of 'work is worship' (p. 17).

The ultimate vision of the education system, as the PCF indicates, is to realise the state's 'human resource potential to its fullest, with equity and excellence' (p. 22) and 'to inculcate values, skills and knowledge that help in the task of nation building as to create citizens with global outlook' (p. 22).

On the other hand, the Karnataka State Curriculum Framework 2007 (KCF) (Department of State Education Research and Training and Karnataka Textbook Society, 2007) aims to focus on curricular offerings that are meant not only for children who continue education beyond the elementary school but also for those who drop out after Grade 10. Thus, it states that the 'aim is to ensure that they have "employable avenues" from Grade 8 itself' (para 3.11). Specifically, it states that the aim of school education is to provide for core curricular areas of language, math, science, social sciences and physical education and co-curricular subjects for necessary life skills and creative abilities. In contrast with the PCF, which aimed at balancing nation building with the development of a global outlook, the KCF states that the purpose of learning should be culture sensitive and schooling should be based on culture of the community. The KCF emphasises the need to ensure that children are taught how to learn rather than what to learn. This resonates with the ideas presented in the Delors report (1996) on the nature of education required in this century. With regards to the methods of achieving these aims, the KCF states that the teachers will have to be prepared in critical pedagogy – to become facilitators rather than suppliers of knowledge – so as to provide opportunities to reflect on political, social, moral and economic aspects. The KCF is relatively bare in terms of proclaiming ideological values that the education system should aim to embrace as well as other means (besides teacher preparation) to achieve the aims.

Discussion

Educational systems are today being seen with great interest because their inter-connections with economic and political systems are well established. There is also a growing frustration that educational goals that have been proclaimed from time to time have not been met and the challenges remain daunting, especially in countries such as India. While the mechanical targets of ensuring universal provision of primary education or bringing gender parity in schools occupy the mindshare of most policy makers, the larger questions about what are the overall aims of education and what is the bigger picture that the education system is helping create are largely ignored in the everyday education activities. However, the importance of understanding the aims of education cannot be overstated because it is this vision that enables the creation of specific objectives, targets, institutions and curricula around which education is organised and delivered. This exploratory study attempted to consider the normative frameworks to understand the various strands that emerge in the discourse on aims of education. The key observations emerging from this synthesis are given below.

1 The manner in which aims of education are articulated show that they are categorised as individual and social aims as well as intrinsic and extrinsic aims. All the normative frameworks provide for all these categories of aims, although in varying degrees. For instance, 'hard law' at both the international and national levels is not as elaborate in specifying the aims compared to the 'soft law'. The extrinsic aims of education are recognised at the international, national and sub-national levels, but they are most heavily laid out at the international level, followed by the national level; and at the sub-national level, it is found that a greater emphasis of aims is on intrinsic benefits. For instance, the extrinsic and social aims of education that are elaborated in the Jomtien Declaration stress that the purpose of education is to counter the entire range of threats and risks posed due to unequal societies and globalisation, while the state curricular frameworks give greater attention to spelling out the individual aims of education.

2 The aims articulated in the normative frameworks are largely high on rhetoric and use clichés without relating these to the operation of the aims into regular practice. This reiterates Koos's view of

aims as 'bootless expressions' (Koos, 1924: 513). The values that have been recognised as worthy of our educational efforts can be largely called the 'universal' values because first, it is rather difficult to identify values that are not universal. Moreover, the normative frameworks are formalised after careful consensus building through a collective process, which may not allow for values that clash with or are different from the 'universal values' to find space. In fact, any policy, treaty or statute addresses the general and the universal values and rarely co-opts the culturally specific values of minorities. There is indeed a process of homogenisation and normalisation seen in the values taken up as aims of education. At the international level, values are derived primarily from the UN Charter and goals of international organisations and at the national level, values largely derived from the Constitution are reinforced.

3 The aims of education speak little about the achievement of curricular competencies. While the 'hard law' is silent about curriculum and gaining adequate mastery over even the foundational competencies such as literacy and numeracy, the 'soft law' provides for them minimally by indicating clearly the goals of achieving basic learning levels and competencies. This excessive emphasis on the 'social' aims in comparison to the 'curricular' aims of education at the normative level needs to be analysed against the empirical practices of schooling in both public and private institutions, which tend to give excessive attention to the achievement of curricular norms and requirements rather than preparing the students to fulfil the social objectives of education.

4 While the possibilities of conflicting aims of education cannot be ruled out, there is an absence of established standards by which conflicts could be resolved. These conflicts are evident in the aims recognised in the normative frameworks, both within and across each other, and there is no indication of any one aim being superior to another. This implies that aims of education provided in the normative frameworks may need to be either seen as a 'menu of options' or subject to the interpretation of the collective and a comprehensive sense that they are trying to convey.

5 The normative frameworks do not necessarily provide clarity on the means and methods of realising the aims. There is a lopsided focus on stating the aims without much outlining of the specific measures that can be undertaken to bring them into reality. This lack of prescription of means can be seen as providing flexibility for a range of possible working arrangements to be tried out for

reaching the aims. However, the lack of such clarity creates a gap and a challenge in implementation.

6   The aims of education also speak to the globalising societies that are increasingly seeing the proliferation of private and voluntary actors in the education ecosystem. The more recent frameworks recognise the role of these non-state actors in education processes, and hence by implication extend the obligation of fulfilling the aims to all educational programmes, irrespective of who is offering them. The frameworks assume that by being a part of the overall project, the non-state actors would have ideologies that match the proclaimed aims and bear the capacities and commitment to work towards their fulfilment. This throws open the questions on whether the public aims of education can be realised with the help of private and voluntary actors, and if so, what the status of public aims in the overall education project is.

7   The normative frameworks do not indicate if there are procedures for evaluating or reviewing whether the aims have been met or at the least how close the existing systems are towards realising these aims. Moreover, the manner in which the proclamations on aims are made indicates that these are like a one-way street – never to be retracted once passed, and the only movement is forward. Thus, the codifications show layers of values added at different points of time, thereby providing a mixture of older and newer aims of education. For instance, nation building and national integration have been our national normative ideals and these have only been supplemented by newer aims of producing human resources required for the changing economy.

Concluding remarks

This exploratory study has mapped the normative framework on aims of education and has analysed it using the available theoretical literature on the subject. This review has not been exhaustive, given that it does not deal with the various disciplinary orientations that have a bearing on studying the aims of education. Future research in this area could consider the applications of proclaimed aims to the curricular, pedagogical and education processes that are implemented through state and non-state actors. Such an inquiry will also help us to understand what is public about the public aims of education and how do different non-state actors working within the education space align with the aims and what is a way of knowing that these aims have been satisfactorily realised.

References

Basu, A. (1982). *Essays in the History of Indian Education.* New Delhi, India: Concept.

Becker, G. S. (1993). *Human Capital: A Theoretical and Empirical Analysis, with Special Reference to Education.* Chicago: University of Chicago Press.

Bhattacharya, S. (2003). 'Introduction', in S. Bhattacharya and C. R. Yagati (Eds.), *Educating the Nation: Documents on the Discourse of National Education in India 1880–1920* (pp. ix–xxvii). New Delhi, India: Kanishka Publishers in association with Educational Records Research Unit, Jawaharlal Nehru University.

Curtis, B. (1983). 'Preconditions of the Canadian State: Educational Reform and the Construction of a Public in Upper Canada, 1837–1846', *Studies in Political Economy*, 10(1): 99–121.

Department of Education, Government of India. (1968). 'National Policy on Education', available at http://mhrd.gov.in/sites/upload_files/mhrd/files/document-reports/NPE-1968.pdf [accessed 18 September 2017].

Department of State Education Research and Training and Karnataka Textbook Society, Bangalore. (2007). 'NCF 2005 Based State Curricular Policy Framework and Guidelines for Curriculum and Textbook Revisions in Karnataka 2006–2007', available at http://dsert.kar.nic.in/ncf2005/KCF2007-EngVer.pdf [accessed 5 September 2017].

Dewan, H., and Mehendale, A. (2015). 'Towards a New Education Policy: Directions and Considerations', *Economic & Political Weekly*, 50(48): 15–18.

Faure, E., Herrera, F., Kaddoura, A., Lopes, H., Petrovsky, A. V., Rahnema, M., and Ward, F. C. (1972). *Learning to Be: The World of Education Today and Tomorrow.* Report of the International Commission on the Development of Education. Paris: Unesco Pub.

Green, A. (1997). 'Education and State Formation in Europe and Asia', in K. J. Kennedy (Ed.), *Citizenship Education and the Modern State* (pp. 9–26). London: Falmer.

International Commission on Education for the Twenty-first Century, Delors, J., and Unesco. (1996). *Learning, the Treasure Within: Report to UNESCO of the International Commission on Education for the Twenty-First Century.* Paris: UNESCO Pub.

Jernegan, M. W. (1919). 'Compulsory Education in the American Colonies: I. New England (Continued) in', *The School Review*, 27(1): 24–43.

Kleinberger, A. F. (1975). 'A Comparative Analysis of Compulsory Education Laws', *Comparative Education*, 11(3): 219–230.

Koos, L. (1924). 'Recent Conceptions of the Aims of Elementary Education', *The Elementary School Journal*, 24(7): 507–515.

Liggio, L. P., and Peden, J. R. (1978). 'Social Scientists, Schooling, and the Acculturation of Immigrants in 19th Century America', *The Journal of Libertarian Studies*, 2: 69–84.

McMahon, W. W. (1999). *Education and Development: Measuring the Social Benefits.* Oxford: Oxford University Press.

Ministry of Human Resources Development, Government of India. (1992). 'National Policy on Education 1986 with Revised Policy Formulations 1992', available at www.ncert.nic.in/oth_anoun/npe86.pdf [accessed 5 September 2017].

———. (2016). 'Some Inputs for Draft National Education Policy', available at http://mhrd.gov.in/sites/upload_files/mhrd/files/nep/Inputs_Draft_NEP_2016.pdf [accessed 28 September 2017].

Ministry of Law and Justice, Government of India. (2009). 'The Right of Children to Free and Compulsory Education Act, 2009', available at http://mhrd.gov.in/sites/upload_files/mhrd/files/upload_document/rte.pdf [accessed 5 September 2017].

Nardinelli, C. (1980). 'Child Labor and the Factory Acts', *The Journal of Economic History*, 40(4): 739–755.

National Council for Education Research and Training, Government of India. (2005). 'National Curriculum Framework 2005', available at www.ncert.nic.in/rightside/links/pdf/framework/english/nf2005.pdf [accessed 5 September 2017].

Schultz, T. W. (1960). 'Capital Formation by Education', *Journal of Political Economy*, 68(6): 571–583.

Sen, A. (1999). *Development as Freedom*. New York: Knopf.

Sirisena, U. D. I. (1967). 'Educational Legislation and Educational Development: Compulsory Education in Ceylon', *History of Education Quarterly*, 7(3): 329–348.

Soysal, Y. N., and Strang, D. (1989). 'Construction of the First Mass Education Systems in Nineteenth-Century Europe', *Sociology of Education*: 277–288.

Srivastava, S. (1998). *Constructing Post-Colonial India: National Character and the Doon School*. London: Routledge.

State Council for Education Research and Training, Government of Punjab. (2013). *Punjab Curriculum Framework School Education 2013*. Punjab: State Council for Education Research and Training.

UN Committee on Economic, Social and Cultural Rights (CESCR). (1999). 'General Comment No. 13: The Right to Education (Art. 13 of the Covenant)', December 8, 1999, E/C.12/1999/10, available at www.refworld.org/docid/4538838c22.html [accessed 5 September 2017].

UN General Assembly. (1948). 'Universal Declaration of Human Rights', December 8, 1948, 217 A (III), available at www.refworld.org/docid/3ae6b3712c.html [accessed 16 February 2018].

———. (1966). 'International Covenant on Economic, Social and Cultural Rights', December 16, 1966, United Nations, Treaty Series, vol. 993, 3, available at www.refworld.org/docid/3ae6b36c0.html [accessed 5 September 2017].

———. (1989). 'Convention on the Rights of the Child', November 20, 1989, United Nations, Treaty Series, vol. 1577, 3, available at www.refworld.org/docid/3ae6b38f0.html [accessed 5 September 2017].

UNESCO. (1990). *World Declaration on Education for All and Framework for Action to Meet Basic Learning Needs*, adopted by the World Conference on Education for All: Meeting Basic Learning Needs, Jomtien, Thailand, 5–9 March 1990. New York: Inter-Agency Commission (UNDP, UNESCO, UNICEF, World Bank) for the World Conference on Education for All.

———. (2000). 'The Dakar Framework for Action: Education for All: Meeting Our Collective Commitments', available at http://unesdoc.unesco.org/images/0012/001211/121147e.pdf [accessed 5 September 2017].

Weiner, M. (1991). *The Child and the State in India: Child Labor and Education Policy in Comparative Perspective*. Princeton: Princeton University Press.

4 Regulatory state and the diversified private

Archana Mehendale and Rahul Mukhopadhyay

The institutional system in school education and regulation

Studies around elementary education in India have foregrounded supply-side constraints and demand-side challenges, to the relative neglect of a deeper understanding of the institutional complexities of the school system that greatly affects educational processes and outcomes. It is only recently that some studies have started directing their attention to the school institutional system and have, in an indirect way, been able to offer some preliminary insights on these institutional dimensions and the regulatory capacity and monitoring capabilities of the prevailing system. Primary among these insights is the idea of a complex institutional structure for education administration that continues to bear the legacy of a colonial supervision system (Sharma, 2000). This structure has also been found to be both under-resourced and burdened with improbable physical targets of coverage (Sharma, 2009; Mukhopadhyay and Sriprakash, 2013). As a recent study indicates, 'attributes of organisational design and fuzzy goal-setting fortify administrative apathy by sustaining the claims of poor work-motivation amongst last mile administrative staff' within the educational administrative structure (Aiyar and Bhattacharya, 2016: 62). In addition, new modes of programmatic delivery have resulted in a blurring of the chains of reporting and accountability across multiple agencies of authority within this structure (Mukhopadhyay, Vasavi, and Ramkumar, 2009). Another insight pertains to the informal norms and processes that, alongside formal rules and procedures, constitute the 'internal dynamic' of the education system (Sharma, 2009). As studies have shown, political linkages of both teachers and subordinate education functionaries with elected representatives create the logic of this 'internal dynamic' and help them bypass official accountability mechanisms (Kingdon and Muzammil, 2003; Beteille, 2009; Vasavi, 2015).

Indeed, the study of institutional complexities becomes even more pertinent in the case of regulation in the sphere of elementary education, encompassing as it does the functions of 'standard-setting', 'information-gathering' and 'behaviour-modification' to control and guide different institutional actors, primarily by the state (Hood, Rothstein, and Baldwin, 2001). Even the few studies focused on regulation show the nature of this institutional complexity in the ways in which intended institutional objectives are subverted by private actors, often in collusion with state actors. In one such study, contrary incentives created by regulatory and procedural norms that are different for government and private schools are seen to engender an informal set of norms and mechanisms that depend on and use the formal policy and regulatory framework. This 'shadow institutional framework' is used by the low-fee private (LFP) unrecognised schools to evade formal regulations mandated by the state (Srivastava, 2008). As Srivastava elaborates,

> the shadow framework was not a formal set of institutions as it was neither formally written nor passed in any legislative or authoritative body, and thus did not have formal legitimacy. Nonetheless, for case study schools as for other LFP schools, the shadow framework gained practical legitimacy on two counts: (1) it minimised uncertainty and provided case study schools with structure in terms of their performance; and (2) it was proven to be the 'way to get things done', not least because the formal framework's perverse incentives made it difficult for schools to operate in accordance with it. Furthermore, and perhaps surprisingly, the shadow framework operated with the knowledge of institutional actors, and was sometimes favoured by them because of those perverse incentives.
>
> (2008: 464)

Other studies reveal how politicians, education functionaries and private school managements are complicit in disregarding regulatory norms for obtaining and continuing school recognition. One study finds that 'comprehensive regulations (. . .) exist "on paper", covering profit, teachers, physical facilities and management. . . (but) the regulations are widely ignored, subject to the payment of bribes' and though inspectors do visit schools, they do not visit classrooms (Tooley and Dixon, 2005: 282). Yet another study on low-fee private schools emphasises how a 'practical legitimacy' arises from processes of negotiation by different stakeholders of their own positions and understanding vis-à-vis these schools (Ohara, 2012). This 'practical legitimacy' then helps the low-fee private schools to negotiate the blurred zones of 'legal legitimacy' that prevail due to contradictory regulatory provisions and a reluctance on the part of the state to enforce regulatory norms in practice.

At one level, it is not as if there have been no efforts by the state to strengthen its own institutional processes. This has been mainly through 'short-route' accountability linkages[1] that envision a more active role for decentralised political structures and school management committees in school governance. Even the recent Right of Children to Free and Compulsory Education Act, 2009 (RtE Act) has underlined powers of oversight of these bodies and often detailed them in rules that have been formulated to give effect to the Act. However, as one state-level study shows, a transition from political to legal accountability is rendered complex when such policies create 'a web of "local authorities" with unclear and overlapping jurisdictions. . . (and) increases the chance of red tape and delays and does little to raise awareness or provide any space for social mobilisation' (Bhatacharjee, Mysoor, and Sivaramakrishnan, 2014: 40). At another level, the regulatory framework for elementary education in India can be said to be both restrictive and over-regulated – the former in terms of legal mandate requiring private participation only on a not-for-profit basis, and the latter in terms of a wide range of government agencies being involved in regulation through a variety of mechanisms.

Alongside such empirical insights, it is also important to assess the regulatory capacity and mechanisms of the existing institutional system within an analytical framework that examines both the changing nature of the state and the non-state as well as the relationship between them. This, in the Indian context, bears special relevance due to the increased and diversified presence of the non-state, mainly in the form of the 'private', which has carried different connotations historically and has also been subject to internal diversity (see, Chapter 1 by Manish Jain in this volume), especially over the last two decades. As we shall analyse, the particular form of the private that has emerged has been more an outcome of regulatory mechanisms that the state has sought to adopt and exercise or refrain from deploying or deployed differentially, both across time and across its sovereign territory.

The next section of the chapter elaborates on the changing nature and relationship of the state and the private in education, particularly over the last two decades. Thereafter, we draw upon specific examples from the Indian context to underline the broader directions that the regulation of school education in India seem to be taking and review these trends with reference to key conceptual ideas emerging from a broader review of the literature on regulation internationally. The concluding section summarises our main arguments.

Changing nature of the state–private relationship

Till around the mid-1980s, both government and government-aided schools were the preferred form of education in India even among large sections of the middle classes (Nambissan, 2010). Since then, both pro-market policies in the economic realm and the newly emerging middle classes benefiting from these policies started altering the equation between the state and the private in the provisioning of education quite remarkably. There are three specific ways in which the state–private relationship has been altered in the realm of school education in the recent decades.

First, there has been a rapid and exponential increase in private enrolments in school education. Different reports over the years indicate that, while even till the mid-1980s attendance in private primary schools was as low as 2 per cent, elementary level enrolments in rural areas reached 10 per cent by the mid-1990s, and almost a quarter of rural and more than 50 per cent of urban children were in private schools by 2005 (Desai et al., 2010). The all-India figures for elementary level enrolments in 2005 were 72 per cent in government and 28 per cent in private schools (ibid.). The continuation of this trend over the next decade is also apparent from a recent report that finds that during the period 2007 and 2013, 'enrollment in government schools (Std. 1–8) declined by about 11.7 million, from 133.7 million to 121 million' while 'the enrollment in private schools went up by 27 million, from 51 million to 78 million' (ASER, 2015: 2). Much of this expansion in private school enrolments has been driven by mushrooming budget private schools in both rural and urban areas. What is also important for our discussions is a 'hierarchy of access' created among the schools in terms of differential access to different social groups (Ramachandran, 2004; Juneja, 2014). As researchers using Hirschman's (1970) notions of 'exit' and 'voice' have observed, in such a hierarchy, families with disposable incomes slightly more than the extremely marginalised groups have been using the 'exit' option in choosing private schools over government schools, while the government schools have become the only option for the 'voiceless' poor and the marginalised (Härmä, 2010).

Second, the nature of 'private' schools has itself changed drastically since the 1990s and studies show how the heterogeneity that characterises this 'diversified private' no longer remains confined to the middle and upper middle classes in India (e.g. Kingdon, 1996). This is important because in India, the broad categorisation of the 'private' and the 'state' has primarily been mapped onto the following types of schools in terms of differences in funding and management: the private unaided, government-aided private schools and government schools. Researchers have, however, noted that such a mapping conflates the differences that exist in reality among schools, including the private unaided segment (Juneja, 2011). The private unaided schools now 'span a vast array of operations with varying fee structures, from low-fee to elite, high-fee schools' and 'may be run by voluntary organisations, missionaries, philanthropic bodies, or individual owners as business enterprises' (Srivastava, Noronha, and Fennell, 2013: 4). In addition, there are alternative schools, progressive schools, and schools run by charitable trusts, new-age 'edupreneurs', and various forms of corporate bodies that run school-chains or school franchisees (see, Chapter 7 by Padma M. Sarangapani in this volume).

The diversified nature of private schools is also manifest in the extent to which these schools adhere to formal regulatory norms; there may be schools recognised by the government, not recognised by the government or not even registered.[2] Similarly, the private unaided schools may offer education for school grades that vary widely across the schools, and may or may not be affiliated to a school board, as required for purposes of public examinations. There is also significant variation in the ways in which such private schooling is offered – in terms of both infrastructure and resources. In a sense, the non-state-run schools, therefore, differ in terms of their motivation, scale and capacities and constitute a largely heterogeneous 'private' category.

The third way in which the state–private relationship has been reconfigured is through a significant expansion in education service providers. As one study notes, such service providers 'have become an increasingly important part of the Indian education ecosystem in the recent years', offering 'a range of services including teacher and management trainings/workshops, curriculum management, and, teaching activities and methodologies' (Garg, 2011: 35). Rapid changes, in both existing forms of school inputs and services, such as textbooks and tuitions, and more recent forms of such services, including in-service training for teachers and school leaders, different forms of student assessment and technology-enabled pedagogical support materials, have redefined the space of the 'private' in school education in fundamental ways. The presence of the 'private' is, therefore, no longer limited to that of provisioning of education in schools; rather, it is manifest in the multiplicity of products and services that mediate both formal institutional spaces of school education and other learning spaces beyond that of the school. Simultaneously, both funding for and delivery of these products and services now occur through complex institutional systems that include social-impact investment via venture capital firms focused on education markets, public–private partnerships (PPPs) of multiple types and informal/shadow institutional frameworks that coexist with the formal institutional structures of schools.

The reconfiguration of state–private relationship over the recent decades should be read alongside the regulatory and policy-related trends that can be said to have gone hand in hand with the former. First, even in a purportedly restrictive regulatory environment, there have been both a remarkable growth of private schools in the recent decades, in terms of numbers and types, and the flourishing of an unregulated private sector. In addition, there has been a diversification in the nature of education 'goods and services' that has come to be financed by and provisioned for through newer and newer non-state institutional mechanisms. However, at the same time, there has been little change in the regulatory environment to address these shifts. Second, policy discourses in India have veered towards a logic of privatisation of schooling and an endorsement of the efficacy of private schooling. This is not only in the face of inconclusive evidence on the overall 'private school advantage',[3] but also in the light of evidence that has underlined the shortcomings and consequent inequitable implications of the burgeoning low-end private school sector. Even the clearly laid out standards for different school inputs and norms on school infrastructure in the RtE Act have proved to be without teeth, with no significant impact on private unrecognised schools that do not comply with the stated norms (Azim Premji Foundation, 2016). Third, what is also visible is an endorsement of contractual models for PPPs in the recent Five-Year Plan documents along with a simultaneous move towards diverse forms of PPP arrangements in school education.[4] This, in the absence of any coherent policy or legal frameworks, appears to be a wilful neglect by the state of cautionary observations that emphasise the need of new regulatory frameworks to bolster the already weak institutional capacities of the state.

Regulation of elementary education in India

Quite contrary to common perceptions, regulation is neither a post-liberalisation, post-privatisation phenomena in India nor has it come about after the enactment of the RtE Act and the state rules notified thereunder. In fact, the responsibility of the state to regulate has been expressed in state education legislations that have existed for several decades. With increasing proliferation of private interests in education and private provisioning of education, the adequacy and effectiveness of the role of the state in regulation (in addition to its role in provisioning and funding) is getting critically questioned. While, in general, state intervention in elementary education has been justified on economic, political and socio-cultural grounds (Boissiere, 2004), the role of the Indian state itself has undergone significant changes since the 1990s. The functions of provision, funding and regulation have been increasingly reconceptualised, and these are now being rendered by a mixed set of actors, viz. state, market and civil society, who are often simultaneously engaged with these functions at various levels. What is evident in this transition, following broader regulatory trends elsewhere referred to by Dale (1997), is a coordinating role of the changed 'regulatory state' under the broader rubric of governance. Dale's suggestion that education markets can be understood by looking at regulation frameworks, including deregulation that entails removal of existing barriers to choice, appears to resonate with the Indian context (see also, Chapter 2 by Christopher Winch in this volume).

The idea of a 'regulatory state' has been discussed by various scholars and there are differences in the ways in which the regulatory functions of the state are constituted across the world (Moran, 2002). According to one scholar, the current trend across countries is more towards the American way of regulation with 'bureaucratic generalists (. . .) everywhere replaced by specialised agencies set up to regulate particular aspects of a formally deregulated and decentralized system' (Dale, 1997: 278). Another trend of regulation which Dale discusses is juridification, which takes away contentious issues from the political realm and places them only for legal scrutiny. He further observes that the strategy of New Public Management and the emphasis on public accountability within this strategy are removing the differences between the public and the private in governance, as both are now functioning within a results-oriented framework. In this paradigm, governments should 'steer and not row' by stressing on quality, competition, performance measures and customer satisfaction and by creating competition among the local schools. Regulations would be required only to correct market inefficiencies and 'restructure the marketplace'.

However, regulation, as it has traditionally been understood in the Indian context, is closely related to the idea of exercising a top-down control within a formally laid-down framework. In the case of the education sector, this control emanates from both the central and state governments. However, the idea of regulation also raises fundamental questions about the rationale and justification of governmental intervention in controlling activities of the 'private', which are factors that in turn understandably influence choice of methods adopted for such intervention and ways to assess if these efforts are successful (Francis, 1993). In the Indian context, these questions revolve around the facts that there is often the operation of a 'shadow institutional framework' that blurs the public–private dichotomy, and that the regulatory methods are, therefore, likely to be influenced by vested interests.

In intent, regulation of school education in India, particularly elementary education, is largely a bureaucratic exercise undertaken within a normative framework laid down by the government with an objective of serving social aims. Education is meant to be a non-profit activity[5] and although private actors enjoy the freedom to establish and run schools,[6] the state has the authority to lay reasonable restrictions in public interest.[7] In the following sub-sections, we examine some of the school regulation frameworks of the state with reference to a few key conceptual issues in regulatory theory. Concurrently, we raise questions pertaining to the nature of contradictions and tensions apparent in both the newer regulatory norms laid down under the RtE Act and the state rules under the same that have supplanted the older regulatory regimes.

The nature of the regulatory framework

The existence of a large corpus of regulatory norms on education in India can be explained from the standpoint of the 'public interest theory' wherein the purpose of regulation is the protection of collective welfare and public aims of education, which may remain ignored by individual consumer choices (Morgan and Yeung, 2007; Prosser, 2010) and may particularly be needed in the context of market failures. This, however, assumes that the regulators (in the case of education, it is the government and its agencies) are technically competent, neutral and without personal interests, thus making enforcement and compliance with regulatory instruments hassle-free. In the case of education, 'what constitutes public interest' can itself be questioned; regulatory bodies may not be disinterested parties in the activity being regulated, given that the government itself is a provider and in competition with the private providers, leaving ample room for corruption and rent-seeking. The growing contestation around state regulation of private schools in India seems to draw its logic from the 'private interest theory', as opposed to 'public interest theory', and stresses a reliance on unfettered market forces due to the inevitability of regulatory capture by vested interests. In fact, an extreme version of such a logic is that no regulation is preferred to bad regulation or over-regulation that might exist in reality in the name of 'public interest'. Another challenge to the 'public interest theory' comes in the form of questions about both the legitimacy and accountability of regulatory bodies, which though competent may not be elected, and could therefore be removed from political oversight (see, Prosser, 1999; Dubash, 2008).

What is also evident in the regulatory framework in Indian school education is that it comprises a large and growing body of statutes enacted by the central and state governments, rules, executive orders and judicial directives, with a host of governmental and quasi-governmental agencies involved in regulation of various matters. This resonates with the idea of 'decentred regulation', which involves a plurality of regulation objectives and multiple regulatory bodies. Further, such regulation has been observed to be increasingly visible in recent times as a mechanism of intentional use of authority to affect the behaviour of different parties according to set standards, involving instruments of information gathering and behaviour modification (Black, 2001). Table 4.1 summarises these multiple agencies and their functions in the Indian context. These agencies and regulatory activities are not necessarily interdependent. For instance, on the one hand, registration of a school by the affiliating agency, including central boards, is incumbent upon the recognition and the no-objection certificate issued by the state government, showing coherence and interdependency between different regulatory provisions. On the other hand, reimbursements granted by the government to private schools for the education of economically weaker and disadvantaged sections are not linked to the school completing the recognition norms under the RtE Act, showing contradictions within the same regulatory provision (Mehendale, Mukhopadhyay, and Namala, 2015).

Compounding this complexity, especially within the context of a 'diversified' private already elaborated upon in a previous section, is the absence of a common regulatory framework applicable to the diverse set of private providers; indeed, often different sets of rules

Table 4.1 Multiple regulatory agencies for school education and their functions

Regulatee	Activity	Regulator/regulatory instrument
Private schools	Establishment and registration of a not-for-profit body	Registrar, Societies Registration Act; Public Trusts Act; Registrar, Companies Act
Private schools	Recognition and derecognition of the school	State government, under the RtE Act and rules
Private schools	Education of children from economically weaker and disadvantaged sections	State government
Private schools	Fee hikes	State governments (in certain states)
All schools	Affiliation to an examination board	State Examination Boards, Central Board of Secondary Education, Council for the Indian School Certificate Examinations
All schools	Curriculum	Central and state governments through the affiliating bodies
All schools	School infrastructure	Central and state governments through RtE Act and state rules under RtE and state legislation
All schools	School functioning	Central and state governments through RtE Act and state rules under RtE and state legislation
Teachers	Eligibility	National Council for Teacher Education (NCTE) and state governments
Teachers	Code of conduct	Appointing authorities such as Central and state governments through RtE Act and state rules under RtE and state legislation and private managements
Teachers	Service conditions	Appointing authorities such as Central and state governments and private managements
Teacher Education Institutions	Recognition	NCTE through its regulations
Teacher Education Institutions	Curriculum	State Council for Education, Research and Training
Teacher Education Institutions	Programmes on Special Needs Education	Rehabilitation Council of India through Rehabilitation Council of India Act, 1992

Source: Authors' own work

and regulations are applicable for different providers. Such a lack of standardisation may be challenged as an application of differential and inconsistent norms. In recent times, the issue of differential standards being applied to government and private schools on matters of infrastructure provision has been questioned as a protectionist measure towards government schools and their exemption from the stringent standards of regulation that are applicable to private schools. Similarly, questions have also been raised regarding certain categories of non-state providers such as minority institutions, residential schools and schools affiliated to international school boards that have been exempted from the regulations under the RtE Act. In the case of minority schools, the exemption is grounded in constitutional provisions protecting such institutions from state interference. However, exemptions of schools from other categories from the regulatory norms of RtE Act needs to be questioned given the elite populations they serve and the diversity of motivations, relevance and contributions of these multiple providers.

Moreover, regulatory norms are laid down and mediated by various sub-divisions within the government machinery, particularly different functional departments. These can lead to gaps and inconsistencies in applicable norms. For example, schools for tribal children established by the state Tribal Welfare Department are not obliged to follow the provisions under the RtE Act or the provisions laid down by the National Council for Teacher Education Act, 1993 on teacher eligibility. Conversely, the norms could also be supplementary as in the case of the child protection norms issued by the Ministry of Women and Child Development, Government of India, which, although binding on schools, are not monitored or regulated by the state departments of education. In addition to the norms promulgated by the government executive, judicial directives have also stipulated norms that are of regulatory nature. For example, the Supreme Court has laid down guidelines pertaining to minimum specifications for school buildings in the case of disaster management and fire safety standards in schools.[8] As education is a concurrent subject in India, in addition to the central legislation, there is also a corpus of state regulatory norms that constitute the bulk of the normative framework on school education. Another kind of 'layering' happens when new rules and regulations are added to older ones on the same subject areas.

In the Indian context, Anant and Singh (2006) have tried to examine where regulation fits within the schema of constitutional governance. They suggest that regulatory commands emanate from the state or bodies delegated with powers by the state and regulation involves

Regulatory state and the diversified private

administering contracts and arrangements that go beyond contract law. Therefore, regulatory activity requires a conglomeration of legislative, executive and judicial functions. In such a scenario, where there is a wide spectrum of regulating agencies or where regulation spans a wide range of functions within the state, each motivated differently, the key question is what principles guide the work of the overall regulatory framework and what benchmarks can be adopted to assess whether regulation is working.

The complexity of this regulatory structure makes it difficult for stakeholders to decipher the applicable standards. Admittedly, there is also the absence of any legal framework, as envisioned under institutionalist theories (see Morgan and Yeung, 2007), which can play a coordinating role and mediate the diverse interests of the multiple stakeholders in a coherent manner. In such a situation, what is often evident is the contradictory impulses of regulation even within the ambit of regulatory agencies of the state. Thus, in practice, there is a proclivity for a defacto deregulation that signals both the increasing complexity of the existing regulatory structure as well as the inadequate capacity of current regulatory institutions to negotiate divergent regulatory claims. Such a defacto deregulation in practice could explain the growth and continued existence of private schools that do not comply with RtE norms within formal structures that are restrictive as well as over-regulated. In the next sub-section, we select a specific example – that of minimum qualifications for teachers – to illustrate the nature of state–private dynamic that is increasingly evident in school regulation.

State–private dynamic in regulation

In the current context of the changing nature of the state–private relationship in India, the regulatory state is required to balance interests among actors located on two axes – the government and citizens on one axis and the market and consumers on the other. These axes underpin fundamental differences between the political and economic aims of education. This can be elaborated with a specific example of regulation on teacher qualifications. With the intention of preserving quality of education and protecting interests of students, the government has empowered the National Council for Teacher Education (NCTE) to prescribe minimum qualification norms for persons to be eligible for appointment as teachers in Grades 1–8.[9] The notification of these norms was done in order to ensure that a minimum quality of teachers and teaching standards are mandatorily adhered to.

The underlying premise that can be said to justify this state regulation is the public interest theory wherein the state upholds its own larger political project of education; and it does so on behalf of those directly consuming the service for promoting larger values of public interest that may remain ignored by individual consumer choices (Morgan and Yeung, 2007; Prosser, 2010).

Such a regulatory power of the state, aligning with the political project of education, is intended to both benefit the education of its citizen-students by imposing 'quality' restrictions on 'who can be teachers' irrespective of the type of school, and act as a controlling mechanism for profit-seeking motives of private schools to hire poorly qualified or unqualified teachers at lower costs. In terms of the latter motive, those supporting the 'efficiency argument' for school reforms and favouring the growth of low-fee private schools have argued that teacher qualifications and education do not help in improving learning outcomes (Bhattacharjea, Wadhwa, and Banerji, 2011; Atherton and Kingdon, 2010), and these arguments have strengthened the resistance from private schools against regulation on teacher qualifications. However, for the regulatory norm under discussion – state-prescribed teacher qualifications – even if the consumers (namely, parents sending their children to private schools) were to align their interests with the private schools and become consenting partners in the consumption of educational services that use unqualified teachers, governmental intervention would still be justified on the grounds of 'public interest'. In such a scenario, the purpose of state regulation would be to protect its normative ideal and the public aims of education, which by implication, the unqualified teachers are unfit to fulfil.

On the other hand, a different picture emerges when the same teacher qualification norm is examined under a 'regulation inside government' framework. 'Regulation inside government' assumes importance in the context of debates on inspections and audits (Hood et al., 1999). This idea is less explored systematically and brings out three important dimensions. First, it entails that the state bureaucracy should aim to shape and control the activities of another part of itself; second, there should be some degree of organisational separation between the 'regulating' bureaucracy and the regulatee; and third, the 'regulator' should have some kind of official mandate to scrutinise the behaviour of the regulatee and change it towards desired regulatory objectives. The NCTE regulates teacher qualification norms for not only the private schools but also the government schools. However, the RtE Act permits state governments to seek exemption from the provision of

Regulatory state and the diversified private 117

hiring qualified teachers because of absence of facilities for teacher training in their states.[10] This one-time exemption allows the states to relax teacher qualifications prescribed by the NCTE norms for not more than five years. Although this extension period has ended for most states that enjoyed this relaxation, the teacher qualification norms are not being adhered to. Thus, 'regulation inside government' remains a challenge for the NCTE, which is unable to regulate the state government, thereby diluting the larger public aims of education that it intends to uphold.

The two preceding examples show how 'public interest' could well be compromised within the ambit of the public actor – in this case the state's own subordinate agencies – while the regulatory framework is able to present, and possibly defend, a normative ideal to arguments presented by vested private interests. However, as in the first example above, such normative ideals (mainly around the notion of public aims of education) and the capacity of the state to ensure the same are increasingly being challenged by the private sector, which has stressed the need for 'goal-governed regulation', where the focus is not on meeting the process requirements of education but on meeting the expected outcomes of education.

Another challenge for the regulatory state that emerges from the process of negotiation between the two axes of 'government and citizens' and 'market and consumers' is the possibility of a deadlock. This is similar to the risks that would be involved in 'stakeholder regulation', as discussed under institutionalist theories, wherein the regulatory framework attempts to balance interests of various stakeholders without there being a prior weightage assigned to these interests. For example, concerns of the state governments having poor teacher educational facilities is accommodated without any sanctions and so are their decisions to appoint unqualified teachers. Thus, the fallout of the deadlock results in lack of implementation of the regulatory framework itself. In other words, if the competing stakeholders' interests (both public and private) are left unattended, say for instance in the case of meeting the teacher qualification norms, there is a possibility that the implementation process of the intended regulation would get paralysed, with the government as a regulator being unable to check the practices on the ground. The gap between the formal regulatory framework and the actual implementation can be viewed as a defacto deregulation by the state, which has wider implications on the method of evaluating the state's capacity to perform regulatory function and the manner of justification for 'decentred regulation'.

Conclusion

In India, the state as a primary guarantor of education has the obligation to provide, fund and regulate. However, in the differentiated and stratified school system that has evolved over the years and exists even today, it is only 'regulation' which is understood to be the commonly performed function of the state across all categories of schools. Moreover, as we saw, the nature of this regulation in education is neither standardised across different types of education providers, nor interdependent or coherent across different levels of the government, agencies of the government or types of regulatory provisions. This complex and layered nature of regulatory framework contributes to the state enjoying different kinds of relationships with different providers.

The state–private dynamic in school education cannot be simplistically defined in a uniform manner because it is nuanced, changing and highly dependent on the nature of the 'private' and the regulatory norms which govern it. These norms are also a reason for legal contestation evidenced in the large number of litigation between the government and different kinds of private actors. The pressure of such court battles is severe, taking up considerable resources and keeping the education bureaucracy preoccupied, sometimes at the cost of other functions. An increasingly 'diversified' private, as has been witnessed in the recent years, and the inadequate capacity of the existing institutional structures of governance to adapt to this changing environment, adds to the woes of the already beleaguered bureaucratic machinery that is expected to oversee regulation. It is, therefore, not surprising that in such a scenario one sees a compromise even in 'regulation inside government' with public goals of education being balanced against more pragmatic federal and fiscal demands as in the case of indefinite deferral of appointment of qualified teachers by some state governments.

What we also noted as a trend in the state–private dynamic is an increasing preference for defacto deregulation. The regulatory framework which is seen to balance contradictory impulses of an understanding of education as a public good and a conception of the rights of citizens to this public good on the one hand, with the understanding of education as a commodity (primarily to further socioeconomic mobility or status) and a conception of those accessing such a commodity as consumers on the other hand, can be characterised as 'overregulation in principle but deregulation in practice'. Notably, current demands for 'goal governed forms of regulation' over 'rule governed forms of regulation' emerge from this very paradox.

Notes

1 These refer to direct claims of clients over public service providers instead of the longer route of political accountability. For more details, see World Bank (2003).
2 The process of registration refers to the organisational form by which a school can be constituted, primarily to underline its non-profit motive. Recognition happens after the school is established and involves application to the concerned governmental authority with detailed documents of various institutional requirements for a school. For details on the various formal procedures for opening a school, see Wadhwa (2001).
3 See Chudgar and Quin (2012) for discussion on 'private school advantage' and evidence to the contrary in India.
4 For more details, see Srivastava (2010) and Srivastava, Noronha, and Fennell (2013).
5 This has been upheld by the Supreme Court of India. See P.A. Inamdar v. State of Maharasthra decided on 12 August 2005 and reported in (2005) 6 SCC 537.
6 As per Article 19(1)(g) of the Constitution of India.
7 As per Article 19 (6) of the Constitution of India.
8 See Avinash Mehrotra v. Union of India (2009) 6 SCC 398.
9 The NCTE has issued detailed norms on the minimum qualifications for being eligible to be appointed as a teacher in Grades 1 to 8. These can be available at http://mhrd.gov.in/sites/upload_files/mhrd/files/upload_document/d_0.pdf [accessed 5 September 2017].
10 See Section 23 of the RtE Act. The following states sought exemption under Section 23(2) of the Act: Assam, Bihar, Chhattisgarh, West Bengal, Orissa, Madhya Pradesh, Meghalaya, Tripura, Nagaland, Uttarakhand, Himachal Pradesh.

References

Aiyar, Y., and Bhattacharya, S. (2016). 'The Post Office Paradox', *Economic & Political Weekly*, 51(11): 61–69.

Anant, T. C. A., and Singh, J. (2006). 'Structuring Regulation: Constitutional and Legal Frame in India', *Economic and Political Weekly*, 41(2): 121–127.

Annual Status of Education Report (ASER). (2015). *Annual Status of Education Report (Rural) 2014*. New Delhi, India: ASER Centre/Pratham.

Atherton, P., and Kingdon, G. (2010). *The Relative Effectiveness and Costs of Contract and Regular Teachers in India*. London: Institute of Education, University of London.

Azim Premji Foundation. (2016). *Right to Education (RTE) Act, 2009 and Private School Closure in India*. Bangalore: Azim Premji Foundation.

Beteille, T. (2009). 'Absenteeism, Transfers and Patronage: The Political Economy of Teacher Labor Markets in India', Unpublished Ph.D. Dissertation, Stanford University.

Bhatacharjee, M., Mysoor, D., and Sivaramakrishnan, A. (2014). 'RTE Grievance Redress in Karnataka', *Economic and Political Weekly*, 49(23): 37–41.

Bhattacharjea, S., Wadhwa, W., and Banerji, R. (2011). *Inside Primary Schools: Teaching and Learning in Rural India*. New Delhi, India: Annual Status of Education Report Centre.

Black, J. (2001). 'Decentring Regulation: Understanding the Role of Regulation and Self-Regulation in a "Post-Regulatory" World', *Current Legal Problems*, 54(1): 103–146.

Boissiere, M. (2004). *Rationale for Public Investments in Primary Education in Developing Countries*. Washington, DC: World Bank, IEG.

Chudgar, A., and Quin, E. (2012). 'Relationship Between Private Schooling and Achievement: Results from Rural and Urban India', *Economics of Education Review*, 31(4): 376–390.

Dale, R. (1997). 'The State and the Governance of Education: An Analysis of the Restructuring of the State – Education Relationship', in A. H. Halsey, H. Lauder, P. Brown, and A. S. Well (Eds.), *Education: Culture, Economy and Society* (pp. 273–282). Oxford: Oxford University Press.

Desai, S., Dubey, A., Joshi, B. L., Sen, M., Shariff, A., and Vanneman, R. (2010). *Human Development in India: Challenges for a Society in Transition*. New Delhi, India: Oxford University Press.

Dubash, N. (2008). 'Independent Regulatory Agencies: A Theoretical Review with Reference to Electricity and Water in India', *Economic and Political Weekly*, 43(40): 43–54.

Francis, J. (1993). *The Politics of Regulation: A Comparative Perspective*. Oxford: Wiley-Blackwell.

Garg, N. (2011). 'Low Cost Private Education in India: Challenges and Way Forward', Dissertation, MIT Sloan School of Management.

Härmä, J. (2010). *School Choice for the Poor? The Limits of Marketisation of Primary Education in Rural India*. CREATE Research Monograph, Pathways to Access series 23. Brighton: University of Sussex.

Hirschman, A. O. (1970). *Exit, Voice, and Loyalty: Responses to Decline in Firms, Organizations and States*. Cambridge, MA: Harvard University Press.

Hood, C., Rothstein, H., and Baldwin, R. (2001). *The Government of Risk*. Oxford: Oxford University Press.

Hood, C., Scott, C., James, O., Jones, G., and Travers, T. (1999). *Regulation Inside Government: Waste Watchers, Quality Police, and Sleazebusters*. Oxford: Oxford University Press.

Juneja, N. (2011). 'Access to What? Diversity and Participation', in R. Govinda (Ed.), *Who Goes to School? Exploring Exclusion in Indian Education* (pp. 205–247). New Delhi, India: Oxford University Press.

———. (2014). 'India's New Mandate Against Economic Apartheid in Schools', *Journal of International Cooperation in Education*, 16(2): 55–70.

Kingdon, G. (1996). 'The Quality and Efficiency of Private and Public Education: A Case Study of Urban India', *Oxford Bulletin of Economics and Statistics*, 58(1): 57–82.

Kingdon, G., and Muzammil, M. (2003). *The Political Economy of Education in India: Teacher Politics in Uttar Pradesh*. New Delhi, India: Oxford University Press.

Mehendale, A., Mukhopadhyay, R., and Namala, A. (2015). 'Right to Education and Inclusion in Private Unaided Schools: An Exploratory Study in Bengaluru and Delhi', *Economic and Political Weekly*, 50(7): 43–51.

Moran, M. (2002). 'Understanding the Regulatory State', *British Journal of Political Science*, 32(2): 391–413.

Morgan, B., and Yeung, K. (2007). *An Introduction to Law and Regulation: Text and Materials*. Cambridge: Cambridge University Press.

Mukhopadhyay, R., and Sriprakash, A. (2013). 'Target-Driven Reforms: Education for All and the Translations of Equity and Inclusion in India', *Journal of Education Policy*, 28(3): 306–321.

Mukhopadhyay, R., Vasavi, A. R., and Ramkumar, N. (2009). *Management of Elementary Education Structures and Strategies*. New Delhi, India: NUEPA.

Nambissan, G. (2010). 'The Indian Middle Classes and Educational Advantage: Family Strategies and Practices', in M. W. Apple, S. J. Ball, and L. A. Gandin (Eds.), *The Routledge International Handbook of the Sociology of Education* (pp. 285–295). London: Routledge.

Ohara, Y. (2012). 'Examining the Legitimacy of Unrecognised Low-Fee Private Schools in India: Comparing Different Perspectives', *Compare: A Journal of Comparative and International Education*, 42(1): 69–90.

Prosser, T. (1999). 'Theorising Utility Regulation', *The Modern Law Review*, 62(2): 196–217.

———. (2010). *The Regulatory Enterprise: Government, Regulation and Legitimacy*. Oxford: Oxford University Press.

Ramachandran, V. (Ed.) (2004). *Gender and Social Equity in Primary Education: Hierarchies of Access*. New Delhi, India: Sage.

Sharma, R. (2000). 'Decentralisation, Professionalism and the School System in India', *Economic and Political Weekly*, 35(42): 3765–3774.

———. (2009). 'The Internal Dynamic', in R. Sharma and V. Ramachandran (Eds.), *The Elementary Education System in India: Exploring Institutional Structures, Processes and Dynamics* (pp. 140–194). New Delhi, India: Routledge.

Srivastava, P. (2008). 'The Shadow Institutional Framework: Towards a New Institutional Understanding of an Emerging Private School Sector in India', *Research Papers in Education*, 23(4): 451–475.

———. (2010). 'Public – Private Partnerships or Privatisation? Questioning the State's Role in Education in India', *Development in Practice*, 20(4–5): 540–553.

Srivastava, P., Noronha, C., and Fennell, S. (2013). 'Private Sector Research Study: Sarva Shiksha Abhiyan', Report submitted to DFID, India.

Tooley, J., and Dixon, P. (2005). 'An Inspector Calls: The Regulation of "Budget" Private Schools in Hyderabad, Andhra Pradesh, India', *International Journal of Educational Development*, 25(3): 269–285.

Vasavi, A. R. (2015). 'Culture and Life of Government Elementary Schools', *Economic and Political Weekly*, 50(33): 36–50.

Wadhwa, M. (2001). 'Licenses to Open a School: It's All About Money', Centre for Civil Society, available at http://ccs.in/sites/default/files/files/wp0001.pdf [accessed 19 March 2017].

World Bank. (2003). *World Development Report 2004: Making Services Work for Poor People – Overview*. World Development Report. Washington, DC: World Bank Group, available at http://documents.worldbank.org/curated/en/527371468166770790/World-Development-Report-2004-Making-services-work-for-poor-people-Overview [accessed 19 March 2017].

5 Recovering the practice and profession of teaching

Padma M. Sarangapani, Rahul Mukhopadhyay, Parul and Manish Jain

Teachers and the work that they do are the most visible part of the school system. While there will be no dispute about the need for teachers in general, expectations from teachers, the scope of their role, teacher preparation, professional status, terms of employment and their quality and efficacy are among the areas of deepest difference in policy and in practice. It is widely recognised that teacher salaries account for about 80 per cent of the government school budget in India. Hence, it is the component of school system provisioning that takes the maximum resources (Dundar et al., 2014; Ramachandran et al., 2015) and is also the most expensive part of school input costs. The Indian state recognises and mandates the need for professionally trained teachers in the school system, regulates the quality of teacher professional development through the statutory regulatory body of the National Council for Teacher Education and mandates salaries of professionally trained teachers. Government school teacher jobs constitute the largest form of government employment in an otherwise shrinking public sector, and along with jobs in the police or public transport, these remain among the few options accessible to educated youth from small towns and rural areas. However, over the last two decades, along with the expansion of the school system and inclusion of a significant percentage of first-generation school goers, there has been a parallel growth in the perception that government school teachers are failing: failing to deliver learning outcomes in their students and failing as accountable moral agents, either through their own incapability (because the profession does not attract talent or because appointments are politicised) or through wilful dereliction and negligence (as the system is incapable of ensuring accountability, and teachers enjoy political protection). This negative image of the immoral, overpaid, underworked or absent government school teacher is widespread in the media (Vidya and Sarangapani, 2011) and in academic writing (e.g. Kingdon and Muzzamil, 2003). It is commonplace to come across bureaucrats asking for solutions to ensure attendance or increase accountability and for a demand of quality interventions that are teacher-proofed or can micro manage teachers and, as if therefore, can enhance learning outcomes in students.

Our approach to quality of education places pedagogy at the centre of educational work of schools (Alexander, 2008; Kumar, 2010). This conception of pedagogy follows the articulations of Winch (1996) of it being 'practice imbued with value' and that of Alexander (2008), who characterises pedagogy as the

> observable act of teaching together with its attendant discourse of educational theories, values, evidence and justifications. It is what one needs to know, and the skills one needs to command in order to make and justify the many different kinds of decisions of which teaching is constituted.
>
> (p. 29)

The starting point is the idea that the quality of the work of the teacher directly affects the quality of the child's education – that is, the education of the child is the consequence of pedagogic effort. Pedagogy is inter-relational; it is carried out by the teacher and is constitutive of the child's epistemic, social and political being. Pedagogic work is an essential aspect of the child's overall socialisation into modern society and formation of citizenship. As Bernstein (2000) notes, pedagogy is both instructional and regulating, and includes the principles of power and social control, entering into and shaping consciousness. The core of education quality is the quality of the overall pedagogic effort made by the teacher, the school, the family and the state, and particularly, of the teacher's work. We make this assertion to draw attention to the fact that the process of education is more than a process of acquiring knowledge and skills; and even the acquisition of knowledge and skills – constructing knowledge; understanding its significance and value; being able to use, create and learn new things; and the emergence of the self as a knower – requires the context created by the teacher, explicitly or implicitly, and the attention she or he brings to the learner, to what is being learnt and to the context (Masschelein and Simon, 2013). Particularly, where children of the poor are concerned, pedagogic effort can enable children to have aspirations, to acquire the capabilities (dispositions, knowledge, skills) and access the social capital needed to achieve these aspirations (Carnoy, Gove, and Marshall, 2007). It is through this that education, as a fundamental human right, becomes a means of personal and social transformation.

Teacher's pedagogic effort is, therefore, not mere facilitation, management or technique. Rather, it draws from and is constituted by their professional identity and their pedagogic theory, which may be a cultural pedagogic theory (Clarke, 2001; Sarangapani, 2003), a folk pedagogy (Bruner, 1996) or a professional/scientific pedagogic theory (Shulman, 1986; Donald, 2002) learnt in pre-service and in-service teacher education programmes. Bruner (1996) offers us a way of thinking about the constitutive elements of a pedagogic theory: beliefs about the aims of education, about the nature of knowledge, about the learner and about the process of teaching and learning. The key advantage of Bruner's approach is that it recognises that pedagogic theories exist prior to professional development programmes and that these personal and cultural theories are built from autobiographical experience and draw from cultural resources (Sarangapani, 2017). This makes it possible for us to recognise and describe pedagogic formation in a range of settings both informal and formal, including the pedagogic practices of tutors, untrained or differently trained teachers, by delving into the belief frameworks that underlie their identities and their practice. We are able to avoid reductionist descriptions that impute to the teacher a lack of thinking, of agency or of investment of self to teaching, as is suggested by descriptions such as 'routinised', 'mechanical', 'ritualised', 'apathetic' and 'deficient'. To be able to discuss and describe the formation of pedagogy through the examination of underlying beliefs and practices in a range of institutional and policy contexts and spaces is particularly important in the Indian case, as we have an intra-disciplinary fracture (apparently irreconcilable) with reference to the formal sources of education theory necessary for teacher formation,[1] a strong influence of cultural pedagogical theories and influential contestations in society (as well as within academia) regarding the need for formal teacher education, or the need, at any rate, of extensive teacher preparation. Drawing from this conception of pedagogy, we can propose explanations for why teachers do what they do, what they do (or do not do), how (and whether) they learn to do what they do and what motivates them to change or adopt new ways of doing things.

Contesting conceptualisations of teachers' work

In this section, we present two alternative and contesting conceptual strands that are prevalent in the current influential discourses on teachers' work. The first of these strands, which we call the 'managerial' approach to teaching, is embedded in the 'new discursive regime' and draws on ideas akin to New Public Management. The second strand locates teachers and their work in historical, institutional and socio-cultural-material contexts, which we call the 'teaching-as-a-profession' approach. In this section, drawing upon Sriprakash and Mukhopadhyay (2015), we engage with recent research on teachers' work to outline these two conceptions, with particular reference to the role of government school teachers.

The 'new discursive regime' (see Introduction, this book) primarily uses ideas of accountability, efficiency and value-for-money to assess teachers' work. Research aligned to the managerial approach has generally put forward a strong critique of teachers and their work in government schools based on these ideas. Accountability of teachers have been shown to be low or almost absent due to political linkages that teachers can exploit for their personal benefits as compared to leveraging such linkages for working towards the larger interests of their profession (Kingdon and Muzammil, 2003; Beteille, 2009). Research on absenteeism among last-mile service providers, in our case teachers, has also provided a strong impetus to the argument of lack of accountability among government school teachers (Kremer et al., 2005; Muralidharan et al., 2016).

Policy solutions emerging from the managerial approach seem to indicate a degeneration of professional values among government school teachers and this strand lays emphasis on the mechanisms of accountability. The solutions suggested by this strand take the form of biometric systems to track teachers' attendance and time-on-task (Duflo, Hanna, and Ryan, 2012; Muralidharan, Niehaus, and Sukhtankar, 2016; Ministry of Finance, 2017), encouraging contractual (and an insecure) employment over regular employment for teachers to make teachers more accountable, hiring such contractual teachers locally as they have stronger community linkages and hence can be made more accountable (Atherton and Kingdon, 2010; Kingdon and Sipahimalani-Rao, 2010; Muralidharan and Sundararaman, 2013) and promoting incentivised pay structures for teachers based on teachers' performance (Pritchett and Murgai, 2006; Muralidharan, 2012). A central proposition of these policy solutions is the cost-effectiveness of these methods when compared to the financial burden on the state for a regular and reportedly unaccountable and under-performing teacher cadre. Teacher-proofing, in terms of both appropriate reorganisation of curriculum and pedagogy and substitutability of a regular teacher cadre by more accountable, even if untrained, relatively cheaper and local candidates, is often included in the solutions.

In its disciplinary assumptions, the managerial-approach-to-teaching aligns primarily with economics and management. This is quite evident in its approach to teachers in the education system as inputs that are substitutable by more cost-effective and supposedly efficient inputs, including para teachers and teacher-proofed classrooms. It is also evident in its understanding of teachers' behaviour as motivated by rent-seeking opportunism of individual rational actors.

The teaching-as-a-profession strand, which locates teachers and the profession in historical, institutional, cultural and social material context, makes the role of teachers central to the educational process and contends that the distinctive professional identity and practice of teachers is constituted both by the knowledge base of the professional community as well as the institutional form in which this community and its work is embedded. Therefore, the institutional limitations of the Indian school system, including the shortcomings of current professional practices of the teaching community, do figure strongly in research aligned to this strand. For example, studies have shown how there is a disjuncture between both policy discourses and educational change efforts and teachers' work, with the former having virtually no space to accommodate teachers' agency in any meaningful form (Dyer, 2000; Batra, 2009; Sriprakash, 2012). As Batra (2005: 4347) observes,

> the contemporary character of a state-led education system often acquires a pretended deafness to the agency of the teacher in the larger process of social transformation in the name of resource and institutional constraints or blind obedience to the 'guruji' in deference to a timeless tradition.

Research aligned to the second strand is also attentive to the historical context within which the disempowered role of the teacher has emerged and consequently been strengthened. Kumar (1991) has pointed this in his idea of the teacher as a 'meek dictator', exercising power in her or his own classroom but powerless within the larger colonial education administrative system. Kumar (1991) attributes emergence of the teacher as meek dictator to the colonial education system that centralised teacher administration and established a break with the pre-colonial role of the teacher as a person in charge of curriculum and pedagogy in her or his own context. This idea of the teacher as a meek dictator has also been observed to resonate with changes in more contemporary times. This is visible in how large-scale in-service teacher training is administered under programmes such as the Sarva Shiksha Abhiyan, with these programmes being defined only in terms of targets to be completed and teachers to be trained anyhow rather than teachers being empowered with professional understanding and skills for the changing socio-cultural context of government schools (Batra, 2005, 2009).

Besides an institutional and historical understanding of teachers' work, the second category of research includes a deeper engagement with the cultural context specific to the Indian school system and the ways in which teachers' beliefs and practices are shaped within such a context. For example, studies by Clarke (2001) and Sarangapani (2003) show how teachers' beliefs and practices draw upon cultural traditions that are more widespread in the larger society and are not aligned to cultural models endorsed by the modern idea of universal education and the school as an institution for propagating such an idea. This is shown to be strongly evident in teacher–student relationships that draw upon notions of 'authority' with reference to the traditional teacher, the family and the existing class structure.

Institutional linkages in this approach explore how for the government school teachers, the changing contexts of pedagogy, society and government schools have barely affected their professional discourse or identity (Mooij, 2008; Sriprakash, 2012). Other studies have extended this argument by examining the socio-material realities of teachers' work and pointing out the contradictions at multiple levels in their everyday work-lives – between ambitious policy objectives and poor resource support, between diminishing professional status and increasing social mobility, and among heightened institutional demands, simultaneous devaluation of professional achievements and identity (cf. Majumdar and Mooij, 2011). Another recent study, which has explored the working conditions of school teachers across nine Indian states, draws attention to the relatively poorly developed status of the management of the teaching profession within the government system. This in turn accounts for many of the occupational problems that teachers have to deal with, for example, the reality that about 42 per cent of elementary schools have a maximum of two teachers only (Ramachandran et al., 2015).

The policy solutions propagated by the teaching-as-a-profession strand include strengthening of systemic aspects of the government school education system with a specific focus on teacher preparation, teacher professional development, continuous personal support and mentoring, and an autonomy and agency for teachers in both larger aspects of curriculum and policy making and more school-level aspects of pedagogy and assessment. What is crucial in this imagination is the distinctive identity for the teaching profession and the normative stand that, irrespective of the professional status and challenges of teachers, only sustained work around practices and belief systems of teachers can lead to desired educational changes that do not short-change the aims of education that should guide a polity such as India, particularly the education of children of the poor.

Problematising commonplaces and issues

In this section of the chapter, we present a few commonplace critical observations about teachers. We show how these problems come to be formulated and analysed differently, based on whether one adopts a framework favouring accountability and efficiency, or a view favouring the centrality of pedagogy and teacher identity. In the first framework, the occupation of teaching itself is seen as involving mainly low levels of skill and techniques, and in the second framework, the occupation is seen as requiring specialised knowledge – theoretical and practical. We present and analyse two cases involving commonplace propositions and show how the same issue can be questioned and problematised differently depending on the framework that one favours.

Case A Teachers with qualifications are mostly neither capable nor motivated.[2]

Question A1: Is it true that teacher education programmes do not attract talented or motivated students?

The managerial-approach-to-teaching answer: Yes, the percentage of those qualifying in the compulsory Teacher Eligibility Test (TET) is abysmally low; it is only about 6 per cent of those who apply. This shows that a disproportionately large proportion of teachers who have acquired professional qualifications are in fact not suitable to be teachers.

The teaching-as-a-profession answer: There is a wide range of quality in Teacher Education (TE) programmes in the country. There is a proliferation of low-quality and fraudulent institutions that have come up in the private sector to cater to the demand for the degree. The statutory institution for regulation, the National Council for Teacher Education (NCTE), is unable to regulate effectively and prevent these institutions from functioning. The state has also neglected the sector with very limited state-funded institutions as compared to the private sector. In the state-funded institutions, which tend to be better in quality, meritorious students are found (see Akai and Sarangapani, 2017). Therefore, students who are interested in becoming teachers are found in better-quality institutions, which also tend to be state-funded (including aided). It would be worth identifying the TE institutions from which teachers who do qualify the TET are educated. Many women who apply to teaching do so on the advice of family members (often men) that teaching jobs will allow them to fully attend to their family responsibilities. The motivations to be a teacher based on interest in the profession, liking to work with students, being inspired by a teacher and so on are secondary reasons cited. However, activities in the TE institution, rigour in preparation and experience of teaching can inspire and create interest and commitment in the profession. While this has been recognised as an aspect of some of the 'new' programmes of teacher education such as the Bachelor of Elementary Education (BElEd) programme of Delhi University, which work on the self and perceptions (Gupta, 2008), it is also found to be true in 'traditional' TE programmes (Latha K., personal communication, 2017).[3]

Case B Teachers in government schools neglect their students.

Question B1: Is it true that government teachers neglect the children they teach?
The managerial-approach-to-teaching answer: Yes, the empirical evidence is that they neglect the children. Time-on-task

studies show us that children are left without supervision for long periods of time (Sankar and Linden, 2014). Teacher absenteeism studies also show us that government school teachers are less likely to be found in schools as compared to private school teachers (Kremer et al., 2005). Private schools can reduce teacher absence as they are better able to make teachers accountable because they do not give them job security and they also have little or no political interference as compared with government schools.

The teaching-as-a-profession answer: No, not all government teachers do. Government school teachers may take legitimate leave, but there is usually no buffer staff to be deployed when they do so, and hence, these classes are unattended (42 per cent of government schools are two teacher schools). In many private schools, while a similar proportion of teachers take leave, the school may have staff who can be deployed to mind classes. Further, in private schools, flexible arrangements may be found so that classes are regrouped based on teacher presence. There are many government school teachers who do not neglect the children they teach, but these teachers are ignored and unrecognised. These teachers are empathetic towards the children on account of the poor home conditions and they do not have negative views about the educability of these children. Such teachers may believe that they need to compensate for the lack of resources and what they perceive to be bad parenting, often on account of poverty. Further, they may believe that the children will drop out and take up jobs early, and they may not expect the children to achieve success in school and break out of poverty through credentials gained in school. Moreover, they may believe that teachers can teach these children to be resilient and self-reliant/independent, develop character and become good citizens. These teachers work from a strong sense of professional identity and may often regard education to be a part of nation building. It is unlikely that we will find such teachers in private schools as they are unlikely to employ teachers with strong professional identities. Government teachers may be working from cultural notions that support identity of teachers as gurus or mothers, etc. (Sharma and Sarangapani, Chapter 12, this book). There is also evidence that as compared to private school teachers and para/contractual teachers, government school teachers have a greater proportion of non-teaching duties (Dundar et al., 2014). This does lead them to spend less time with children and many teachers report feeling 'guilty' on this account (Parul, field notes).

Question B2: Why would teachers neglect children who they are responsible for to educate and for which they are paid?

The managerial-approach-to-teaching answer: Teachers work only if they are made accountable and their results are measured. Government teachers do not work and neglect their students because government systems have poor accountability. In comparison, private schools make teachers accountable, and hence, teachers of private schools do not neglect their children.

The teaching-as-a-profession answer: Teachers who are of the view that the children they teach have a low educability, on account of their caste or poverty, are not likely to make an effort to teach their children, as they believe that these children are unlikely to benefit from their efforts. A teacher may hold this view because she or he is casteist and holds cultural notions/folk pedagogy that children from certain castes cannot be educated. She or he may also hold this view because of her or his own efforts and lack of success in educating children from marginalised and poor communities. Teachers from both government and private schools working with tribal and scheduled caste students and students from very poor or low-income families are likely to hold similar 'folk notions' regarding the process of learning and the aims of education. Their aims of education are likely to differ for different social groups. We are likely to see neglect or 'domesticating pedagogy' in both these kinds of schools.

Question B3: Would contractual appointments and accountability systems, such as the systems found in private schools, be a solution?

> **The managerial-approach-to-teaching answer:** Yes, it is found that para teachers and contractual teachers in the government school system are more regular and produce better results as compared to tenured government school teachers (Atherton and Kingdon, 2010).
>
> **The teaching-as-a-profession answer:** While para teachers and contractual teachers may produce better results and regularity in comparison to permanent teachers in the short term, in the long term, the former are likely to be more demotivated and show no difference (Dundar et al., 2014). Teachers with strong professional identity and professional ethical formation may exercise internal professional accountability, may not require external accountability and may even respond negatively and feel disempowered by external accountability (Green, 2011). Teachers working in private managements who treat education as a 'service' and treat teachers as dispensable labour are likely to experience stress and dissatisfaction. Such schools are likely to have a high turnover of staff.[4]

Conclusion

As the formulations and counter-formulations show us, while there may be agreement or acceptance of phenomena such as 'teacher absenteeism' and 'absence of teacher accountability', how these are 'read', the evidence that is marshalled, the interpretations that explain these phenomena and the solutions that emerge differ both widely and deeply in their understanding of why things are the way they are and what must be done about them.

These contestations regarding teachers' professional identity and practice, particularly what is not working right, why and how to set it right, are high stakes. The financial implications are significant. The costs of teacher education and teacher pay carry significant financial implications for the state and the players in the education market. Teacher education is an expensive activity, with the programme design demanding a student to faculty ratio of 10:1. Further, improving quality, increasing time spent in teacher education and other factors involve greater investment. Teacher pay not only accounts for the major part of any financial outlay of education (state or private) but also is a recurring expense. There are claims that teacher wages in the government sector are disproportionately high and that the market rates of teachers are about 25 per cent to 35 per cent of what government teachers are paid (Jain and Dholakia, 2009). In addition, and perhaps more fundamentally, the two approaches differ on education aims and priorities.

In this chapter, we profiled a key actor in the educational reform process – the teacher – and examined the ways in which different conceptions around the work of teachers and the idea of teaching itself have been shaped in the recent decades. Ideas coming from the 'new discursive regime' are found to be similar to those that come from the 'New Public Management' discourse in education in other countries and the educational reforms centred around the ideas of accountability, efficiency and cost-effectiveness. On the other hand, another set of ideas has focused on the centrality of pedagogical beliefs and practices of teachers and the reforms centred around teacher preparedness and teacher education. Recently, the managerial view of teachers and their work has begun taking this latter view more seriously as the most influential measurement report, the Programme for International Student Assessment (PISA), has drawn attention to the importance of teachers in accounting for the so-called Finland advantage.

As we argued, the idea of teaching as a profession is inextricably linked with the fundamental aims of education, and a reordering of teaching inevitably has long-term consequences for these fundamental values. A technical approach to teaching, as being endorsed by the 'new discursive regime', could well probably have short-term benefits in terms of visible problems of teacher accountability and learning outcomes. However, this would be at the cost of understanding education only as a means to the acquisition of knowledge and skills, often in a limited individualistic sense, rather than as a means of enabling children to engage with constructing knowledge, thinking critically and acquiring capabilities to transform one's own condition and that of the society at large. In addition, one should note that the pedagogic models associated with the technical approach do not provide any unambiguous argument for the overall efficacy of these models, even in terms of student learning outcomes. Indeed, the approach seems to devalue the very idea of any pedagogic model and that of a professional teaching community in favour of other substitutable inputs that can efficiently deliver knowledge and skills.

On the other hand, an approach focused on a recovery of the practice and profession of teaching seeks to build an organic link, in terms of normative values, between what constitutes teaching and what constitutes education. The role of the teacher, her practices and belief systems are held to be central in achieving a conceptual understanding of education and its realisation in the school system, which goes much beyond the diminished version in which education is imagined in the technical approach to teaching.

Notes

1 We are referring here to differences *within the discipline of education* on what constitutes teacher knowledge and how teachers are to be educated. [There is also a contestation on the nature, form and status of education knowledge (and education as a discipline) between educationists and other disciplines. Sarangapani (2011).] With reference to these intra-disciplinary differences, we tentatively identify these two approaches: (a) the old school – behavioural objectives approach, which draws and builds on the work of Bloom (1956) and Taba (1962) and adopts an overall competency approach to teacher development and (b) the new school – informed by cognitive constructivist theories of learning, which draws on the foundational disciplines of philosophy and sociology and foregrounds the construction of self and the beliefs of teachers and, more recently, which has brought in the idea of 'pedagogical content knowledge' (Sarangapani, 2011).
2 This could also involve related propositions such as the following: (a) Teacher education is not useful and does not result in well-prepared teachers. (b) The teaching profession does not attract talent. The teaching profession also does not attract those who really want to be teachers. It is the last-resort profession taken by those who do not get into other jobs. (c) Talented people do not want to join teacher education programmes. It is more important for teachers to be talented than it is for them to have gone through teacher education programmes. Hence, entry into the profession should be deregulated to allow for talent to enter the profession directly, without training. (d) Most government school teachers do not have good knowledge of their subjects and fail in tests given to them on their subject content. (e) Teacher recruitment does not ensure that appointments are merit based.
3 Latha K., who is researching beginning teachers in Bangalore city, has found this in her analysis of interviews with 25 beginning teachers recalling their reasons for joining the profession and their experiences of Pre-Service Teacher Education (PSTE).
4 The two cases, Case A and Case B, are developed as a heuristic device to explain the two frameworks that can be used to assess teachers' work in distinctly different ways.

References

Akai, H., and Sarangapani, P. M. (2017). 'Preparing to Teach: Elementary Teacher Education at a District Institute', *Economic and Political Weekly*, 52(34): 47–55.
Alexander, R. (2008). 'Education for All, the Quality Imperative and the Problem of Pedagogy', Create Pathways to Access. Research Monograph No. 20. April 2008. Institute of Education, University of London.

Atherton, P., and Kingdon, G. (2010). 'The Relative Effectiveness and Costs of Contract and Regular Teachers in India', Centre for the Study of African Economies (CSAE) Working Paper Series 2010–2015, University of Oxford.

Batra, P. (2005). 'Voice and Agency of Teachers: Missing Link in National Curriculum Framework 2005', *Economic and Political Weekly*, 40(40): 4347–4356.

———. (2009). 'Teacher Empowerment: The Education Entitlement-Social Transformation Traverse', *Contemporary Education Dialogue*, 6(2): 121–156.

Bernstein, B. (2000). *Pedagogy, Symbolic Control and Identity: Theory, Research, Critique*. Lanham: Rowman & Littlefield Publications Inc.

Beteille, T. (2009). 'Absenteeism, Transfers and Patronage: The Political Economy of Teacher Labor Markets in India', Unpublished Ph.D. Dissertation, Stanford University.

Bloom, B. (1956). *Taxonomy of Educational Objectives*. New York: David McKay.

Bruner, J. (1996). *Folk Pedagogy: From the Culture of Education* (pp. 44–65). Cambridge, MA: Harvard University Press.

Carnoy, M., Gove, A., and Marshall, J. (2007). *Cuba's Academic Advantage: Why Students in Cuba Do Better in School*. Stanford: Stanford University Press.

Clarke, P. (2001). *Teaching and Learning: The Culture of Pedagogy*. New Delhi, India: Sage.

Donald, J. (2002). *Learning to Think: Disciplinary Perspectives*. San Francisco: Josey Bass.

Duflo, E., Hanna, R., and Ryan, S. P. (2012). 'Incentives Work: Getting Teachers to Come to School', *The American Economic Review*, 102(4): 1241–1278.

Dundar, H., Beteille, T., Riboud, M., and Deolalikar, A. (2014). *Student Learning in South Asia: Challenges, Opportunities and Policy Priorities*. Washington, DC: The World Bank.

Dyer, C. (2000). *Operation Blackboard: Policy Implementation in Indian Elementary Education*. Oxford: Symposium Books.

Green, J. (2011). *Education, Professionalism and the Quest for Accountability*. London, New York: Routledge.

Gupta, L. (2008). 'Making of a Teacher', 3 April 2017, available at www.india-seminar.com/2008/592/592_latika_gupta.htm.

Jain, P., and Dholakia, H. R. (2009). 'Feasibility of Implementing the Right to Education Act', *Economic and Political Weekly*, 44(25): 38–43.

Kingdon, G. G., and Muzammil, M. (2003). *The Political Economy of Education in India: Teacher Politics in Uttar Pradesh*. New Delhi, India: Oxford University Press.

Kingdon, G. G., and Sipahimalani-Rao, V. (2010). 'Para-Teachers in India: Status and Impact', *Economic and Political Weekly*, 45(12): 59–67.

Kremer, M., Chaudhury, N., Rogers, F. H., Muralidharan, K., and Hammer, J. (2005). 'Teacher Absence in India: A Snapshot', *Journal of the European Economic Association*, 3(2–3): 658–667.

Kumar, K. (1991). *Political Agenda of Education: A Study of Colonialist and Nationalist Ideas*. New Delhi, India: Sage.

———. (2010). 'Quality in Education: Competing Concepts', *Contemporary Education Dialogue*, 7(1): 7–18.

Majumdar, M., and Mooij, J. (2011). *Education and Inequality in India: A Classroom View*. London: Routledge.

Masschelein, J., and Simons, M. (2013). *In Defence of the School*. Leuven: Education & Society Publishers.

Ministry of Finance. (2017). *Economic Survey 2016-17*. New Delhi: Government of India.

Ramachandran, V. (2008). 'Primary Education, Teachers' Professionalism and Social Movement: Motivation and Demotivation of Government School Teachers in India', *International Journal of Educational Development*, 28(5): 1–3.

Muralidharan, K. (2012). 'Long-Term Effects of Teacher Performance Pay: Experimental Evidence from India', *Society for Research on Educational Effectiveness*.

Muralidharan, K., Das, J., Holla, A., and Mohpal, A. (2016). 'The Fiscal Cost of Weak Governance: Evidence from Teacher Absence in India', Policy Research Working Paper 7579, World Bank Group.

Muralidharan, K., Niehaus, P., and Sukhtankar, S. (2016). 'Building State Capacity: Evidence from Biometric Smartcards in India', *The American Economic Review*, 106(10): 2895–2929.

Muralidharan, K., and Sundararaman, V. (2013). 'Contract Teachers: Experimental Evidence from India (No. w19440)', National Bureau of Economic Research.

Pritchett, L., and Murgai, R. (2006). 'Teacher Compensation: Can Decentralisation to Local Bodies Take India from the Perfect Storm Through Troubled Waters to Clear Sailing?' India Policy Forum, Global Economy and Development Programmes, *The Brookings Institution*, 3(1): 123–177.

Ramachandran, V., Chatterjee, P., Ravi, A., Linden, T., Beteille, T., Dey, S., Goyal, S., and Mehta, C. (2015). *Teachers in the Indian Education System*. National Synthesis June 2015. New Delhi, India: NUEPA.

Sankar, D., and Linden, T. (2014). *How Much and What Kind of Teaching Is There in Elementary Education in India? Evidence from Three States*. South Asia: Human Development Sector; no. 67. World Bank, Washington, DC.

Sarangapani, P. M. (2003). *Constructing School Knowledge: An Ethnography of Learning in an Indian Village*. New Delhi, India: Sage.

———. (2011). 'Soft Disciplines and Hard Battles', *Contemporary Education Dialogue*, 8(1): 67–84.

———. (2017). 'Sources of Practice and Theory in Education', Paper presented at the Philosophy of Education International Conference. Azim Premji University. Bangalore, January 9–11, 2017.

Shulman, L. (1986). 'Those Who Understand: Knowledge Growth in Teachers', *Educational Researcher*, 15(4): 4–14.

Sriprakash, A. (2012). *Pedagogies for Development: The Politics and Practice of Child-Centered Education in India*. Dordrecht: Springer.
Sriprakash, A., and Mukhopadhyay, R. (2015). 'Reflexivity and the Politics of Knowledge: Researchers as "Brokers" and "Translators" of Educational Development', *Comparative Education*, 51(2), 231–246.
Taba, H. (1962). *Curriculum Development: Theory and Practice*. New York: Harcourt, Brace & World.
Vidya, K., and Sarangapani, P. M. (2011). 'Is Education Nobody's Economic and Political Weekly*, 46(42): 59–76.
Winch, C. (1996). *Quality and Education*. Oxford: Wiley-Blackwell.

6 Notes on quality in education[1]

Padma M. Sarangapani

What do we mean by 'quality in education'? How do we make an assessment of quality in education? And why should we want to do so? This chapter addresses these questions as they are relevant to the current Indian school education. 'Quality in education' has to do with *making an assessment of the worthwhileness of an institution or a programme or a system of education.* Assessment implies normative judgement. The purpose of the discussion on quality in education is definitely linked to the need to make such normative judgements and what follows as a consequence of judging quality. But it means first of all that a programme of education will have to be described in a manner that is relevant from the point of view of assessing its worthwhileness. This requires both senses of the concept of quality as it applies to education – quality as the characteristics of a thing (noun) as well as quality as a measure of the degree of excellence (adjective) (see Kumar and Sarangapani, 2004). The first requirement of assessing quality, therefore, is being able to describe programmes of education so that they can be understood and assessed comprehensively from the point of view of all those characteristics that are relevant to understanding their educational qualities and worth and render them comparable to each other.[2] Such a description and comparison allow for the possibility that educational programmes may vary both in terms of type and degree. That is, they may differ in terms of what they do as well as the degree to which they do it and how well. The normative dimension of quality applies to both types of characteristics – what and how much, that is, type and degree.

I draw primarily on the works of J. P. Naik (1975) who examined this concept at a time when a national policy on education was being drawn up for India, following the Kothari Commission on Education, and Christopher Winch (1996) who was examining the concept that had resurfaced in policy discourse under the influence of neo-liberal,

New Public Management and market-oriented policies in education in the United Kingdom of the late 1990s. These two conceptual analyses of quality, separated by about three decades and located in two very different politico-economic periods and contexts, signify the essential tension that attends the quality debates in India since the 2000s. Naik's work aimed at arriving at an approach that could inform the construction of a national education system which is able to provide relevant quality education for all. Winch's work was engaged with the quality in education in relation to key issues and approaches that emerge from quality discourse of the market where concepts of effectiveness, efficiency and accountability are central. For Naik and Winch, the public character of education is central and necessitates the discussion of quality. They proactively seek to shape the contours and scope of this concept as useful in the context of public systems of education, arriving at dimensions which are remarkably comparable.

'Quality in Education' – a comprehensive, master concept?

Naik wrote his book *Equality, Quality and Quantity* in 1975. This was about 10 years after the publication of the Education Commission's report (Government of India, 1965). In his book, Naik reflectively engaged with the education *system* as it was unfolding in the country after colonisation and provided perhaps the first systematic discussion of the concept of quality as is relevant to education. Naik probably intended that his discussion of equality, quality and quantity and the 'system' encompass the entire range of education from pre-school to higher education. In many sections of the book, there is a suggestion of this – especially in his concerns regarding the relevance of current curricula and the form and status of secondary education, post-secondary vocational courses of study and the linkage of education to employment.

Naik writes:

> In evaluation of the 'quality' of an educational system as a whole or of any of its components (such as teachers or textbooks or a specific method of teaching and evaluation), it becomes necessary to discuss the following issues among others:
>
> 1 Ends and means – The significance and relevance of goals of education from the point of view of (a) the development of the individual in relation to himself, nature, and society; and (b)

development of the society itself. Moreover, since means are as important as ends, the methods used to achieve the goals of education will have to be subjected to the same rigorous scrutiny.
2 Capacity: Very often, one is required to take a view about the potential of a given education system to achieve its content, structure, personnel, organization and finance.
3 Level of performance (or standards): Here the main issues discussed related to the actual performance of the system from time to time on the basis of given criteria and techniques of measurement adopted.
4 Efficiency: This involves consideration of the relationship between the actual performance of the system and its potential.
5 Comprehensive Evaluation: . . . to take a *comprehensive* view of the education system or of one or more of its components from *every* point of view.

(Naik, 1975: 40–41, emphasis in original)

Dissatisfied with discussions that use only the terms 'quality', 'standards' and 'efficiency', Naik defines 'quality' as a comprehensive or master concept and includes in it consideration of the following independent variables:

1 Significance – the judgement of the worthwhileness of the ends and means of an educational system.
2 Relevance – the relationship between the ends and means and individual and social goals of development.
3 Capacity – the potential of a system to achieve its goals.
4 Standards – the level of attainment of students in a given system.
5 Efficiency – the relationship between the actual performance of a system to its potential.

(ibid.: 41–42)

Naik's approach is insightful and significant. He saw the need for any discussion of quality to include a judgement of the ends and means of education – both in regard to significance and to relevance. Further, he explicitly included social goals separate from individual goals (which also include social ends) and clearly visualised both kinds of purposes to be achieved by education – the development of individuals and the development of society itself – the latter would be in relation to equality. The dimension of relevance seems to have come up in relation to Naik's concern that a universalised system of education needs to revisit its goals and broaden its aims and curricula to include productive capabilities that are not narrowly focused on 'white collar' and 'non-manual' forms of employment.

We can regard this 1970s formulation of 'quality' in education as one that arose out of the Indian context and out of the need to comment on the status of the system of education in India in order to chart policy thrust areas. We may also note that when 'quality' entered formal policy discourse as separate from the concern of 'access' in District Primary Education Programme (DPEP), it was *not* the master concept that Naik had in mind, but only with reference to achievement of 'minimum standards' (Sarangapani, 2010) and efficiency.

Winch (1996) is perhaps the only existing systematic discussion of the current notion of quality – which we must acknowledge has entered into education as a part of the ascendency of neo-liberal politics and the increasing application of market and management principles to public services. Winch accepts the validity of the key notions of 'accountability' and 'interest groups', which are central to the neo-liberal approach to public services, but argues that they are integral to liberal democracy and the increasing democratic scrutiny of public services. Further, he takes the view that engaging with the concept of quality can reshape discussions of educational worthwhileness in meaningful ways. For Winch, the discussion on quality becomes essential on account of the public character of education. First, Winch engages with the idea of accountability. The neo-liberal arguments for accountability emerge on account of the utilisation of taxpayers' money in education. Winch extends this to include not only the stewardship of finances but also the political and moral dimensions. Accountability is a valid dimension of quality as students and teachers give their time and effort for education, and hence there is a need to ensure that this time and effort is not wasted. This form of the principle of accountability also applies to pupils' accountability to each other and to the teacher, as well as the teacher's towards the children and the government's towards the teachers and so on. The concept of 'interest groups' is shown to be far more complex than the dichotomy between consumers and producers, which is the terminology of the market. It includes those being educated (learners), those responsible for those who are being educated (often parents or caregivers), state, taxpayers (both individuals and corporate bodies) and government.

Winch develops his examination of quality across five dimensions which effectively constitute a framework for quality in education:

Notes on quality in education 143

1. Aims – as education is a purposeful activity. Winch argues that education must be recognised as a complex activity and that there is a need to take a broader view of aims than is common in the liberal tradition and include economic growth and social cohesion as valid purposes. In other words, the criteria for assessing the educational worthwhileness of aims need not be narrowly confined to the liberal tradition but may accommodate wider interests. Winch points out that the aims of education need to be arrived at through political processes and need to reflect the political consensus achieved. The broadened notion of interest groups informs both the educational aims – allowing for diversity – as well as accountability.
2. Curriculum – the plan for the accommodation and achievement of diverse aims.
3. Standards – the existence of an appropriate measuring rod or criteria of judgement. Winch argues strongly that at least in some areas, for example academic achievement, which is an important outcome, there can be consensus on the standards that should apply, that these standards can be used and performance judged against them and compared.
4. Practice – the pedagogic work of the school and the teacher, both of which are recognised as being educational because they are not merely technique, but are imbued with value.
5. Accountability – the scope and practice of accountability is redefined with reference to financial, political and moral requirements and in relation to different interest groups.

In a later essay on quality, Winch (2010) argues that outputs (measured against standards) cannot, by themselves, constitute a judgement of quality. Not only does this mean that they must be discounted in relation to what they have added (or 'value add'), they must be taken *along with* the process through which they have been achieved.

In Winch's conception of quality in education, schools located within a system (which includes political processes) are the sites of providing education, and it is with reference to schools that quality in education needs to be understood. Winch discusses the problem of trying to comprehensively arrive at a judgement of quality of any institution, through any conceivable method. It would never be able to meet either the logical requirements of how one can arrive at such a judgement, nor would it meet the requirement of objectivity – given the time constraint and the processes through which it would be expected to function. Having said this, he finds that systems such as inspectorates, rather than trying to meet formal requirements of assessing standards, may serve a useful function if they are focused on parts and on particulars, such as institutions, rather than trying to provide comprehensive commentaries on quality (learning standards and quality, teaching quality, etc.).

A striking similarity in the manner in which both Naik and Winch develop their conceptions of quality in education is the centrality of the idea of a 'national system of education' – that is, education as a political project for which the state commits taxpayers' money and in which the state sees the formation of a public good. For both Naik and Winch, the state is a democratic state which sees universal benefit in education. This automatically requires them to see education as a complex process and to problematise the notion of 'aims of education' as being politically contestable and in need of being broadened to respond to diverse interests. This not only means due consideration of social and economic aims in addition to individual ones but also of vocational in addition to liberal aims. Naik separates significance and relevance as two criteria against which aims must be judged.

Naik and Winch identify the planning process dimension for quality. Naik however looks at this in terms of capacity, which includes provisioning, while for Winch, provisioning is not significant but curriculum is. Both curriculum and practice are somewhat underplayed in Naik's conception, which seems to have a greater focus on availability in the system of schools, classrooms, materials and teachers. The possibilities of substandard learning quality (e.g. rote memorisation) or pedagogy do not receive his attention. Winch separates the idea of standards from the performance against standards; Naik uses the term 'standards' only to mean achievement or performance level. Winch successfully makes arguments against epistemic pessimism vis-à-vis standards, along with a later argument that this alone, without knowledge about process, cannot inform one about quality. Furthermore, Winch's arguments are restricted to (performance on) the academic subjects. They do not extend to include learning outcomes such as self-concept of learner in relation to the academic subjects. Winch has a more nuanced approach to the understanding of practice and also a recognition of the 'value' and 'dispositional forming' dimensions of education, and the need to see outcomes in relation to the process through which they were achieved rather than in isolation. Naik's efficiency may be mapped onto the dimension of accountability, although the latter is more directly related to democratic requirements while the former seems to flow more directly from administrative or bureaucratic needs and only indirectly from democratic needs. Both agree that quality cannot be reduced to only standards or achievement on standards and accountability or efficiency. While Naik seems to believe that a comprehensive evaluation of quality is possible, Winch does not quite take up the question of what this may entail, but instead focuses on aspects such as school evaluation (which he finds problematic) and sees merit in focused assessments of particular dimensions. For both, educational worthwhileness has both an individual or personal and a social dimension. Naik is particularly concerned about the problem of equality – he effectively seems to arrive at a similar concern that equality requires diversification and the ability of a system to respond equitably to different interests, without attaching status and preference. The unit of analysis seems to be at the political system level – as being the logical point at which aims of education are negotiated and arrived at, and a system put in place for their achievement. We may also notice that the school as an institutional arrangement for the provisioning of education may have an educational sanctity in Winch's formulation (although he does not make this explicit). However, the school is surprisingly invisible in Naik's system.

Krishna Kumar's (2010) writing on quality is in response to the contemporary discourse which he feels is built around thin ideas of 'outcomes', 'transparency', 'accountability' and 'competitiveness'. He argues that these are neo-liberal agendas and are not the dimensions which are salient in giving activities their *educational* quality. Instead, his proposal is for teacher autonomy and dispositions and the ability to address inequality in society. The autonomy of the teacher (and by extension, the control that a learner has) is over the teaching–learning situation. This amounts to an understanding of where educationally relevant authority rests and how it is shared with teachers and children. The second dimension is to do with the skill and disposition building capacity of education in relation to equality. How does education address disadvantages that accrue on account of inequality (e.g. language, gender) and thereby increase freedom by removing restraints? This is different from the opposition of quality (as excellence) with quantity, which is in relation to competitiveness. Kumar's characterisation of quality is at the level of the school and at the level of the system. Both the key dimensions he chooses as characterising a programme of education, school or system for an understanding of its quality are significant for the Indian context, that is, the authority of the teacher in relation to the system and control of the child, and the school's or programme of education's explicit ability to address and deal with inequality in Indian society. From Kumar's paper, it is difficult to decide whether he intends that these should be taken as individual school characteristics or the characteristics of pedagogy that vary from institution to institution or as systemic characteristics which vary at the level of educational systems – more likely all three. The two characteristics seem to have the quality of indicators – of the 'quality or health of an education system'.

Kumar also seems to approach educational outcomes as 'valued' on account of their being primarily positional rather than possessed of intrinsic worth. They may have intrinsic worth as well, but that in itself is not key to or the crux of the quality question. He seems to be suggesting that educational effort should be directed at addressing inequalities which may alter the acquisition of positional goods through processes of schooling. He, therefore, seems to be more concerned with the need to ensure that social goals are met in the process of education rather than *through* any intrinsic qualities of education. His formulation does not include content and process considerations in education quality, but it does allow that one could make judgements of worthwhileness based on participation and achievement to be examined on the axis of achieving equality.

Discussing an approach to quality that may be relevant to the Indian context, Alexander (2008) identifies pedagogy as central to educational worthwhileness. Pedagogy is imbued with purposes and meanings and is not mere technique. Further he argues that a *full* understanding of pedagogy is necessary to be able to characterise fully how going to school and being taught produces education.

> Teachers develop procedures for regulating the complex dynamics of pupil-pupil relationships and the equality of law, custom, convention and public morality in civil society. . . . Further, teachers and teaching convey messages and values which may well reach beyond those of the particular learning tasks which give a lesson its formal focus.
>
> (ibid.: 31)

Alexander tries to make an argument for acknowledging culture, and therefore, to begin with description and later move to judgement. He also regards the act of teaching as only one facet. The 'act' of teaching takes place in the 'form' of lessons and is 'framed' by space and resources, student organisation, time, curriculum and routine, rules and rituals. Further, pedagogy has an ideational dimension. At the level of the classroom are the ideas that enable teaching (about students, learning, teaching, curriculum); at the system level are ideas that formalise and legitimise teaching (about school, curriculum, assessment and other policies); and at the cultural or society level are ideas that locate teaching (about community or family attitudes and mores, culture, and self or identity). Although Alexander argues for an approach to understanding pedagogic quality in culturally sensitive ways, he does privilege interaction between teachers and pupil and the use of language in the classroom as especially important in education and in giving pedagogic experiences an educational worth from the point of view of students' learning. As such, it is not clear what is gained from invoking the concept of culture in the study of quality of education. Instead, one may agree that context (in the sense of a political system) is important as aims and purposes of education would differ from context to context. What he calls 'culture' perhaps could be better understood as one of several competing ideologies on the what and why of worthwhile education, schools and pedagogy.

Neither Kumar nor Alexander starts with a comprehensive approach to quality in education, but both prefer to focus on what they regard as essential and central in making an activity educationally worthwhile. Although the idea of purposes of education is important in their formulation of what would contribute to understanding quality, the scope of their conception is not developed in response to any democratic requirements nor the public character of education. Again, although they are concerned with the aims and purposes of education, neither has a view about the need for standards or accountability or efficiency dimensions. Yet, they do arrive at a conception of quality which extends to include systemic considerations, intentions and ideas, aims and curriculum, along with actual practice, but which is nevertheless anchored on teachers and teaching. What is significantly missing is the question of accountability and efficiency. Alexander directly articulates a point that is implied in Winch, that there are levels of needs within a system for assessments of quality, and one need not approach conceptualising quality, nor assessing it, as if the same information as well as the same standards of objectivity and reliability be applied across all levels. Dhankar (2007) offers a formulation of quality which looks at three dimensions: the education ideals and values that guide the system and are of the nature of being social aims such as equality and justice; sociopolitical concerns such as sensitivity, autonomy and reason; and economic contribution. Education outcomes are conceptualised at the individual level. In contrast to the observation made by Mehendale in Chapter 3 (this book) on aims, most of these outcomes are academic in nature, drawing on the key activities that occupy most of the school curriculum and are the concern of the timetable and examinations. These approaches to quality are compared in Table 6.1.

Table 6.1 Comparison of quality frameworks

Quality dimension	Naik (1975)	Winch (1996)	Kumar (2010)	Alexander (2008)	Dhankar (2007)	Global Monitoring Report 2005
Aims of education, individual and social	Significance of means and ends and relevance of means and ends – individual and social	Aims – political process	Addressed to alleviate effects of inequality Neither significance nor relevance of aims – not intrinsic educational worth of aims	At both ideational or intent and formal and actual manifested	Selection of aims – social and personal	Literacy and numeracy for all
Provisioning or planning	Capacity, includes conception of curriculum but also planning and provisioning of infrastructure and teaching as well as access			Societal, cultural, systemic or school, institution and classroom, and also teacher and teacher education		Enabling quality, but not itself indicative of quality
Curriculum		Curriculum – the plan for pedagogic activities for achieving educational aims				
Standards and assessment	Meeting standards	Standards and outcomes	–	–	Standards for quality of learning	Both are important
Pedagogy: 'Valuable' practice	–	'Valuable' practice	Teacher authority and pupil control; 'value'-based and moral	Practice imbued with educational purpose and value		Trained teachers
Accountability or Efficiency	Efficiency	Accountability	–	–	Standards for processes	Accountability to community and cost-effectiveness

Source: Author's own work

The exploration of the conception of quality through these five studies draws our attention to the need for a wider and inclusive concept that allows all five dimensions to be examined and assessed: (i) aims of education, (ii) provisioning (infrastructure) and curriculum, (iii) standards and assessment, (iv) pedagogy, (v) accountability. The concept of quality then appears to be, as Naik noted, a 'master concept'.

Historical interlude

While it is true that 'quality' has been invoked as an educational ideal in Indian post-independence policy discourse, it has been used more for rhetorical purposes as a portmanteau term to draw attention to the content and process of education and the differences created by differential provisioning. Naik's seminal work on quality discussed earlier in this chapter did not contribute as a framework for policy planning. Access and provisioning and universalisation of elementary education were the primary concerns of the state, but from the District Primary Education Programme period onwards (i.e. about 1995 onwards), quality began to find mention as an aim of policy and state action in education (Sarangapani, 2010). The shift to include quality has been noted and critiqued from different viewpoints in three essays carried in *Contemporary Education Dialogue Special Issue on Quality* (CED, 2010). Velaskar (2010) finds that the centrality of the idea of 'equality of educational opportunity' as an aim is displaced and 'quality', which is the replacement, has a reduced and tokenistic commitment to equality. Pappu and Vasantha (2010) criticise the class biases in existing conceptions of quality, especially with regard to childhood, the place of work in the life of the child and assumptions regarding the role of the parents. Sarangapani (2010) finds the formulation of 'quality' in large-scale programmes in elementary education limited, equated with either achievement levels alone or with standards of provisioning, and with an undue emphasis on the dimension of efficiency (cost-effectiveness). It also seems as if the concept of quality was to be applied only to government schools (schools for the poor) and one could then approach it with a reduced and circumscribed expectation vis-à-vis the aims of education as having to deliver literacy and numeracy.

The quality debate has continued in this last decade; empirical research on quality continues to be constructed around selective indicators of provisioning or outcomes and retain focus on schools for the poor (see Table 6.2). The key question now being asked is how government or private schools fare in comparison with each other on various metrics of quality, such as outcomes and achievement.

Table 6.2 Education quality and indicators

	Study	Schools observed	Unit of analysis	Qualities examined and indicators selected
1.	Govinda and Varghese (1993)	Rural government schools, MP	School (class IV)	(1) Achievement test in Class IV
2.	Anitha (2005)	Rural government primary schools, Karnataka	School (class IV (teacher and practice)	(1) Standards achieved in numeracy and literacy tests (2) Teachers' pedagogic practice types (3) Teachers' attitude and definition of education objectives (4) Average length of school day (5) Student attendance
3.	Mehrotra and Panchamukhi (2006)	All types of schools by villages Rajasthan, Madhya Pradesh, Uttar Pradesh, Bihar, West Bengal, Assam, and Andhra Pradesh and Tamil Nadu	School	(1) Enrolment by gender (2) Teacher absence (3) Infrastructure, especially toilets for girls (4) Mono or multigrade classrooms (5) Pupil teacher ratio (6) No. of working days
4.	Kramer and Muralidharan (2006)	20 states, rural areas, government and private schools	School	(1) Teacher absence (2) Rating on infrastructure index (3) Incidence of teacher dismissal for negligence (4) Multigradedness (5) Teacher–pupil ratio (6) Class size (7) % of teachers engaged in teaching (8) Level of starting English (9) Pupil achievement

5.	Srivastava (2006)	2 Uttar Pradesh private schools	School	(1) Parental views
6.	Tooley, Dixon, and Gomathi (2007)	Urban zones in Hyderabad	School	(1) Teacher absence (2) Teacher activity (3) Pupil teacher ratio (4) Infrastructure (5) Equity (gender in enrolment) (6) Medium of instruction (7) Parental preference
7.	Tooley and Dixon (2007)	Government, private, unaided recognised and private unaided unrecognised, east Delhi	School	(1) Teacher absenteeism (no. of teachers absent on a given day) (2) Class IV teacher activity (3) Infrastructure (inputs) (4) Philanthropy (equity) (5) Gender in enrolment (equity)
8.	Jalan and Panda (2010)	Rural government primary schools, West Bengal	School	(1) Achievement test (2) Attendance (3) Dropout Explanatory variables: school and teacher characteristics, school supervision, teacher training and other government programmes, community participation
9.	Education Initiatives (2010)	Government schools in 20 states	School (as represented by classes IV, VI, VIII)	(1) Results on achievement tests for language and maths (2) School infrastructure (3) Teacher practice (4) School characteristics

Source: Author's own work

Two dimensions have dominated recent studies of quality – outcomes as measured by achievement test scores of children in mathematics and language and provisioning, which are inputs in the form of school infrastructure. Pedagogy has been studied in very few studies. In general, a limited view of teachers' work, primarily reduced to mere teacher presence (or absence) and 'time on task' are taken as adequate metrics of teachers' work. Given the salience of the private versus government comparisons for many of these studies, it is to be expected that parental preference and teacher absence are more frequently documented. Equity concerns, mainly in the form of enrolment of girls and SC/ST students in private schools, have been examined. More recent studies continue to focus on education outcomes as the most important quality dimension for comparison between institutional types as well as for equity concerns.

'System' – 'school' – 'class': what is the unit of analysis?

The usage of 'quality of education' implies that the term applies to a programme or course or relatively long-term deliberate engagement with learners, with particular institutional arrangements, organisation, involvement of people, including teachers, activities of teaching–learning and assessment. In other words, a 'system or programme of education' is an instantiation of the provisioning of education, and the characteristics which are relevant to the question of quality of education involve the characteristics of this: why, where, who, what, how and how much. It would therefore include ideas or intent, planning and practice.

What is the relevant unit of analysis for quality of education? Is it the 'education system' which is assessed and described for its qualities (understood as a political system with a particular view of and commitment to education)? Is it an individual school? Is it a school understood in terms of the sum of its practitioners and practices? Is it a system of schools under an education administrative structure (e.g. government schools)? Or is it a school along with its management or board (e.g. a private school)? Is it a board of education with all the schools that it oversees and regulates? Or is it a department of education, with all types of schools that it regulates? Is it a political system that gives itself an act such as the Right to Education?

The studies summarised in Table 6.2 all approach quality as a feature of a school and more particularly, as a feature of a type of school management: government or bureaucratic management or private management. The conceptual studies that have been used to develop the quality master concept, however, suggest that quality of education is produced and managed not only by the school by itself, but by the larger organisation within which the school is embedded, from which the school derives its educational programme or provision vision or plan – what, what type, where, how, how much, for whom, by whom, when, how long. The 'school' is a particular spatial unit with institutional arrangements, teachers, classrooms and children, the location of practice and the site where the day-to-day of education takes place. However, as we can see from the dimensions of quality (and the idea of a 'programme of education'), 'school' may not by itself contain all that is relevant to understanding the educational characteristics of a programme of education, in the provisioning of which, it is a part, and it has a part to play.

An organisation which creates a programme of education not only translates aims into plan, curriculum and practice, but also, at least in the Indian case, may be forging a working consensus on the aims of education that would be its guiding purposes. Such a system may coincide with a school, in the case of a private school managed by a trust or set up by an entrepreneur. But it may also encompass a set of schools – in case there is a trust managing several schools, which may be at several levels, or a chain of schools and so on. In the case of government-run schools again, for example the Morarji schools in Karnataka, which are all run by a society, would constitute such a system. In other words, it is a 'system of education' which would contain all the dimensions and characteristics that have been discussed under the concept of quality – aims, capacity, curriculum, standards, practice, accountability – and not the unit of the school per se.

However, the unit of 'school' may be particularly important in understanding practice and teachers' work, and we also realise that there may be a special status for the school as an institution that needs to be understood and factored in separately into our considerations of educational worthwhileness. We could argue that aims, capacity or provisioning, curriculum, standards, practice and accountability are all relevant at the levels of system, school and individual teacher or classroom and ask whether those aspects which are 'more than school' and contributing to system could be located in the governance structures, for example administration, management, board.

While we may be certain that the assessment of quality of education would be for an education system, would we be able to provide an assessment of *quality of education* of a school or teacher? We may provide an assessment (or more likely a partial assessment) of one of the characteristics, as clearly system, school and teacher are not independent of each other but are interacting sites, and their characteristics are likely to be understood only if we allow for interaction and mutual influence. Each is constitutive of and constituted by the other. For example, the schools' accountability for the appropriate use of teachers' effort may be determined, or at least constrained, by systemic factors.

The key argument in favour of the school is that it is the 'school' and not 'organisation' that is the legal unit (recognised by RtE, requiring a No Objection Certificate [NOC], etc.), and also it is the school that has a physical existence. Further, educational purposes which are under consideration in this discussion of quality are realised through a process of schooling and by going to school. Both the individual and social aims of education that are the purposes of programmes of education are realised through schooling. Schools, and not individual classrooms, are given the responsibility of providing educational programmes. The 'classroom' is a part of this programme, albeit an important part. Some questions that need to be clarified are regarding whether the school can be understood in terms of the sum of its classrooms or average classroom, and in terms of the sum of its individual students and their achievements or their average achievement. So also the system is important in how it enters into and shapes the educational worth of a programme of education offered by a school. Perhaps the relevant unit is 'school with teacher in system'.

Conclusion: questions on quality of education in the current Indian context

In the light of the above discussions – both relating to how we conceptualise quality of education and the overview of existing studies on quality – we can now ask the question: What do we want to know about quality in the current Indian context and why?

Most approaches examine a selection of metrics such as (i) student academic achievement – by gender, rural, urban, caste; (ii) infrastructure; (iii) teacher qualifications, gender; (iv) presence of and use of teaching learning materials; (v) teacher presence and time on task; (vi) access, enrolment, completion, absence. A set of indicators would need to be developed that would enable us to examine and assess the dimensions of (i) aims of education; (ii) provisioning, design, capacity; (iii) curriculum; (iv) standards and achievement; (v) pedagogy; (vi) accountability. Related to this is the question of what accounts for the quality that is seen or found. Is it finances, ideology, culture or history? A quality as master concept approach using the five dimensions

Notes on quality in education 155

developed by Naik and Winch could be the basis of studying empirically the range of educational institutions in a society to understand what qualities of education are on offer and why there are differences. The Indian education system has always been a very diversified system beginning from the period of British colonisation. Historians of the early phase of the development of schools have noted the presence of many providers – private, missionary, government and government-aided, as well as more than one medium of instruction – vernacular or English. Further, schools differed in the level of education they offered – one distinction being primary, middle and high, as well as the curricula they offered – vocational or 'academic' and also were sometimes segregated for gender, as well as residential or non-residential. Schools were also affiliated to different regional boards of education which prescribed different curricula as well as provided different certifying examinations. This variety has only increased since independence. There may be several different boards of education and language policies within boards (especially vis-à-vis the place of English versus mother tongue). Minority institutions are regulated differently. In addition to the department of education, traditionally, the social welfare department has also had an involvement in education – setting up special schools for tribal children or SC children. More recently even within government, there may be different types of schools – government (municipal), model, Sarvodaya, Morarji, Navodaya, and in addition, several government-supported pan-Indian school systems such as Kendriya Vidyalayas or schools of societies of public sector undertakings, such as Atomic Energy Schools. Similarly, the private sector of schools is diversified, not only in terms of the level of fees charged, but also in terms of management structures and multiplicity of schools, as well as school chains, including schools run by NGOs and by other private entrepreneurs which may not even be recognised as schools. This is a considerable variety in types of schools and complex relationships to state departments of education as regulatory authorities and boards of examination as certifying authorities. Our understanding of the educational characteristics of this range of schools is very limited. Often, only very broad typologies are offered and followed in existing studies, using very broad categories such as government, private, or only by medium of instruction, or only in terms of rural, urban, and thus giving us very limited understanding of the variations in the characteristics of these institutions and the quality of the education they provide.

Our conception of quality and the tools we develop to study quality could enable us to map the range of school and institutional forms.

It could enable us to arrive at the significant aspects of similarities and differences between schools and provide us with the possibility of revisiting whether the current dominant typology of government and private, or government, government-aided and private is a significant one from the point of view of educational quality. We would be able to investigate the question of who goes where and why. What is the basis of the differentiation of clientele of different schools? To what extent and in what form do 'quality' considerations enter into school selection? To what extent do non-quality-related attributes of schools – positional attributes, cost and so on – contribute to school selection?

In the context of RtE, there is an increased pressure on the state to provide access to schools, for the state to regulate schools more actively as well as for all schools to now provide access to underprivileged social groups and thus become more heterogenous. The impact of these on the diverse types of schools – their response to the RtE clauses as well as the manner in which the RtE may reconfigure their educational characteristics – are also important subjects of study.

Finally, as regards the aims of education, it may be that the aims of education are being renegotiated in public and private spaces, so that the diversity of schools may need to be understood in relation to aims, and 'achievement standards' alone may not enable us to understand school diversification as a social phenomenon in relation to educational aims. It may also enable us to reflect on the extent to which schools have moved away from the aims of the traditional education system that catered to the middle class and are negotiating both the aims of education and curricular requirements that are emanating from policy and boards of education and those that are emerging from politics and from parent communities. The neo-liberal climate too has led the governments of some states to deregulate schools to a greater extent. The manner in which this has produced or contributed to the emergence of new aims in education can also be examined. In the course of this investigation, we may be able to separate those characteristics and aims that are found desirable on account of their educational value and those that are found desirable for other reasons – convenience and status being some possible values. These distinctions are important in understanding and interpreting 'school preferences' and 'school selection' by parents.

Notes

1 This chapter is a revised version of my unpublished 'Notes on Quality', dated 17 December 2010, discussed at the workshop on Comparative Study of Schools, 17–18 December 2010, Tata Institute of Social Sciences, Mumbai.

2 It is probably worth noting at this point, that there may be characteristics of programmes of education which are not important from the point of view of their educational worth, but which, nevertheless, may account for or be important in understanding their social role and value.

References

Alexander, R. (2008). 'Education for All, the Quality Imperative and the Problem of Pedagogy', Create Pathways to Access Research Monograph No. 20, University of London, Institute of Education.

Anitha, B. K. (2005). 'Quality and the Social Context of Rural Schools', *Contemporary Education Dialogue*, 3(1): 28–60.

Contemporary Education Dialogue (CED). (2010). *Special Issue: Quality*, 7(1). Guest Editor Rohit Dhankar.

Dhankar, R. (2007). 'The Idea of Quality in Education', unpublished paper presented at International Conference on Quality in Education, Organised by Digantar and ICICI-SIG, Jaipur 11, January 12, 2007.

Education Initiatives. (2010). *Student Learning Study*. Ahmedabad: Education Initiatives.

Government of India. (1965). 'Report of the Education Commission', (Kothari Commission).

Govinda, R., and Varghese, N. V. (1993). *Quality of Primary Schooling in India: A Case Study of Madhya Pradesh*. Paris: International Institute of Education Planning, available at http://unesdoc.unesco.org/images/0009/000960/096038eo.pdf [accessed 8 December 2010].

Jalan, Jyotsna, and Panda, Jharna. (2010). *Low Mean and High Variance: Quality of Primary Education in Rural West Bengal*. Calcutta: Centre for Studies in Social Sciences.

Kramer, M., and K. Muralidharan. (2006). 'Public and Private Schools in Rural India', available at http://scripts.mit.edu/~varun_ag/readinggroup/images/d/dc/Public_and_Private_Schools_in_Rural_India.pdf [accessed 18 February 2018].

Kumar, K. (2010). 'Quality in Education: Competing Concepts', *CED*, 7(1): 7–18.

Kumar, K., and Sarangapani, P. M. (2004). 'History of the Quality Debate', *Contemporary Education Dialogue*, 2(1): 30–52.

Mehrotra, S., and Panchamukhi, P. R. (2006). 'Private Provision of Elementary Education in India: Findings of a Survey in Eight States', *Compare: A Journal of Comparative and International Education*, 36(4): 421–442.

Naik, J. P. (1975). *Equality, Quality and Quantity: The Elusive Triangle of Indian Education*. Mumbai: Allied Publishers.

Pappu, R., and Vasantha, D. (2010). 'Educational Quality and Social Inequality: Reflecting on the Link', *CED*, 7(1): 94–117.

Sarangapani, P. M. (2010). 'Quality Concerns: National and Extra National Dimensions', *CED*, 7(1): 41–57.

Srivastava, P. (2006). 'Private Schooling and Mental Models About Girls' Schooling in India', *Compare: A Journal of Comparative and International Education*, 36(4): 497–514.

Tooley, J., and Dixon, P. (2007). 'Private Schooling for Low Income Families: A Census and Comparative Study in East Delhi, India', *International Journal of Educational Development*, 27: 205–219.

Tooley, James, Dixon, Pauline, and Gomathi, S. V. (2007). 'Private Schools and the Millennium Development Goal of Universal Primary Education: A Census and Comparative Survey in Hyderabad, India', *Oxford Review of Education*, 33(5): 539–560.

Velaskar, P. (2010). 'Quality and Inequality in Indian Education: Some Critical Policy Concerns', *CED*, 7(1): 58–93.

Winch, C. (1996). *Quality and Education*. Oxford: Wiley-Blackwell.

———. (2010). 'Search for Educational Quality: The Dialectic of Inputs and Outputs', *CED*, 7(1): 19–40.

Part II
Empirical studies

7 Hyderabad's education market[1]

Padma M. Sarangapani

In international education development discussions on education market solutions for access to quality education, Hyderabad was made famous by James Tooley's studies of 'budget' schools in the Muslim-dominated areas of the city. Tooley began in the early 2000s with a study commissioned by the Centre for British Teachers (CfBT) to investigate the market potential for English-language teaching (Tooley and Dixon, 2003a). He has claimed to find evidence that the needs of the poor for quality education are served best by an education market, that private providers in this market produce better quality compared to the state, and that market discipline works effectively and produces value for money while state regulation is corrupt and produces inefficiencies and distortions (Tooley and Dixon, 2003b, 2006; Tooley, Dixon, and Gomathi, 2007; Tooley et al., 2010; Tooley, 2009, 2010).

We (Sarangapani and Winch, 2010) had critiqued Tooley's studies, which we found did not provide adequate contextual details that are crucial to interpretation, confused educational opportunity with education and lacked a conceptual definition of quality that would guide selection of appropriate metrics. Jain, tracing the category of 'private' and 'public' (Chapter 1, this book), has drawn attention to the continued presence of private players in education from the colonial period, including 'public private partnership' in the form of state grants-in-aid to privately managed schools. This has drawn attention to the need to unpack the ideas of good education that are held by different sections of society – parents, schools and the state (Chapter 2, this book).

A study of quality in one education *mandal* of Hyderabad was designed to take a more contextual, historical and 'ecological' approach to understanding the education market, school diversity and quality (see Introduction, this book). The analysis of the concept of quality as relevant to assessing educational worthwhileness, presented in Chapter 6 (of this book), was used as the framework to guide the selection of indicators of quality. Quality, as argued in Chapter 6, is best understood as a multidimensional, composite concept having the dimensions of educational aims, provisioning, curriculum, standards and learning outcomes, and pedagogic practice, and the sixth related dimension of accountability and efficiency.

One educational mandal in the city of Hyderabad was selected, which presented both a very diverse demography, as well as a range of types of schools (as listed in the DISE). A census approach was adopted to be able to study all types of schools with a common set of tools and to be able to understand the types of schools and school quality that are available. A similar survey was also planned in Delhi and Kolkata. In Delhi, we were less successful in gaining access to all the schools (Chapter 8, this book). In Hyderabad, on account of the support we received from the education department, we were very successful in accessing almost all schools (with a few exceptions, see next section on the schools).

The rich data has allowed us to build a new commentary on a range of schools through which the educational needs of Indian children are currently being met and on the interaction of school quality with social class, caste, religion and language. The findings of the study, which are presented in this chapter, validate the value of the approach of this study in understanding school diversity and the educational market in relation to the segmented and stratified Indian society. It allows us to explore questions such as who goes where and why, the relationship of the cultural capital of the home to school quality, the management of market-based accountability and the relationship of pedagogic forms to class formation.

The chapter begins with an introduction to the city of Hyderabad and the 84 schools that were surveyed. Findings are presented in two parts. First, the school managements and their clientele are presented. This is followed in the second part by a presentation of the schools and school quality.

The context

Hyderabad was the capital of undivided Andhra Pradesh and, since 2014 when the state was divided, has continued as the capital of the new state of Telangana.[2] The city is over 400 years old and has a sizeable Muslim population (over 30 per cent) (Census of India, 2011). Between 1995 and 2005, the leadership of the ruling Telugu Desam party promoted the use of information technology (IT) and the city as friendly to the IT sector and multinational corporations.

The neighbouring district of Rangareddy, which the city straddles, was renamed 'Cyberabad' by the then chief minister Chandrababu Naidu, signalling political parties' view of the importance of IT in the development of the city and the state. Over all, a pro-liberalisation image was cultivated and private sector enterprise was encouraged. The state also pioneered the entry of the private sector in public services, particularly in health, pioneering schemes such as Arogyasree health insurance, and introducing e-governance in many sectors (Mooij, 2003).

The state of undivided Andhra Pradesh was also notable for the very large number of privately run engineering and medical colleges and a thriving private coaching industry aimed at cracking competitive entrance examinations ranging from elite exams such as the Joint Entrance Examination (JEE – entrance to the Indian Institutes of Technology) to various state exams. Some of these successful coaching chains, after 2000, reinvented themselves as schools, starting from class VI, with the stated aim of enabling students to succeed in the entrance tests through gruelling regimes of preparation in mathematics and science in particular. Suffixing the words 'techno' or 'concept' to their name, they have built a new brand identity in the private fee-paying school sector. The brand identity signals their unique value and pedagogy in the market, comparable to the earlier brand types of 'public' and 'convent' which were popular in the 1970s and 1980s and stood for English medium education. In 2000, the regulations governing private schools were revised, deregulating the pay scales of teachers employed in the private sector. A minimum of 40 per cent of the earning of the school through fees and other sources was to be spent towards teachers' salaries.[3] The city of Hyderabad also saw a sudden mushrooming of private low-fee-paying schools in the same period.

Between July 2011 and October 2011, 84 schools identified in one education mandal 'A' of Hyderabad city were surveyed. Mandal A was selected as the latest District Information System for Education (DISE)[4] indicated that it had many types of schools: a reasonable number of government and aided schools, a range of private school types and a madrassa. A group of 12 researchers with education training spent time every day for over four months, locating and visiting schools and studying them using a set of seven tools.[5]

Mandal A is known for a busy retail commercial hub nestled at its centre (see Figure 7.1). Busy arterial roads run through it connecting the city of Hyderabad to new developments. The area includes a range of socioeconomic groups, from upper middle classes – professional, government bureaucrats and police – to low middle class, working class and a few slums with migrants from the northern districts of

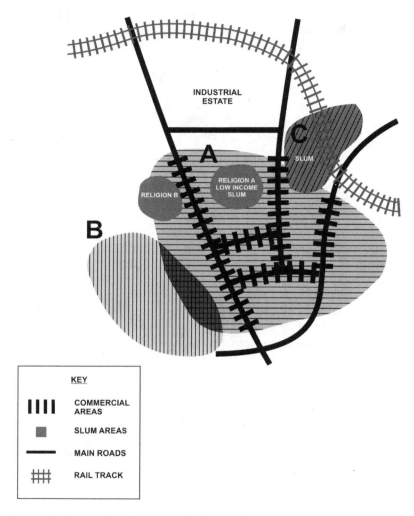

Figure 7.1 Rough layout of the mandal surveyed
Source: Author's own work

the state. The population includes old residents of the city as also newer migrant communities and from diverse linguistic and regional backgrounds and localities, with a concentration of Muslims and Christians. One side of the mandal is an old industrial estate whose character is now changing as manufacturing is moving outside the city. Another side is an upper middle class residential area of Hyderabad, a third side is a slum and informal sector manufacturing and tinkering mainly for the automobile industry. A fourth side extends into the new lower middle class development areas. Driving through the mandal, it is difficult to miss the schools, coaching centres and tuitions houses amidst the shops and restaurants, all crowded along the main roads. With their brightly coloured walls and boardings with the school name and photographs of top student ranks in the most recent class 10 examinations, the schools position themselves to catch the eye of passersby, much like any shop selling its wares in the market place.

The schools

Mandal delimitation in the city is a difficult task given the continuous nature of areas and layouts. Further, mandal limits do not coincide with other boundaries such as election wards or municipal wards. Some schools listed on DISE had been closed, and many not listed were found. Actual government schools also were at variance with the records as schools listed separately had been 'consolidated' in fact. Another practical anomaly is that most private schools are listed twice, separately as elementary and secondary schools. The total schools finally identified were 84, including a few which were on the borders of the mandal.

School types, spread and year of establishment (Table 7.1): Of the 84 schools surveyed, 11 per cent were run and funded by the government and 6 per cent were aided schools. The mandal had a large proportion of private unaided recognised schools (57 per cent), of which a large proportion were low-fee-based schools (70 per cent of the unaided recognised schools) and 20 per cent were unrecognised private schools. This included many high-fee-based schools, 11 low-fee-based schools and 3 charitable schools (refer to Table 7.1).

The schools were spread unevenly over the mandal. The low-fee-paying schools, aided schools and charitably funded schools were mostly found in residential areas. In and around the slum areas were schools funded by charitable or religious institutions. Mainstream private schools and particularly new private schools were clustered on roads in and around the main market and commercial areas. A large

Table 7.1 Schools in Mandal A, B and C and year of establishment

	1(a) Location				1(b) Period (decade of establishment)								
	Mandal A	A/B	Mandal C (slum)	Grand Total		1930s	1950s	1960s	1970s	1980s	1990s	2000s	2010s	2011 ni
A) Government	8		1	9	11%		3	1	1			4		1
B) Aided	5			5	6%	1	2	1	1					
Government-aided	3			3	4%		2		1					
Government-aided and charities (religious mission, CSR, grants)	2			2	2%	1		1						
C) Private Unaided Recognised	45		3	48	57%		1	1	3	16	14	12	1	
Charities (religious mission, CSR, grants)			1	1	1%							1		
Fees and charities (religious mission, CSR, grants)	2		1	3	4%					1		2		
High-fee-based	10			10	12%				1	3	3	3		
Low-fee-based	33		1	34	40%		1	1	2	12	11	6	1	
D) Private Unaided Unrecognised	12	6	2	20	24%					2	3	7		1
Charities (religious mission, CSR, grants)	1		1	2	2%						1	1		
Fees and charities (religious mission, CSR, grants)		1		1	1%							1		
High-fee-based	6			6	7%								6	
Low-fee-based	5	5	1	11	13%					2	2	5	1	1
E) Madrassa (unrecognised)	1		1	2	2%					1		1		
Grand Total	71	6	7	84		1	6	2	5	19	17	24	7	2

Source: Author's own work

number of the low-fee unrecognised schools were in the periphery of the mandal. Most (but not all) of these unrecognised schools were known to the mandal education officer who even had the phone number of the school owner. We had naively assumed that the low-fee-unrecognised schools would try to run and hide from officialdom. We found 55 per cent of these schools were easy to access and open with all aspects of the study. Some 15 per cent were difficult to access and gave us limited access to information and data. About 11 per cent of schools obstructed our entry, using delaying tactics and rudeness to keep us out, declaring that local education officers had no authority over them, or being elusive and obstructionist. By contrast, 30 per cent of recognised private schools and 40 per cent of unrecognised private schools were very difficult, elusive and obstructionist and required extraordinary persistence to gain limited access and information for the analysis presented here.

The oldest schools in the area were two girls' schools, established by a Hindu reformist mission in the 1930s with the aim of promoting girl's education in the memory of the daughter of a founding trustee. Both of these schools, after independence, became aided schools. One of them had closed down by the time of the study while the other was thriving under the patronage of a caste group women's trust. Between 1950s and 1970s, most of the schools in this mandal were government schools and government-aided schools. After 1980s (and until 2000s) no new government schools or government-aided schools were added to the mandal. Instead, there was a spurt of private schools, with as many as 16 from the 1980s and growing at a steady rate of over 10 schools added in each decade. In the year of our survey, as many as 7 new schools were added to the mandal, of which 6 were high-fee-paying schools. A few new government schools were added in the Sarva Siksha Abhiyan (SSA) decade of the 2000s in low-income and slum areas of the mandal.

We found that 93 per cent of the schools were co-educational. One recognised and three unrecognised schools catered to children with special needs. All the private recognised and 90 per cent of the private unrecognised schools were English medium. Eight of the nine government schools had an English medium section in addition to Telugu and Urdu mediums. The aided schools were all required to be Telugu medium. Three of these aided schools' managements had started fee-paying English medium schools under the same recognition license! There were only four other schools that were not English medium – all of these schools were funded by charities. Two of these were Urdu madrassas. One Telugu medium school was an evening school centre funded by a Christian mission. One Telugu medium school was a shishumandir affiliated to the RSS and funded by a Hindu mission for which education in the mother tongue was an ideological choice.

Size, catchment and stability (Table 7.2): The size of schools varied widely, from fewer than 50 students (five schools) to between 2,000 and 3,000 students (one school). Of the schools surveyed, 20 per cent had enrolments less than 100 and 35 per cent had enrolments less than 150. An enrolment of about 400 seemed to be a 'tipping' number for stability, giving an average class size of 33 in 12 levels. About 38 per cent of schools had enrolments greater than 400, with three schools being very large with enrolments greater than 1,500. Based on the reports of the school heads and the enrolment trends of the last few years, it seemed that 15 per cent of the schools were well established, sought after and with growing enrolments. About 42 per cent were maintaining their status. While 25 per cent were struggling to keep their enrolment intact and collect fees regularly, 14 per cent were shrinking and losing their enrolment.

About 70 per cent of the schools drew their catchment from the local areas, and about 15 per cent drew their clientele from a wider area using buses and vans. Among high-fee-paying schools, 11 per cent drew their clientele from the entire city. Almost without exception, the low-fee-paying schools had local clientele. One high-fee-paying school, which had been started by a charismatic mathematics teacher with a local reputation, also had a largely local clientele. Some 58 per cent of the schools had the full range of levels from pre-primary to the 10th class. All private schools except three followed this model. The three exceptions had only upper primary and secondary (i.e. class 6 to 10) and were among the 'coaching type' schools with a focus on class 10 exam results in mathematics and science. These schools admitted students selectively – they did not want to be distracted by the educational requirements of the early classes or the liabilities of low-performing students.

Small schools: Of the sample, 29 schools had an enrolment of less than 150. Of these, 17 were low-fee-based (38 per cent of 45 low-fee-based schools and 90 per cent of the unrecognised low-fee-based schools). Among small schools (with enrolments less than 150), 21 out of the 29 were found to be struggling to survive or with shrinking enrolments; this included all the 17 small low-fee-based schools. The only small schools that were steady or even growing were the ones that were government-funded or which had the support of charities (7 out of 9 such schools). Aided schools, which had not secured any other sources of funds, were struggling and shrinking – 15 of these

Table 7.2 School enrolment size and growth status

	2(a) School enrolment band												2(b) Enrolment growth status					
	0–50	50–100	100–150	150–200	200–300	300–400	400–500	500–1,000	1,000–1,500	1,500–2,000	2,000–3,000	nil	Growing	Steady	Struggling	Shrinking	nil	Total
A) **Government**							2							9				9
B) **Aided**		1	2	1	4	1		1					1	1	1	2		5
Government-aided		1	1	1										1	1	2		
Government-aided and charities (religious mission, CSR, grants)			1					1					1					
C) **Private Unaided Recognised**		1	7	2	5	3	9	9	6	2	1	3	11	19	12	6	3	48
Charities (religious mission, CSR, grants)									1				8	1	1			10
Fees and charities (religious mission, CSR, grants)			1					1		1				17	11	6		34
High-fee-based		1	6	2	5	2	8	4	3			3	2	1				3
Low-fee-based				1		1	1	4	2	1	1		1					1
D) **Private Unaided Unrecognised**	5	7	2	1				2	2			3	1	4	8	4	3	20
Charities (religious mission, CSR, grants)		2											1	3			2	6
Fees and charities (religious mission, CSR, grants)	1														6	4	1	11
High-fee-based	3	5	2									1		1				1
Low-fee-based	1		1					2				2			2			2
E) **Madrassa (unrecognised)**		1	1											2				2
Grand Total	5	12	12	4	9	4	11	10	8	2	1	6	13	35	21	12	3	84

Source: Author's own work

small schools that were running on fee had children in classes from preschool up to the 10th. These schools had multigraded classes: a teacher would be surrounded by students of different classes sitting in groups whom she or he taught, rather tutored, by turn.

The managements and the clientele

In terms of their gross features, the schools in the market had considerable variation. This section draws attention to the schools' financial status, managements' business plan, educational ideology and the socioeconomic status of the clientele.

Managements (Table 7.3): The department of education (DEO) had mainly three kinds of managements: the primary school, the high schools and the SSA-slum school. There were 10 distinctive types of private management forms identified, which proved to be useful in understanding aspects of the financing, academic identity and education qualities of schools. Each of these management forms represented a distinctive education ideology – defining their purpose in being in education and their educational imagination and their intentions. Inherent was also an image of their clientele – as representing either a particular community (socioeconomic-religious) that they wished to serve or a particular economic group defined by the amount and regularity with which they would be able to pay a fee.

Corporate management was characterised by hierarchical control in matters such as teacher appointments, curriculum, textbook selection, assessment and reporting, and even daily lesson plans, across all branches from the central control office. New corporate schools were more professionally run while old corporate schools used family to extend and keep control. In general, these family trust schools regarded education as a good for the community and saw their school as serving the needs of a local community and the nation. Most of the older family trust schools were now managed by the second generation of the family and included some family members who had qualified as teachers and were active in teaching and managing the schools as heads. If not, the family kept direct control of the school with their daily presence. Some 61 per cent of all fee-based schools were started by entrepreneurs. As many as 95 per cent of such entrepreneurial schools were low-fee-based schools, and 46 per cent of these were started by teacher entrepreneurs. Typically, they had started their career as teachers for some other private school in the same local area and had decided to set up their own school. They frequently cited the desire not to work for someone else and to be independent as the

Table 7.3 Management types and sources of funding

Broad management category		Specific management type	Government-funded	Government-aided	Government-aid and charities*	Charities	Fees and charities	Low-fee-based	High-fee-based	Total	
1 Government (district education office)	9	Primary	9							5	11%
2	2	High school								2	
3	2	initial SSA-funded slum school								2	
1 CSR-philanthropy	1	Trust (CSR)				1				1	1%
2 NGO-expert specialised group	2	NGO					2			2	2%
3 Religious organisations	12	Charity (religious)				1				1	1%
4		Mission			1	3	1			5	6%
5 (Hindu, Islamic, Christian)		Religious trust			1		1	2	2	6	7%
6 Family trusts	7	Family trust		3				3	1	7	8%
7 Individual entrepreneurs	41	Teacher entrepreneur						18	1	19	23%
8		Tuition teacher-entrepreneur						5		5	6%
9		Entrepreneur						16	1	17	20%
10 Corporates	12	Corporate						1	11	12	14%
			9	3	2	5	4	45	16	84	

Source: Author's own work

Note: * Charities include religious missions, CSR and grants.

key motivator for this move. Eight had established their reputation as maths and science tutors and had broken away to start their own schools when they were confident of their tuition clientele. Four were women teachers and said they made the change because they wanted to pursue their educational ideas. Eight of these schools had achieved a stable enrolment of 400.

Schools established by tuition teachers and business entrepreneurs tended to cater to the lowest socioeconomic groups (mostly groups 4 and 5 explained in the next section). The five which had been started by tuition teachers were very small schools and ran like home tutorials. Another 17 schools were started as businesses by entrepreneurs, including three women. Most had opted for the school business as a means of earning a living, thinking that it would be relatively easy to establish and run schools. They had acted on the advice of a friend or relative and often because they had the use of space – an apartment or house. One of them had seen the advertisement for a school for sale in the newspaper and had decided to buy it. There were at least seven cases of the school registration and recognition having been bought by the current management. In some cases, management held more than one registration under different names, though there was only one school. Of the 50 privately managed schools which did not charge high fee, 19 were managed by families, typically a husband–wife team, and 12 were managed by women. Close to 50 per cent of the schools were run like family enterprises in order to make ends meet.

A total of 12 schools had religious purposes and ideals. These institutions drew on religious connection. Six of these were for the poorest of the poor of the area. One was a Christian charity catering to children who were not able to attend regular school, five were directly under a religious mission (Christian convent, mosque (madrassa) and the RSS (Saraswathi Sishu Mandir)) and offered religious instruction along with formal schooling. Their teachers worked at very little or no pay out of a religious commitment to serve the poorest of the poor of their community. Six were run by religious trusts (including a Christian convent mission which had a minority status) and offered faith-based modern education for the religious communities they served.

There was one professionally run non-fee-paying school by a CSR-funded trust with a non-religious approach to working with the poorest of the poor. This organisation had similar schools in several parts of the city. Two NGO-run special schools raised funds for their work and involved parents and volunteers in running the school.

As can be seen from these descriptions of management forms, each involved an implicit business plan based on a niche being created through their unique educational offering and aims of attracting a clientele group with the ability to pay, and pay regularly, by appealing to their perceived aspirations. For a large number of schools that had not reached the magical turnaround number of about 400 enrolment, existence could not be taken for granted. Many were struggling to survive, and many were shrinking. Low-fee-paying schools, in particular, mostly survived through a family effort and involvement, much like any small business. These distinctions in educational management forms enable us to develop a more nuanced understanding of managing finances and client–vendor relationships. Some of the specific attractions in operation were being a successful neighbourhood tutor or reputed teacher, being an institution of a particular religion, offering special education for children with learning difficulties, and, in the case of high-end schools, the lure of competitive success. These were all aspects of the client–vendor relationship over and above the fee. This combination enables us to understand the niche carved out by the school or served by it, and gives us insights into the education on offer in that institution.

Clientele

We were able to elicit fairly detailed accounts of the occupational profiles of parents (Table 7.4). These categorised into five economic–occupational groups that were then used to categorise the school clientele (Table 7.5). Groups 1 and 2 represented the elite, well-to-do and educated end of the spectrum (white-collared, professional or businessmen). Group 3 represented 'pink-collared' occupations involving low but regular income, including primary school teachers, accountants, supervisors, skilled workers such as plumbers. Group 4 represented blue-collared jobs including domestic workers, fruit and vegetable vendors, manual labourers. Group 5 represented the poorest of the poor, dalits and very poor Muslims, with occupations such as ragpicking and scavenging.

In general there was a noticeable homogeneity of clientele across schools. High-fee-paying private schools were patronised by clientele from Groups 1–2, low-fee-paying schools catered to Group 4. Interestingly, and significantly, this was also the group that was largely found in the government schools – both primary and high schools. The poorest of the poor (Group 5) were not served by either the low-fee-paying schools or the government schools. It was the charities – mainly religious and one CSR school – that served children from this group. There were only three schools that catered to a range of

Table 7.4 Occupational profiles of parents

SE-occupational groups	Employment types
Group 1 (elite, upper middle class)	Software engineers, doctors, professionals, bank professionals, elite government servants
Group 2 (upper middle, middle class)	Businessmen, lawyers, small businessmen, shop owners, hostel owners
Group 3 (lower middle class)	Low-paid services (electricians, plumbers, accountants), supervisors, clerks, shop employees, company employees, tiffin centre or mess employees, private or primary school teachers
Group 4 (working class)	Domestic workers, watchmen, daily wage labourers, rickshaw pullers, mechanics, fruit vendors, white wash painters, bakery and hostel maintenance workers, carpenters, saree embroidery workers
Group 5 (poorest of the poor, dalits and poor migrants)	Ragpickers, scavengers, scrap collectors, people in sporadic and unreliable employment

Source: Author's own work

socioeconomic groups – extending from Group 1–4. One of these was run by a religious trust and was meant only for students from one community. The other two were special schools dealing with a specific disability and run by an NGO. That is, they were heterogenous with regards socioeconomic profile, but homogenous from another point of view, religion and disability, both of which are important dimensions of stratification and hierarchy and inequality in Indian society.

Unrecognised schools were largely catering to either the highest or the lowest of the economic and occupational groups. Both these groups of clientele seemed to be less concerned about recognition. The high-fee-paying groups were all part of chains with a huge demand and well positioned to protect their students' interests regardless of recognition. For the poorest of the poor, the matter of recognition seemed to be irrelevant. The private unaided recognised schools, with enrolments between 400 and 1,500, established in the 1980s and 1990s, were stable and well established and were all catering to clientele in Groups 3 or 4. A large number of schools (35: 25 PUR and PUU) catered to Group 4. Of these, 16 schools were very small and struggling. In many

Table 7.5 School clientele

	Groups 1–2	Group 2	Groups 2–3	Group 3	Groups 3–4	Group 4	Groups 4–5	Group 5	Groups 1–4	Groups 2–4
Charities (religious mission, CSR, grants)							4	1		
C) Private unaided recognised							1			
D) Private unaided unrecognised							1	1		
E) Madrassa							2			
Government						7	1	1		
Government-aided						5		2		
Fees and charities (religious mission, CSR, grants)			1		1				1	1
C) Private unaided recognised			1		1					1
D) Private unaided unrecognised									1	
Low-fee-based	3	4	2	2	9	21	2			1
C) Private unaided recognised	1	4	2	2	9	14	1			1
D) Private unaided unrecognised	2					7	1			
High-fee-based	13	2			1					
C) Private unaided recognised	7	2			1					
D) Private unaided unrecognised	6									
Grand Total	16	6	3	2	12	31	7	3	1	2

Source: Author's own work

Group 1 – elite, upper middle class: software engineers, doctors, professionals, bank professionals, elite government servants

Group 2 – upper middle, middle class: businessmen, lawyers, small businessmen, shop owners, hostel owners

Group 3 – lower middle class: lower-paid services (electricians, plumbers, accountants), supervisors, clerks, shop employees, company employees, tiffin centre or mess employees, private or primary school teachers

Group 4 – working class: domestic workers, watchmen, daily wage labourers, rickshaw pullers, mechanics, fruit vendors, white wash painters, bakery and hostel maintenance workers, carpenters, saree embroidery workers

Group 5 – poorest of the poor, dalits and poor migrants: ragpickers, scavengers, scrap collectors, those in sporadic and unreliable employment schools catering to Groups 4 and 5, teachers reported that children worked before and after school hours – girls typically helped their mothers who were domestic workers and boys worked in mechanic shops, fruit and vegetable vending and local hotels.

Quality dimensions

With this background understanding of the providers and consumers in the education market, the school managements and their clientele, we now profile and analyse the schools along the five quality dimensions and accountability.

Aims

Each school evolved in its business niche to develop its unique selling proposition (USP) which defined its academic identity for itself and for its clientele.

'We serve the needs of a particularly constituency of the community.' These schools were run by charitable or religious groups, and their constituencies were girls from a particular religious group or the poorest of the poor of a particular group. By 'learning *hukumat*' and being able to pass exams privately, providing a Christian education to make girls God-fearing and learn to love Jesus, becoming good citizens and working for nation building, students were socialised into community values and enabled to the extent possible to take advantage of opportunities through education. As the school was integrated into the community and saw this as its purpose, their ability to collect fees was limited.

'We serve the poor' was key to the education identity of 19 schools. The needs of the poor were interpreted as 'access to modern education' (in 8), 'access to English medium education' (in 2) and included learning social norms of obedience and adjusting to society. 'Access to education to develop character, resilience, confidence, independent thinking and problem solving' was the aim in 6 schools that were aided or charitable. In government schools, multiple aims were seen, depending on the teacher. For some, the aim was 'domesticating and civilising the poor'. Other teachers saw their work as either serving a community need or serving the poor to develop confidence and independent thinking.

'We give affordable good education and unlike the greedy corporate schools, we want to develop children for the country, we enable "dullers"[6] (sic) to pass by training them in hard work and discipline' characterised about 13 of the low-fee-based schools. Many of these schools struggled to cajole parents to pay fee and often humiliated their children by making them stand outside and miss classes or even examinations. This group did not promise 'results' and 'high marks' in the 10th exam. They often referred to how they accepted children who had been rejected by other schools and enabled them to pass. At the higher end of this spectrum of affordable good education, the management (often teacher-entrepreneurs) also spoke of all-round development, the importance of English and good marks in mathematics and science.

Corporate schools promised 'training for success in competitive exams' and focused on preparing students for professional courses and with analytical and conceptual thinking in mathematics and science. Reflecting emerging trends in career aspirations of this class, some of these corporate schools were including more 'all-round development' in their educational aims. 'All-round development with values' was the articulated aim of well-established schools serving Groups 1 and 2. 'We develop personality through scientific testing' was the claim of another. 'Not an engineer or doctor but an IAS officer who can hire any engineer or doctor' suggested that these schools were preparing students for a wider range of white-collar employment opportunities.

There were schools that did not articulate or formulate any specific educational ideal that defined them (8 recognised and 3 unrecognised). All of these were struggling and shrinking, low-fee-based schools run by entrepreneurs and teacher-entrepreneurs. Several of these schools were facing a management crisis following a family crisis. In one case, the school had lost its mooring in the last few years as the head had run into financial crisis after investing all her money into making a film with her son. These managements were focused on just staying afloat, and retaining their students. Three of these schools ran like tutorial centres, with flexible timing for students and teachers based on mutual convenience and multigrade grouping based on how many teachers and how many students turned up. As one of the entrepreneurs put it, for this fee, no good education can be provided.

Provisioning

In this mandal, 42 per cent (i.e. 35 schools) of the schools functioned in spaces that could be designated as 'institutional' spaces. These were buildings constructed on plots earmarked for schools – government, private and aided. This included 8 of the 9 government schools, 2 of the schools run by religious missions and all the CBSE-affiliated schools.

Among these schools, the majority (25 of 35) were old schools in the area, all established before the 1980s. They had spacious classrooms, were generally well ventilated and well lit, with well-positioned blackboards. They also had play areas or open areas, and a few of them had good playgrounds.

Eleven schools functioned in commercial spaces. Here, the building was typically shared with shops and other commercial establishments. There was no open area in such schools and children had to remain in the classrooms all through the day. Another 31 schools ran in residential spaces – independent houses – and in 11 of these, the owner also lived in the same space. Half of these were small houses which had no open space at all, and children had to remain in their classrooms all through the day. Classrooms were accessed one through the other, and noise from one spilled into the other rooms. They were very cramped, and children were huddled on benches close to each other. Often, the blackboard was small and placed in a corner of the room. There were 6 schools, 2 recognised and 4 unrecognised, which ran in places that were unsafe, badly lit and ventilated, poorly maintained and congested: the basement of a building, the roof top of a small house with open brick partitions and tin roof, and sheds in an open ground with construction activity going on around. All recognised schools claimed they had an agreement with a local municipal park or ground for PE, but said that it was unsafe to take children there daily. Twenty-two schools had very poor maintenance – these were all schools catering to the poor and the poorest of the poor (50 per cent of the government, 20 per cent of the private aided, unaided and unrecognised schools).

'While in government and aided schools teacher staffing was easy to understand and establish, in the private schools this was more difficult. These schools had a range of people working, from various types of management and administrators to teachers, quasi- and part-time teachers, maintenance staff and family members. The mornings were usually busy times during which making alternative arrangements for the classes of absent teachers was a major activity. Schools with student strength of more than 200 seemed to have sufficient buffer of adults who could be deployed to supervise the classes. In smaller schools, arrangements were flexible and fluid and children were grouped based on teacher availability. The government schools were not provided with cleaners, but in all schools, teachers had pooled money to employ a person to clean the premises and manage the midday meal. In private schools, managements said they had a staff turnover of about 4 to 5 teachers each year. Teachers said they preferred not to work in the corporate schools in spite of better pay as they preferred schools where they could develop a better relationship with the school head and take leave as and when they needed it. For women in particular, such flexibility and understanding from management was important.

Curriculum

Of the 84 schools surveyed, 74 followed the state curriculum and textbooks. Of these, 7 pursued what may be considered an abbreviated curriculum as they were focused on exam preparation alone and used guidebooks only. Three of the corporate schools claimed to be offering an 'enriched' curriculum, drawing on the SSC, CBSE and ICSE curricula as also competitive exams and private olympiads. Five others were known for their competitive exam preparation curriculum and materials, and the state board textbooks were incidental. As regards diversified and enriched curricula, only the CBSE schools in the area followed this as was mandated and regulated by the CBSE. In other schools, this was a function of infrastructural resources and ideology or educational imagination. Over half (46 of 84) of the schools had a timetable with only subject teaching every day, the only variation being morning assembly which tended to be short and was conducted over a PA system with all the children standing in their own classrooms. Seventeen schools offered a limited range of additional activities: primarily computer classes, intraschool competitions with a school head and 'houses' and participation of a few children in mandal-level interschool events. Eighteen schools offered very diversified curricula that included music, dance and art; activities in clubs; and school excursions. Such varied curricula were provided in 73 per cent of the schools catering to Groups 1 and 2, 15 per cent of the schools catering to Groups 3 or 4 and 24 per cent of the schools catering to Groups 4 and 5. These schools were more likely to be the ones started by family trusts (60 per cent) or teacher entrepreneurs (50 per cent). Schools started by tuition teachers or entrepreneurs were more likely to be limited to only subject teaching (88–100 per cent).

Forty-four of the private schools prescribed additional textbooks and materials. This seemed to be linked to the schools' profitability for the owner or entrepreneur, but the exact relationship could not be determined. Twenty-eight schools extended school hours to offer tuition, tutoring and coaching. In corporate schools, students came two hours earlier and stayed back for two additional hours for coaching. Schools that did not extend hours had periods in the timetable blocked for supervised study.

Pedagogy

An understanding of pedagogy was synthesised drawing on five dimensions: (i) teachers' expectations and aims for the children they were teaching, (ii) their expectations of students' homes, (iii) the method they were employing to teach, (iv) the method they employed to make students learn and finally (v) the prevalent form of discipline and moral regulation. At least one class each in primary and middle school were observed and teachers were interviewed. The schools and teachers observed were assigned specific characteristics along each of the five dimensions, and the observations were then synthesised into eight broad pedagogic forms.[7]

In all except 5 schools in which we were able to observe pedagogy in two or more classes, we found the same pedagogic form, suggesting that pedagogy was largely determined by the institution and the individual teacher had relatively limited authority to decide methods of teaching and of learning. The corporate schools provided micro teaching plans. The high-fee-based schools required progressive pedagogies to realise their own educational ideals, and these were fostered through professional inputs, guidance and timetabling. In schools where drill or textbook pedagogies were followed, there was generally little supervision of what teachers did, being limited to occasional suggestions by the school head. Much of the institutional conformity seemed to come about through self-selection of teachers joining these schools or following existing practices.

A very high variability of pedagogic forms within the same school was noticed only in aided and government schools attended by children in Groups 4 and 5, where pedagogy varied from domesticating type to elaborated, dialogic and progressive pedagogies depending on the individual teacher and her ideological stance and interpretation of the value of education for the children. The government and aided institutions exercised no influence or control on what teachers did or how they did it.

Overall there seemed to be a strong relationship between the social class of the clientele and the pedagogic form of the school, with domesticating, massified pedagogies for the poorest to progressive, individualised pedagogies for the richest (see Table 7.6).

Most of the low-fee-based private unaided, unrecognised schools catering to Groups 4 and 5 had pedagogies for citizenship and basic literacy for the poor. It was common to hear teachers remind children that they were from poor homes. Rarely were textbooks seen in these classrooms. Usually, the blackboard was small, badly maintained and

Table 7.6 Pedagogic forms by funding type and clientele groups

	Funding type							Clientele group											Grand Total	
	Charities***	Fees and charities	Government-aided	Government-aided and charities	Government-funded	High-fee-based	Low-fee-based	Groups 1–2	Groups 1–4	Group 2	groups 2–3	Groups 2–4	Group 3	Groups 3–4	Group 4	Groups 4–5	Group 5	nil		
No information	1	1				2	5	3			2				1			1	7	8%
Special education	1															1			2	2%
Religious	1		1PD**		3		9										1PD		1	1%
Basic citizenship or domesticating													1		8+1PD	4	1PD		13	15%
Dialogic (mother tongue)	2R*		1+1PD		1V		1	1							1+1PD	2	1PD		7	8%
Guidebook and drill		1	1		5		13	13		1				6	14			1	21	25%
Textbook and repetition				1			13					1	2	4	6				13	15%
Textbook and understanding		1		1		2	3	1		4		1		1					7	8%
Competitive exams and swotting						9	1	8		1				1					10	12%
Textbook and all-round development (English medium)	1					3		3								1			3	4%
Total	5	4	3	2	9	16	45	16	1	6	3	2	2	12	31	7	3	1	84	

Source: Author's own work

Notes:
*: R – Religious
**PD – Teacher-dependent pedagogy varies between dialogic and harsh domesticating. The same school is classified under 'basic citizenship and domesticating' and 'dialogic (mother tongue)' but is counted once in the total.
*** – Charities includes religious charities and missions, CSR and philanthropic grants.

rarely used. The teachers defined what needed to be learnt. They rarely made eye contact with the children and mostly marked things for students to copy out in their notebooks. Supervision was negligent and sporadic. The authority of the teacher was personalised, discretionary and total. In a few aided schools and government schools, individual teachers adopted a 'domesticating' pedagogy, where children learnt little more than obedience: to keep quiet and still. Teachers could be heard speaking roughly to them and mocking their poverty, saying that their parents could not clothe or feed them and that they were in school for the midday meal. Teachers seemed to expect that this group would drop out of school soon.

In the low-fee-based recognised school group, rote or drill-type pedagogies were found in 74 per cent of the schools. Teacher-entrepreneurs schools were more likely to have drill pedagogies – while most of the class was conducted in a chorus format, attention was individuating (not individualised). Teaching was cursory, but a lot of time was spent on making children learn by repetition and constant checking on individual children. In the teaching phase, portions to be memorised would be marked out while in the learning phase, children were expected to repeat and repeat. In the entrepreneur or tuition entrepreneur schools, many of which were shrinking and had crowded classrooms, teachers did little more than supervise rote learning.

There were usually little or no expectations of home support, and the home was believed to have negative influences on the children. Children in these small crowded classrooms – their large school bags on their desk and their books on top of the bags – frequently fought with each other, knocking or jabbing each other and making noise. Most of the teachers' efforts were in maintaining discipline and order. Corporal punishment was frequently resorted to in these schools. It was common for a teacher to be holding the child's ear while correcting her book, twisting it each time a mistake was found. The teachers shared and drew authority from the textbook and examination; the parents and children feared the shame of failure in examinations. Some of these schools supported 'dullers' – children who had been pushed out of other schools on account of failure – to pass examinations through more supportive attention.

Schools and parents had a tense relationship, centred mostly on the regularity of fee payment and the possibility of their children being humiliated publicly by having their names called out, being made to stand outside the classroom or even being sent home. The school had to manage relationships with parents to retain their patronage and ensure fee could be collected regularly, occasionally making concessions such as reduced fee or free education for one sibling. The interactions with parents were completely controlled by the school head or some delegated authority. Teachers and parents had little or no direct interaction except for occasional parent–teacher meetings in which they exchanged complaints about the students' need to study more, be disciplined, work hard and give up bad habits of watching too much TV. The child was a shared moral project. Sharma (Chapter 10, this book) draws on her ethnography in a north Delhi village to provide a finegrained understanding of this side of private managements.

Among the low-fee-based schools were a group of older institutions that favoured pedagogies that were textbook-based, but also involved understanding. In these schools, teachers spent time teaching in addition to also supervising and ensuring learning. Though the form was not dialogic, children could ask questions for clarification and bring new information into the classroom. They answered in their own words rather than simply repeating the textbook verbatim, and these answers were accepted and in some cases even appreciated. These schools had more all-round development in their curricula, and children had sports and games and some art and music activities. Attention to children was more individualised. In these schools, even if parents did not have much cultural capital, particularly of English, they could be expected to send children to school with all necessary resources and punctually.

In the more high-fee-based schools that catered to children of professionals and wealthy businessmen, the home provided the necessary cultural capital for learning English. Pedagogy was oriented to all-round development. Teaching was elaborate and interactive, and students were expected to learn to express themselves and understand. The textbook and exam were important, but students also were expected to participate in other activities, including sports, art, craft and music, and develop overall self-confidence. Revision involved variation and positive feedback and encouragement. Discipline involved self-control, with appeal to reason or values, sometimes religious.

In swot pedagogies found in the corporate schools, conceptual abilities found favour over rote learning or memorisation in mathematics and science. Students were expected to be able to apply what they had learnt to solve new and tricky problems at high speed. Although in English medium, they were less focused on achievement in English or self-expression. The pedagogy provided individuated attention in a competitive environment, with frequent assessments and grading and tracking progress. Discipline was achieved through the strict management of students' time within the school and even at home. Parents and teachers closely co-operated in this effort. Teachers were expected to call homes at 4.30 a.m. to check if children were up and studying.

Dialogic pedagogy was also found in mother tongue education schools catering to the poor and the poorest of the poor where there was no home support for schooling. Teachers in these schools viewed the home with empathy, acknowledging the stress experienced by children on account of poverty and violence in the home. The teachers in these schools were keen to develop the children's resilience, independence, self-confidence and ability to learn and stand on their own feet. They felt being able to read for understanding rather than rote learning was important because these children had to rely on their own abilities to make anything of their lives. They did not have either any cultural capital at home or parental resources to get them ahead in life. Reading for understanding was important as they would need to make sense of things on their own. Children could be heard asking questions and arguing with teachers. The teachers did not seem to think that the children would make their futures through paths that involved school academic success (examinations). They expected them to drop out and enter the workforce early. Progressive pedagogy seemed to be relevant to provide life skills to students who could not hope to continue in school, though these life skills seemed different, even opposite, to the skills and attitudes needed for success at school, such as obedience, memorising and reproducing textbook knowledge. Sharma and Sarangapani (Chapter 12, this book) discuss the formation of these pedagogies in government school teachers, through the personal resources of the teachers.

Accountability

The pedagogic forms have variations corresponding to those found between schools in the accountabilities between parents, students, teachers and managements in relation to the quality of pedagogic effort and work. Kapoor (Chapter 9, this book) draws attention to the role of school ethos in constituting the culture of quality and its inherent accountabilities. Two other forms of accountability were related to monitoring by the state to hold schools accountable for quality of provisioning and the control that managements were able to exercise over their teachers' attendance and work.

The mandal education officers had easy and direct access to the state board–affiliated schools, the government schools and also the unrecognised low-fee-based schools, many of which (though not all) were known to them. However, they complained of the total inaccessibility of the CBSE-affiliated schools, which claimed immunity from local state regulatory officers. The private schools of the mandal were members of an association that seemed to manage their relationships with the government. There were no regulatory activities during the period of our study; all the schools were up to date with the renewal of recognition, and there were no tensions around the unrecognised high-end and corporate school branches. Many of these schools had not been visited by regulators in many years.

Three aided schools listed in DISE seemed to have 'disappeared' and the mandal officers had no idea of their whereabouts. One school had not sought renewal of recognition that year, openly stating that the process was so time-consuming and harassing that they had decided to become unrecognised. None of the schools had as yet been subjected to a Right to Education Act–based recognition check. It may be reasonable to conclude that whatever basic quality – particularly of infrastructure, hygiene and safety – was found in the schools was ensured not by state regulation but by either the educational ideology of the management or by the market. Meeting parental expectations was a driving factor in the ability to retain clientele who could vote with their feet. Managements sometimes managed to effectively silence parents through the guilt of unpaid fee or the 'non-performance' children.

The relationships of accountability between managements and teachers varied with school finances. A laissez-faire relationship was found in government and aided schools in which teachers were left to perform as they felt fit – high commitment as well as negligence manifested in these schools. In the low-fee-based schools, there was a relationship of 'adjustment' in which (women) teachers worked for low pay and schools adapted and managed when teachers took leave as and when they needed it. Women teachers in particular seemed to value the flexibility in their working hours, not having to take too much work home, and the leave policy.

A few schools were run professionally and treated their teachers as professionals. They had staff rooms; teachers were reasonably well paid and given responsibilities and duties in the school. The staff turnover in these schools was low. Here, teachers felt respected and valued for their competence. In the corporate managed and swot schools, teachers were generally well paid but micromanaged. Their time was strictly controlled. While they were respected as professionals, they were also expected to function at high levels of efficiency and put in a lot of additional time on following fixed lesson plans, conducting numerous tests and grading. It was only in these corporate schools that teachers spoke of being held accountable and the management as being demanding and closely monitoring their work. Teachers from other schools also referred to this feature of corporate schools and cited it as a key reason for not wanting to work there even if the pay was better.

On the whole, this suggested that, even in private schools, the authority of the management in holding teachers to account varied depending on a number of factors. Teachers were able to negotiate more flexibility in lieu of pay. In general, it is true that in private schools, classes were rarely left unattended. However, it was not clear that the adult in the class was the teacher. Many private schools had a range of quasi-teachers and family pitching in. Each morning, an important duty in the private school was checking which teachers were absent and deputing others to substitute for them. There seemed to be buffer staff available in most schools for such arrangements. This was not found in government schools, and in case teachers were absent, their class was left unattended. On the whole, it did not seem that private school teachers were taking less leave than government school teachers. At the same time, even in government schools where teachers were not held to account in the same way, the teacher's own professionalism could operate, producing commitment to work.

Conclusions

The heterogeneity and diversity of schools in Hyderabad city seems to be developing on account of the features of the state system as well as of the market – indeed, on account of the complementary action of the two sectors taken together. From 1970s to 1980s is a turning period in education, with the cessation of state investment to open government schools or new aided schools and the beginning of the growth of private schools. There is heterogeneity and diversity seen in the schools, and this maps closely to the socially stratified character of Indian society. The education market has grown along the class and community stratification. To this, we can add new dimensions of stratification: disability and intelligence – children with disabilities (impairments or learning difficulties) and 'dullers' (i.e. lower 'intelligence'). The threat of slipping down the social hierarchy is only too real when one views the strata of schools that these 'academically non-performing children' are able to access. School clientele stratification is suggestive of a sorting taking place in school selection along the lines of class, community, disability and intelligence (as measured by scholastic tests). This study was conducted just before the RtE clause pertaining to 25 per cent reservation for students from economically backward families

Hyderabad's education market 187

was operationalised in Telangana schools. It thus provides us with a baseline reference against which we can track whether this homogeneity is disrupted in future. English medium is the default option, and opportunities for education in the mother tongue (Telugu and Urdu) are severely limited, only for the poorest of the poor and in government or charitable settings.

The typology of managements that was found in the area surveyed provides a new lens to understand both school quality and financing, and gets us a sense of the niches in the market that are developed and occupied by different schools. Schools for the poor run by entrepreneurs were mostly 'shrinking' and unstable small schools, raising questions regarding their stability. Pedagogic cultures in these schools were basic literacy and citizenship for the poor, or drill. Relationships with the students' homes, on the whole, were tense and combative, with the schools having to find a balance between keeping an upper hand over the parent and extracting the fee while not losing their clientele. Among those which were able to set aside such consideration were schools that had a community religious affiliation with their clientele. Teacher-entrepreneur–run schools had less rote-based pedagogies, and although they were textbook cultures, these schools also enabled thinking and had expectations of concept development. While there were several schools for the poor which were based on shaming students – domesticating them or treating them as immoral – there also seemed to be widespread support for and parental investment in schools that put students through difficult regimens preparing them for competitive examinations. These schools seemed to be more desirable to parents. An invisible segregation seemed to be operating in which more competent students, or at least those who could cope with the regimen, were put into these high-pressure schools while less competent ones – the 'dullers' – were being sent to schools that could coach them sufficiently to pass examinations. The poorest of the poor were served by charitable institutions, particularly religious ones from all the three major faiths – Christianity, Islam and Hinduism. These schools, along with some of the aided schools and government school teachers, also espoused pedagogies that promoted autonomy, thinking and student confidence, all practised in the mother tongue. In fact, few of the government schools and none of the low-fee-based schools catered to this group of students. Religiously motivated trusts and institutions figure in the private school space.

The view of educational aims and pedagogic forms found in different schools serving the needs of different social classes provides us with unique empirical evidence of Bernstein's class reproduction and the formation of consciousnesses through the pedagogic work of schools (Bernstein, 1991, 2000). At the lower end is the aim of students becoming one of the masses, developing obedience and conformity and being controlled by the official text (which is rote learnt); this is for the lower social groups. At the upper end is the possibility of becoming an individual with autonomy, decision-making and self-expression, engaging with knowledge for understanding and creation. In other words, strongly classified and framed at the lower socioeconomic end and weakly classified and framed at the upper end of the socioeconomic spectrum. The availability of dialogic pedagogic for the development of capabilities of literacy and reasoning, developed in mother tongue education, may seem an aberration. However, it is instructive to note that this pedagogy comes without access to official knowledge (which includes English) and is meant for those who were expected to drop out of school and who would need to be independent and self-reliant to make a life on their own.

The types of non-state interests in starting schools have evolved over the decades. Until the 1970s, initiatives were community-oriented, yielding place to entrepreneurs from the 1980s onwards. However, there are differences in quality even in the single dimension of educational aims in this group between schools established by teacher-entrepreneurs and business entrepreneurs. Given how many of these schools are small and struggling, not only quality but also the institutional formation and stability of these schools are issues that cannot be ignored in discussions of their ability to serve the needs of the poor. Moreover, in addition to level or quantum of fee charged, the ability to collect fees regularly is a major concern for these institutions, leading to tense relationships with parents and resort to shaming children as a way of 'disciplining' parents. Where fee collection tension is mitigated, it is by the simultaneous operation of charitable and communitarian considerations.

The diversity of school types and quality as reflected in their aims suggests that the calculus includes considerations of clientele being served – economic and communitarian, school finances as well as the type of management. There are multiple niches in the market ecosystem that these schools occupy. Considerations of these niches, rather than 'private versus aided versus government' or 'recognised versus unrecognised' differentiations, provide us with greater insight into the educational purposes and activities of the schools. Within any given bracket, being recognised or unrecognised per se did not help to distinguish any aspect of education quality between schools.

We thus obtain a unique and valuable understanding of the diversity of institutional forms and qualities by unpacking the categories of 'private' and 'government' to reveal the nature of managements and leadership, their reasons for being in the business of running schools, the core finances of their operations and how they produce and manage quality in their institutions (or fail to do so). Without doubt, this is an education market, but understanding the market – pricing, clientele, quality and accountability – requires more than what neo-liberal theory provides in terms of understanding both the market or the state.

Notes

1 This chapter and the next one are based on our study Sarangapani et al. (2013), which was funded by the Sarva Siksha Abhiyan, Ministry of Human Resource Development (Government of India, New Delhi), thanks to the late Anita Kaul who saw value in the effort. The survey was carried out by a dedicated team comprising Rekha Pappu, Sakshi Kapoor, P. Anuradha, K. Ramgopal, Amar, Saroj B., Bhagyalakshmi V., Praveen Reddy and G. Sreeramulu.
2 The period of our survey, 2011–2012, was marked by several *bandhs*, or shut-downs, called by political groups campaigning for the formation of a separate state of Telangana to be carved out of Andhra Pradesh, leading to schools being closed on several occasions during the period of our work.
3 Andhra Pradesh Educational Institutions (Establishment, Recognition, Administration and Control of Schools Under Private Management) Rules, 1993, cited in Tooley and Dixon 2003a, http://cdn.cfbt.com/~/media/cfbt corporate/files/research/2003/r-private-schools-for-the-poor-india-2003.pdf
4 The District Information System for Education (DISE) (www.dise.in), maintained by the NUEPA, is an online record of all schools in India since 2008. The records available at the time of planning our study were for 2009–2010. DISE had not begun the practice of including data for unrecognised schools.
5 Tools: School fact sheet, morning assembly observation, school documents, interview with school leadership (head, trustee, management), classroom observation and teacher interview. We gathered information in some schools on children's performance on internal tests and examinations. However, we did not administer an achievement test. The study of quality, thus, does not include the parameter of learning outcomes. Analysis was done using MAX-QDA for coding and synthesis allowing each school to be described along a set of parameters that were evolved. For a full description and the tools, see Sarangapani et al. (2013).
6 This is probably 'dullards'.
7 For a full discussion of the pedagogic forms, see the full report of the study.

References

Bernstein, Basil. (1991). 'Social Class and Pedagogic Practice', in *Class, Codes and Control*, Volume IV. London: Routledge.
———. (2000). *Pedagogy, Symbolic Control and Identity*. London: Routledge & Kegan Paul.

Census of India. (2011). 'Hyderabad Religion 2011', available at Census2011.co.in [accessed 14 November 2015].

Mooij, Jos. (2003). 'Smart Governance? Politics in the Policy Process in Andhra Pradesh, India', Working Paper 228. London: Overseas Development Institute.

Sarangapani, P. M. et al. (2013). 'Baseline Survey of the School Scenario in Some States in the Context of RTE: Study of Educational Quality, School Management, and Teachers. Andhra Pradesh, Delhi and West Bengal', Unpublished report submitted to the Sarva Siksha Abhiyan, MHRD, New Delhi, India.

Sarangapani, P. M., and Winch, C. (2010). 'Tooley, Dixon and Gomathi on Private Education in Hyderabad: A Reply', *Oxford Review of Education*, 36(4): 499–515.

Tooley, J. (2009). *The Beautiful Tree: A Personal Journey into How the World's Poorest People Are Educating Themselves*. Washington, DC: The Cato Institute.

———. (2010). 'Could for-Profit Private Education Benefit the Poor? Some a Priori Considerations Arising from Case-Study Research in India', *Journal of Education Policy*, 22(3): 321–342.

Tooley, James, and Dixon, Pauline. (2003a). 'Private Schools for the Poor: A Case Study from India', London: CfBT Research and Development, available at http://cdn.cfbt.com/~/media/cfbtcorporate/files/research/2003/r-private-schools-for-the-poor-india-2003.pdf.

———. (2003b). 'An Inspector Calls: The Regulation of "Budget" Private Schools in Hyderabad, Andhra Pradesh, India', *International Journal of Education Development*, 25: 269–285.

———. (2006). 'De Facto Privatisation of Education and the Poor: Implications of a Study from Sub-Saharan Africa and India', *Compare: A Journal of Comparative and International Education*, 36(4): 443–462.

Tooley, J., Dixon, P., and Gomathi, S. V. (2007). 'Private Schools and the Millennium Development Goal of Universal Primary Education: A Census and Comparative Survey in Hyderabad, India', *Oxford Review of Education*, 33: 5539–5560.

Tooley, J., Dixon, P., Shamsan, Y., and Schagen, I. (2010). 'The Relative Quality and Cost-Effectiveness of Private and Public Schools for Low-Income Families: A Case Study in a Developing Country', *School Effectiveness and School Improvement*, 21(2): 117–144.

8 Schools, market and citizenship in Delhi

Manish Jain

Introduction

Conceptual chapters in the earlier section of this book have urged us to move beyond narrow frames to examine the question of quality and have articulated a more complex layout for this purpose. As mentioned in the introduction to the previous chapter on Hyderabad, Delhi was another site of the comparative study to explore issues of education market, school diversity and quality. The study deploys the framework of quality outlined in Chapter 6 and the frame of citizenship to present and make sense of the findings in Delhi.

Citizenship is added as a frame to make sense of schools and the education market for two reasons. First, citizen formation is a major goal of education in liberal democracies (Gutman, 1999: 13). Second, both the material and pedagogic dimensions of education, the terms by which children are included and excluded in educational spaces and the relationships and pedagogies that are forged and negotiated in schools, signify distinct meanings of citizenship (Balibar, 2015: 62–65). Such a frame allows us to situate contemporary contestations over education and citizenship with reference to material and discursive operations of power even as we retain the normative dimensions to conceptualise education, quality and citizenship.

This chapter is organised in three sections. With its focus on contemporary Delhi, the first section provides a contextual background of Delhi, its political economy, recent contestations over reconfigurations of its urban space and its educational landscape. It also gives a brief account of the site of study and the challenges of access. The second section of the chapter presents the findings of the study about school managements, their clientele, spaciousness and maintenance. The third section is centred on the pedagogic dimensions of quality followed by concluding remarks.

Situating Delhi

Being the capital of post-colonial India assigns a distinct status of power to Delhi, but three tiers of governments – namely, the central government, the Government of the National Capital Territory of Delhi (GNCTD) and the municipal bodies – complicate issues of governance, overlapping jurisdictions, responsibilities and accountability.[1] Delhi has had an elected state legislative assembly and government since 1993, but the central government continues to control the police through the Ministry of Home Affairs and land acquisition and development through Delhi Development Authority (DDA), which is answerable to the Ministry of Urban Development (Ghosh et al., 2009: 32). Within the domain of education, this overlap and control is also manifested in educational provision.

The earlier unified Municipal Corporation of Delhi (MCD) and the currently trifurcated MCD are responsible for public provisioning of primary schools, but they are 'poorly equipped' due to lack of adequate budgetary support (Planning Commission, 2009: 68, 255). These primary schools act as feeder schools for the middle, secondary and senior secondary government schools established by the Directorate of Education (DoE), GNCTD. The Sarvodaya schools under the DoE have pre-primary to secondary and senior secondary stages.[2] One can find distinct hierarchies of private and public schooling with sharp stratifications within each category, along with the presence of a large number of unrecognised schools in Delhi (Menon, 2014: 125–128; Menon, 2017: 454; Mooij and Jalal, 2009: 144). Government schools dominate in terms of enrolment at the middle stages, but the share of the private sector increases at the secondary and higher secondary stages (Planning Commission, 2009: 257).

Absence of adequate planning and provision for schools by state government combined with control over land by central government via DDA has led to severe shortage and overcrowding of government schools, specially at the secondary and senior secondary stages (Menon, 2017; Saxena, 2013). The state response has been to provide more schools by converting existing schools to sex-segregated two shifts and opening more schools within the existing school space. This has led to 'slumming and dilapidation' with government teachers complaining that they are no longer 'educators' but have been reduced to be 'herdsmen' (Menon, 2017: 454–456).

This overcrowding and slumming of government schools and increasing privatisation and absence of regulation of unrecognised schools can be better appreciated if we look at the changing political economy of Delhi. Industries, trade and public employment were the main centres of economic activities until the 1980s. Despite the decline of the manufacturing sector in recent times, the residential areas near the remaining industrial zones and estates are sites of 'flexible and shape-shifting economic activities', providing employment to rural workers who live in dormitory-like conditions (Chakravarty and Negi, 2016: 11). During the emergency (1975–1977), many inner-city slums were resettled in new areas in a bid to 'clean' and 'decongest' the city (Tarlo, 2003). From the 1980s, Delhi witnessed significant increase in population due to migration. During 1991–2001, the majority of migrants to Delhi came from Uttar Pradesh and Uttarakhand (46 per cent) and Bihar (23 per cent) (GNCTD, 2006: 3–4) and added to the growing demand for educational facilities (Planning Commission, 2009: 255). A large number of these migrants joined the informal economy and settled in unauthorised colonies, slums, *jhuggi-jhopri* clusters and urbanised villages.

This period was marked by two simultaneous developments with different meanings and consequences for citizenship. The bourgeoisie environmental litigation led to judicial orders resulting in the closure of factories, evictions and resettlements of about a million people to the urban fringes. The increasing assertiveness of the middle class to redefine the urban space to create a world-class city also expressed itself in their increasing involvement in urban governance through resident welfare associations (RWAs). This process, combined with privatisation of public spaces, emergence of middle-class 'plotted' localities, gated colonies and communities, led to the consolidation of class solidarities and deepened new cultures of consumerism, privatisation and individuation. At this juncture, the figure of the slum-dweller, the migrant from the rural and non-metropolitan space, came to signify a possible criminal who illegally encroached on and dirtied the urban space and from whom the middle-class 'citizen' needed to reclaim his or her right to leisure by dispossessing and invisibilising the urban poor (Batra, 2002; Baviskar, 2002; Bhan, 2009; Srivastava, 2015).

The middle-class proclivity to privatisation, consumption and investment was reflected in the increasing demand for private schools, many of which were set up in new localities, with land leased by DDA. In contrast to these privileged urban middle classes, the state's 'neglect' of public provisioning of schools, evident in their shortage, insufficient infrastructure and absence of attention to children in the crowded government schools, 'forced families towards individual, household-centric family responses for realising urban hopes from education' by enrolling their children in schools which may be private yet not elite

(Menon, 2014; Mooij and Jalal, 2009: 141; Menon, 2017: 457–458). The promise of English medium and attention to children, with the 'tacit understanding' that government is unable 'to come up with an alternative that is acceptable to the parents of children' in unrecognised schools, allowed them to proliferate (Mooij and Jalal, 2009: 153–154).

Delhi's diversity is also manifested in the significant number of schools operated by its religious minorities (Muslims, Christians, Sikhs and Jains) along with various cultural–linguistic minorities like Bengalis, Malayalis, Tamils and Telugus.[3] Like Hyderabad, Delhi too has been a site of research for James Tooley (Tooley and Dixon, 2007, 2012) and of the transnational advocacy of school choice and vouchers led by the Centre for Civil Society (CCS) (Nambissan and Ball, 2010). The city is also witnessing the operation of public–private partnership (PPP) in the entry of different NGOs and charities like ARK who have adopted some municipal schools and initiated projects like Nanhi Kali, which has been resisted (Gupta and Ahmad, 2016; Lok Shikshak Manch, 2012; Mooij and Jalal, 2009: 147). A variety of actors – ranging from corporate social responsibility (CSR) initiatives like Teach for India (TfI), venture philanthropy such as Central Square Foundation (CSF) and NGOs like Pratham – operating in Delhi devalue public education, vilify public school teachers, undermine 'the need for rigorous teacher education' and promote a model of their skilled volunteers replacing professionally trained teachers (Banerji, 1997: 2062; Menon, 2014: 128–134).

The study site

In the NCTD, DoE and MCD use different geographical delimitations to classify areas. Census and District Information System for Education (DISE) divide Delhi in nine districts. From these nine districts, one district which bordered Uttar Pradesh was selected as the site for research as its socioeconomic and demographic profile, percentage of Muslims and SC population, density and literacy did not significantly vary from the figures for Delhi. The selected district had a range of educational institutions, from high-end private schools to unrecognised schools (i.e. different management types).[4] Within this district, a geographically congruent area was delimited for research on the basis of detailed profile sheets prepared from school reports available from DISE data, list of recognised schools at DOE website and visits to the possible research sites. The delimited area corresponded to the socioeconomic, religious and educational management diversity of Delhi and this district. This delimited area included a resettlement colony, jhuggi jhopri areas, slums, unauthorised colonies, notified urban villages, planned DDA colonies and multistorey buildings of gated communities with parks and gardens. It had representation of Delhi's different religious and linguistic minorities. Some of these areas had also witnessed anti-Sikh riots in 1984.

Access to schools and data gathered

Initially, the entire population of 150 recognised schools was to be surveyed within this delimited area, along with at least 21 unrecognised schools which were noted in the course of visits to the study site.[5] Despite repeated requests, DoE refused permission to carry out research in its schools, though MCD granted permission. In the initial phase of the research, some private schools granted access, but later several unaided (private) schools also refused access to researchers. In the light of these constraints, the number of schools and the delimited area were revised to maintain geographical congruity and a representative sample of schools. But still, the representation of the different types of schools in the survey did not match their share in the population (Table 8.1).

Table 8.1 Classification of schools covered in Delhi

School type	Population of school type	Population as % of total schools selected (150) for survey	No. and % of schools surveyed from population of school type	% of school type surveyed from total schools (50)
DoE	31	20.66%	2 (6.45%)	4%
DoE aided	1	0.66%	None	Zero
DoE private unaided	25	16.66%	11 (44%)	22%
MCD	56	37.33%	26 (46.42%)	52%
MCD aided	None	–	None	–
MCD private unaided	16	10.66%	8	16%
Unrecognised	21	14%	3	6%
Total	150		50	33.33%

Source: Compiled by the author

School provisions

School types, establishment, size and symbols

The oldest school of the area was an MCD school established in 1948, followed by another such school in 1949. Both these schools were established in the areas designated as 'villages' in Delhi. Of the 26 MCD schools surveyed in the study, 15 were established in the 1970s and 1980s as the new areas were populated or their population swelled and resettlement colonies were established in this area. Before 1990, only 4 private unaided schools were recognised, and in the next decade 1989–1999, 7 such schools were recognised. About 25 per cent of schools surveyed were established in the 1980s. This is also the period when about half (4/7) of the big private schools surveyed in this study, with classes from pre-primary to senior secondary stage, came into existence. One such private school was a new branch of a school established in another district. In contrast, small private recognised schools having classes from pre-primary to middle school did not show any particular period as significant for their establishment or growth. All the three unrecognised schools (PUUR) were established during 2000–2005, which shows their recent origin. Many private recognised schools had a time gap of five years between the year of establishment and the year of recognition. Almost all DoE recognised private unaided schools were on the main and wider roads in middle-class localities whereas the MCD recognised private unaided schools, which were officially permitted to operate up to class 5 only, were established in the resettlement colony and notified villages.

Of the 50 schools surveyed, 25 were co-educational. In addition, 2 MCD schools had a co-educational section in Urdu or at the pre-primary stage. Of the 3 co-educational MCD schools, 2 were Urdu schools while one was an Adarsh Vidyalaya (ideal school). All the private recognised schools (19) and private unrecognised schools (3) were co-ed schools. As the clientele of small private recognised schools (having classes up to the middle level) and MCD schools have significant overlap, preference for separate schools for girls and boys cannot be simply explained with reference to the socioeconomic status of parents.

All the 26 MCD schools were primary schools. Of these, 14 schools also had the pre-primary stage and 10 were exclusively for girls. Two MCD schools and one unrecognised school (PUUR) were multigrade schools. Two of these three multigrade schools had school size of less than 100. One private recognised school had only primary classes,

Schools, market and citizenship in Delhi 197

whereas 3 had pre-primary as well. Five private recognised schools had both pre-primary and middle stage. Three private recognised schools had middle stage in addition to the primary stage. Of the 12 private recognised schools, 5 schools did not have recognition for pre-primary stage whereas 6 schools were operating middle sections without recognition in violation of existing regulations. The big private recognised schools started classes from pre-primary stage and went up to secondary or senior secondary stage. All these 7 schools, like the 2 DoE schools, were affiliated to CBSE.

Out of the 50 schools surveyed, 21 schools (42 per cent) were Hindi medium, 14 (28 per cent) were English medium schools and 10 schools (20 per cent) had both Hindi and English medium. All the private recognised schools with classes from pre-primary to secondary or senior secondary stage were English medium schools. Six of the 12 private recognised schools with classes up to the middle level were English medium, while 4 had both Hindi and English medium. Of the 26 MCD schools, 19 were Hindi medium schools. No MCD school was a fully English medium school, and two schools had an English medium section along with a Hindi medium section. No English medium section was found in Urdu medium schools. Two MCD schools had sections with Telugu and Tamil medium. Telugu medium school had less than 100 students and was a multigrade school. Only MCD schools had Urdu medium. Private unrecognised schools either had both Hindi and English medium or only English medium.

One-fifth of schools surveyed (10/50) had less than 300 students. Eleven of 26 MCD schools (42.30 per cent) ranged from 100 to 500 students. Nine of 26 MCD schools (about one-third) may be considered as big schools with school size above 800 to 1,500. In contrast, 10 of the 12 private unaided recognised schools – that is, 83.33 per cent schools with classes up to primary or not beyond elementary level – had a school size ranging from 101 to 500.

Information about the presence of religious and nationalist symbols was recorded for 44 schools. Of these, only 4 show distinct religious identification (2 Hindu, 1 Muslim and 1 Sikh). But what is noticeable is the significant presence of Hindu and nationalist symbols combined together. This category occupies almost two-thirds (29/44, 65.90 per cent) space. Nationalist symbols were noticeable in the form of pictures or posters of national leaders and freedom fighters, extracts and quotations from their writings and speeches, pictures of the national flag, the national anthem and pledges. Hindu symbols were most visible through prayers (Gayatri mantra, Saraswati vanadana), pictures, posters and statutes of Hindu gods and goddesses, small temples in the school premises (e.g. at reception), religious symbols (Om) and pictures of Saraswati (Hindu goddess of learning). This suggests that Hindu religious symbols were seen as congruent and continuous with nationalist symbols and not as distinct or in conflict with nationalist symbols. Two schools had both Hindu and Muslim symbols along with nationalist symbols, and another 7 schools had only nationalist symbols. Thus, nationalist symbols independently or in combination with other religious symbols were present in 38 of 44 schools (86.36 per cent). It may be worth noting that the number (16/23) and percentage (69.56 per cent) of government-run schools (MCD and DoE) with both Hindu and nationalist symbols is quite high considering constitutional provisions that bar imparting any religious education in government-maintained educational institutions. These practices may be read as passive forms of religious education that naturalise Hindu symbols and ethos as norms in the educational institutions. One school each had photographs of Gautam Buddha and Sikh gurus. In a private unrecognised school run by a Muslim management, reference to god, Allah and Ishwar were made in the prayer, and it did not give a clear sense of religious orientation and being aimed at any specific group. Islamic prayers were offered in one MCD Urdu medium school which catered to Muslim students.

School clientele and provisions

In this section, we examine the relationship between social class position of parents and the educational institution attended by children. We also use spaciousness, maintenance and availability of other provisions to evaluate whether there is any significant difference between private and public schools on these material parameters of quality. Through an examination of concerns expressed by teachers about children from socioeconomically weak groups, we will also discuss the issue of social distance and teacher attitudes in private and public schools.

School types and clientele

Occupations, employment, social class, caste, religion and educational backgrounds of the students' families were ascertained from school managements to understand the nature of their clientele. These were listed and categorised into four groups (Table 8.2).

The numbering of these groups can be taken to represent a rough social stratification and hierarchy with Group 1 being engaged in

Table 8.2 School clientele profiles

Group	Occupation and education
Group 1 ('elite' or upper middle class)	Post-graduate; earning Rs. 0.6–1.5 million; professions of doctor, businesspersons, lawyers; four-wheeler vehicle
Group 2 (middle class)	Graduate; service class; school teachers, small businesspersons; two-wheeler vehicle
Group 3 (lower middle class)	Class 5 to 12; Class IV employees, small shop owners, skilled jobs, clerks, watchmen or security guards, factory workers, butchers, drivers, plumbers, mechanics, welders, electricians, police constables, painters; bicycle
Group 4	Uneducated; earning 3,000–5,000 per month; daily wage earners, domestic help, unskilled jobs, packet making, unemployed, rickshaw pullers, *dhobis*, hawkers, barbers, orphan children

Source: Compiled by the author

professional jobs or owning businesses with substantial income and education. Group 2 comprised educated families with regular income from service or business and assets. Group 3 was a mixed group where parents were not educated beyond school, had regular jobs but at the lower levels of the hierarchy in offices and factories or worked as skilled manual labour. Group 4 represented the poorest of the poor in this classification and mapped onto migrants, people without any regular income who performed unskilled labour. This classification was then applied to the schools to cross-tabulate schools by clientele type against other relevant variables such as school size, levels, management type, spaciousness, maintenance and cleanliness.

Examination of the school type and the clientele (Table 8.3) confirms the often-repeated observation from other studies that only children from poor labour households attend government schools (Mooij and Jalal, 2009; Menon, 2017: 458). Among MCD schools which shared information about the social background of their students, more than one-third (9/24) were accessed by students coming exclusively from Group 4, that is, migrant families with irregular income and unskilled jobs. Of the 24 MCD schools, 15 schools (62.5 per cent) had students from both Groups 3 and 4. Almost 4 of every 5 (83.33 per cent) private recognised schools operating up to class 8 received students from Groups 3 and 4. No school in this category had only Group 4

Table 8.3 School type and clientele

School type / Clientele	MCD	DoE	PUUR	PUR PP-MDL	PUR PP-SEC/SS	Total
Groups 1 and 2	–	–	–	–	1	1
Groups 3 and 4	15	1	2	10	–	28
Group 4	9	1	1	–	–	11
Groups 1, 2 and EWS	–	–	–	–	3	3
Groups 2 and 3	–	–	–	1	2	3
Groups 1, 2 and 3	–	–	–	–	1	1
Groups 2, 3 and 4	–	–	–	1	–	1
No information	2	–	–	–	–	2
Total	26	2	3	12	7	50

Source: Compiled by the author

clientele. Two unrecognised schools also had students from Groups 3 and 4, and one private unrecognised school had clientele only from Group 4. Four out of 7 private recognised secondary or senior secondary schools reported students coming from Groups 1 and 2, that is, from professional and educated families with regular income, which gave them a largely homogenous character. Three such schools also had Group 3 students.

About 25 per cent of schools (12/50) had a small school size of less than 300 enrolled students from Groups 3 and 4 only. Of the 39 schools exclusively accessed by students from Groups 3 and 4, 23 schools (58.97 per cent) did not have a school size greater than 500. Seven MCD schools had sizes of 501–1,000, but only one of these was cramped and three of these had poor maintenance. In comparison, all the four private recognised schools with sizes of 101–300 had poor or very poor maintenance. Schools that enrolled students from Groups 1 and 2 had bigger size (above 1,000) which points to their financial viability.

School types, spaces and clientele

BUILDINGS

About 85 per cent of schools (43/50), including all government schools and bigger secondary or senior secondary private recognised schools, operated from buildings meant for schools. One-third of private recognised schools with primary or middle stage operated from residential buildings owned by them. In some cases, the buildings were shown as rented to avoid the possibility of government takeover of these buildings along with the school. Private unrecognised schools also operated from either residential buildings or commercial buildings. One such school had a nursing home on the ground floor while the school operated from the first floor. Three of the four residential buildings and the one commercial building were very cramped in terms of space. Interconnected rooms in residential buildings provided quick access to one classroom through another, along with spilling of sound. Ventilation was often poor and lighting was also usually not natural and poor in quality.

SCHOOLS AND SPACIOUSNESS

As Table 8.4 shows, 20 of the 43 institutional buildings were found to be very cramped (7) or cramped (13) in the study. Of these 20 buildings, 10 were MCD schools. About a quarter of institutional buildings (12/43, 27.9 per cent) were 'spacious' and another one-third (15/43, 34.88 per cent) were 'Ok' in terms of spaciousness. Seven of the 26 MCD school buildings were 'Ok' whereas 8 (30.8 per cent) were 'spacious'. Taken together, it indicates that about two-thirds of the MCD schools could be deemed satisfactory in terms of space. Spacious MCD schools outnumbered private unaided recognised schools operating up to class 8 (2/12, 16.67 per cent). Six of 12 such schools were classified as 'Ok' (50 per cent). All private unaided recognised schools of senior secondary level were unmistakably 'Ok' and 'spacious'. In

Table 8.4 School type and spaciousness

School type / Spaciousness		Very cramped	Cramped	Ok	Spacious	No information
MCD		2	8	7	8	1
DoE			2			
PUUR		2	1			
PUR	PP-MDL	3	1	6	2	
	PP-SEC/SS		1	2	4	
Total = 50		7	13	15	14	1

Source: Compiled by the author

comparison, both DoE schools were cramped. All the private unaided unrecognised schools were also very cramped or cramped. These findings indicate that within public schools, MCD schools provided greater space whereas DoE schools were overcrowded as found in other studies (Menon, 2017; Saxena, 2013). Smaller schools, whether private recognised schools with primary or middle stage or private unrecognised schools, operated with less space than private schools with secondary and senior secondary stage.

SPACIOUSNESS, MAINTENANCE AND CLIENTELE

If the number of very cramped and cramped schools attended by Groups 3 and 4 are taken together, it constitutes about two-third of total schools (13/20, 65 per cent) in this category (Table 8.5). In terms of numbers, it is lower than the 'Ok' and 'spacious' schools (15/29, 51.72 per cent) attended by students from these groups but is proportionately higher in percentage terms. Comparison with schools attended by Groups 1 and 2 students show that they are invariably 'Ok' and 'spacious'. From these observations, we may conclude that while students from Groups 3 and 4 were more likely to study in cramped spaces leading them to jostle for space to sit, read and write, students from better-off social groups are not likely to face such challenges.

Table 8.5 Clientele and spaciousness

Clientele / Spaciousness	Very cramped	Cramped	Ok	Spacious	No information
Groups 1 and 2				1	
Groups 3 and 4	6	7	9	6	
Group 4	1	4	2	4	
Groups 1, 2 and EWS				3	
Groups 2 and 3			3		
Groups 1, 2 and 3		1			
Groups 2, 3 and 4			1		
No information		1			1
Total	7	13	15	14	1

Source: Compiled by the author

Schools, market and citizenship in Delhi 203

Of the 43 institutional buildings, a substantial number (25/43, 58.14 per cent) had satisfactory maintenance and cleanliness and 17 (39.53 per cent) had very poor or poor maintenance and cleanliness. Two-thirds of residential buildings (owned or rented) also fared badly on this criterion. In terms of school type, more than half MCD schools (14/26, 53.84 per cent) did well (ok, good and very good), but 11 of 26 (42.30 per cent) such schools had poor or very poor maintenance. Almost similar proportions of poor and very poor (5/12, 41.66 per cent) and ok to good cleanliness (58.33 per cent) were witnessed in the case of small primary and middle level private recognised schools. It is worth noting that almost one-third of MCD schools had either good or very good levels of cleanliness, but no PUR up to class 8 was very good. Both DoE schools were poor in terms of cleanliness, which may be attributed to overcrowding, shortage and contractualisation of cleaning staff (Saxena, 2013). Most big private recognised schools were found to be reasonably clean with acceptable levels of maintenance. No distinct trend with regard to maintenance can be observed in the case of private unrecognised schools.

A distinct correlation that may be observed is the relationship between spaciousness and maintenance and cleanliness in schools (Table 8.6). There were 14 institutions (28 per cent) which were either very cramped or cramped and were simultaneously very poor or poor in terms of maintenance. This correlation was further underlined as 16 (32 per cent) institutions characterised as 'Ok' and 'spacious' also had 'good and very good maintenance'. With reference to school type,

Table 8.6 School type, spaciousness and maintenance

School type / Spaciousness and maintenance	Very cramped or cramped and very poor or poor maintenance	Spacious or ok and good and very good maintenance	Cramped and good maintenance	Spacious and poor maintenance
MCD	7	7	1	3
DoE	2			
PUUR	1	1	1	
PUR PP-MDL	3	3		
PP-SEC/SS	1	5		
Total	14	16	2	3

Source: Compiled by the author.

this data shows that for MCD, PUUR and PUR schools up to middle school, the correlation holds true as the number and percentage of poorly maintained cramped spaces and spacious well-maintained schools is equal. As observed above, private recognised schools of senior secondary level were both spacious and well maintained. The only cramped and poorly maintained private recognised school was a secondary level school of smaller size (less than 600 students). This school was also a drill pedagogy school.

Students coming from Groups 3 and 4 were not necessarily found to be studying in institutions with deplorable quality of maintenance and cleanliness. Of the 50 schools students from these groups attended, 17 (34 per cent) had poor or very poor maintenance and cleanliness but 21 (42 per cent) had satisfactory or good maintenance and cleanliness. Distinct correlation of social group with better maintenance and cleanliness emerged in the case of Groups 1 and 2. This means that students from higher positions in the social hierarchy are guaranteed better provisions.

OTHER PROVISIONS

Almost all MCD schools (24/26) and private recognised schools of senior secondary level (5/7) had playgrounds. Playgrounds were available only in half of private recognised schools with classes up to the middle level. Ramps were made in almost 60 per cent of MCD schools but were not observed or reported elsewhere except in one DoE and middle level private recognised school. Both DoE schools had libraries in separate rooms, and 16 of 26 MCD schools had libraries in some form. Only a quarter of MCD schools had separate rooms for teachers, and in 4 of the 24 schools where a separate room for the school head existed, it was used for multiple purposes. Senior secondary level schools (DoE and PUR-SS) were more likely to have separate science labs than those operating up to the primary or middle level. While computers were present in various categories of schools, computer-aided learning was available in 25 per cent and 50 per cent of private recognised middle and senior secondary level schools, respectively. Certain other curricular provisions and facilities were present only or largely in private recognised schools and were most likely absent in government-run schools (MCD and DoE). These include music room, dance room, school transport, counsellor, medical room, craft, canteen and yoga. Besides these facilities, language lab, gym, swimming pool, horse riding, squash court, tennis court, basketball court and recreation room were also found in one private recognised senior secondary school.

School's biases or concerns?

The concerns expressed in the English medium private schools about the families and children belonging to disadvantaged social groups (Groups 3, 4 and EWS) can be broadly classified in three groups. Of the 48 problems reported for these children, 21 (43.7 per cent) are in the category of the families' failure to take an interest in children, their education, school and to provide a supporting educational environment with respect to English or homework. The second set of concerns (8/48, 16.7 per cent) may be classified as perceptions about dysfunctionality or immoral character of the families as manifested in domestic violence and conflict, alcoholism, single mothers and coming from a 'slum' that acts as a code to express various pathologies and anxieties. These two sets of pathologies together with the third set of issues such as illiteracy, ignorance and financial problems of the family (9/48, 18.7 per cent) were reported by private unaided English medium schools as resulting in a variety of problems among students (9/48, 18.7 per cent) such as irregularity, problems of adjustment, incomplete homework, lack of interest in studies and even increase in theft.

The range of concerns expressed with regard to the families and children belonging to Groups 3 and 4 were repeated in the non-English medium schools with the addition of other concerns and noticeable difference in emphasis. If we follow the threefold classification used above, we find that concerns related to education (42/121) occupy more than one-third of the space. Within it, the families' inability to provide support to studies had the highest frequency (11), followed by lack of concern about children and education (8) with absence of English and failure to contribute to school (6 each) being other significant concerns in this category.

Within the second set of concerns (27/121, 22.3 per cent), which we classified as perceptions about dysfunctionality or immoral character of the families, domestic violence and conflict (11) and alcoholism (8) emerge as significant issues. Their frequency is much higher in non-English medium schools than in English medium schools. Financial concerns (poverty and unemployment) are about half (11/24) of the third category of concerns (24/121), and this is almost similar in weightage (4/9) as in English medium schools. What is significant to note are the addition of small size of families and the necessity for mothers (4 each) to engage in wage labour, which leaves little space to help children to study.

A new set of issues are also raised in the non-English medium schools. These relate to neighbourhood community (6/121) and encompass forcible entry of drug addicts and criminals in the school, gambling, theft and garbage. Irregularity of students (10) is a major concern among various issues cited with reference to students (20/121) along with incomplete homework. Absence of uniform, cleanliness and hygiene and sexual deviance are new anxieties expressed in these schools and were absent in the list of concerns expressed in English medium schools.

The first set of concerns mentioned in both English and non-English medium schools may be interpreted in two ways. A more generous interpretation would point to the expectations by school about the role of family in socialising and preparing children for academic success. Alternatively, these concerns may be seen as an expression of a deficit model of poor families that constructs them as apathetic towards their own children (Sharma, 2016: 280). It assumes possession of certain cultural capital as necessary for academic success and sanctions persistence of social inequalities. It is easier to read the second set of concerns as middle-class stereotypes about poor families (Talib, 1992: 87; Dalal, 2015: 37) and the boundaries that distinguished this *other* and the self that expressed hostility towards those on the lower rung of the social hierarchy. But greater frequency of domestic violence and alcoholism and impact of the mother's wage labour as concerns in non-English medium schools may also be seen as awareness of the challenges faced by children from such families, which interpretation needs to be probed further.

Pedagogic forms, school types and clientele

Like Hyderabad, a composite of seven pedagogic forms was developed.[6] Unlike Hyderabad, emphasis on teaching for success in examination or corporate connection or swot-type micro-managed regimentation were absent in Delhi. There were classes in Delhi where teachers engaged in long monologues and explained things on their own. Findings and discussion about pedagogies of the 82 classes observed in 48 schools of Delhi have been classified at two levels, class and school.[7] Given the significant differences in the pedagogies in classes within a school, such schools could be classified as pedagogic form 7 (see fn 8), but such a classification would not have given an idea about the diversity of pedagogies practised within and across school types. It also would have failed to do justice to these diversities. Disaggregated data at class level could give a far richer understanding of what was happening in the classrooms. At the same time, attention to only class-specific pedagogy would not have given us any sense of the dominant pedagogic type in a school or the institutional pedagogic culture.

As shown in Table 8.7, no classes in MCD schools were practising domesticating pedagogy, which focused on production of very

Table 8.7 Pedagogy in classes

School type / Pedagogy	MCD	DoE	PUR (PP+PR, PR, PP+PR+MDL and PR+MDL)	PUR (PP-SEC/SS)	PUUR	Total classes
Domesticating (P1)	–	–	1 (33.33%)	–	2 (66.66%)	3
Drill and guidebook (P2)	11 (39.28%)	–	14 (50%)	1 (3.57%)	2 (7.14%)	28
Textbook and repetition (P3)	12 (46.15%)	3 (11.53%)	6 (23.07%)	4 (15.38%)	1 (3.84%)	26
Textbook and understanding (P4)	6 (100%)	–	–	–	–	6
Student understanding and experience (P5)	9 (75%)	–	–	3 (25%)	–	12
Dialogic, encouraging independence (P6)	6 (85.71%)	–	–	1 (14.28%)	–	7
Total	44 (100%)	3 (100%)	21 (100%)	9 (100%)	5 (100%)	82

Source: Compiled by the author

basic skills of literacy and numeracy with corporal punishment. Three such classes were observed in PUR (PP-MDL) and private unrecognised schools. Guidebook and drill pedagogy that asked students to reproduce the answer given by the teacher or in the textbook and focused on memorisation with expectation of negative home influence constituted more than one-third (28/82, 34.14 per cent) of the total classes observed. For these two pedagogies that operate with notions and practices of domesticated citizenship and obedience, this is a significant proportion. Close to another one-third (26/82, 31.70 per cent) among the observed classes employed pedagogy where the textbook reigned supreme and both teaching and learning revolved around it. Progressive pedagogies (P5 and P6) that provide space for children, their experiences and views and expect them to go beyond textbooks and teachers were being practised in less than a quarter of the classes (19/82, 23.17 per cent). Teachers who practiced these pedagogies in the classrooms had a non-threatening and affectionate attitude towards all children. Children felt free and comfortable in their presence. Such teachers used a polite tone, were concerned about the well-being and learning of their students and believed in the capacity of all children to learn. This smaller share of progressive pedagogies in the total number of classes observed during this study means that in almost three-quarters of classes, love, care, belief in the dignity and capacity of all children were absent.

The distribution of these pedagogies in classrooms across different types of schools (Table 8.8) shows some interesting observations. The number and percentage of drill pedagogy classes was much higher in PUR (PP-MDL) schools (14/28, 50 per cent) than in MCD schools (11/28, 39.28 per cent). A much larger number of MCD schools practised textbook and repetition pedagogy (11/26, 46.15 per cent) than all levels of PUR schools put together (10/26, 38.46 per cent). Textbook and understanding pedagogy that involved long monologues by the teacher to explain the chapter with occasional use of textbooks and experiences and responses of students to develop conceptual understanding was found only in MCD schools. All classes in DoE were textbook and repetition pedagogy. What is of significance is the very high share of MCD schools in pedagogies that focused on students' understanding and experience (9/12, 75 per cent) and dialogic pedagogy encouraging independent effort (6/7, 85.71 per cent) and the absence of such pedagogy in PUR schools operating up to the elementary stage. This becomes all the more noteworthy as the students who access MCD schools are from Groups 3 and 4 only. We have noted before (Table 8.3) that this same group also enrols in PUR (PP-MDL)

Table 8.8 Pedagogic forms across school type

School type Pedagogy	MCD	DoE	PUR (PP+PR, PR, PP+PR+MDL, PR+MDL)	PUR (PP-SES/SS)	PUUR	Total schools
Domesticating (P1)	–	–	1 (50%)	–	1 (50%)	2
Drill and guidebook (P2)	4 (26.67%)	–	8 (53.33%)	1 (6.67%)	2 (13.33%)	15
Textbook and repetition (P3)	6 (50%)	2 (16.67%)	2 (16.67%)	2 (16.67%)	–	12
Textbook and understanding (P4)	2 (100%)	–	–	–	–	2
Student understanding and experience (P5)	1 (50%)	–	–	1 (50%)	–	2
Dialogic, encouraging independence (P6)	2 (100%)	–	–	–	–	2
Different pedagogies (P7)	11 (84.61%)	–	–	2 (15.38%)	–	13
Total	26 (100%)	2 (100%)	11 (100%)	6 (100%)	3 (100%)	48

Source: Compiled by the author

schools. This difference in presence and absence of progressive pedagogies in two types of educational institutions having similar clientele calls for critical reflection on claims about the failure of the public schooling system and the superiority of all kinds of private schools, including unrecognised schools.

If we retabulate the share of different types of pedagogies within a school type, a new set of insights emerge. P1 and P2 together, classified as 'domestication and citizenship', constitute 80 per cent of all pedagogic types for private unrecognised schools and 71.42 per cent for pre-primary to middle level private recognised schools. This is almost three times the share of such pedagogy in the case of classes in MCD schools (P2, 11/44, 25 per cent). We have noted above (Table 8.7) that MCD schools had a high share of textbook and repetition pedagogy (11/26, 46.15 per cent) among all types of schools. But within MCD, the share of this pedagogy was about one-fourth (12/44, 27.27 per cent). More than one-third of classes observed in MCD schools were of progressive character. It is important to note that this 'progressive' pedagogy was being practised in schools where children do not come with 'cultural capital'. This progressive pedagogy (P5, P6 put together) had a significant share (4/9, 44.44 per cent) in the case of private recognised schools with classes from pre-primary to secondary or senior secondary.

After taking note of class-specific pedagogies across different school types, we may now turn our attention to the pedagogic regimes at the school level. Table 8.8 shows that guidebook and drill pedagogy (P2) has the highest share (15/48, 31.25 per cent) among different types of pedagogic forms and is closely followed by higher-order pedagogies (P7, 13/38, 27.08 per cent) and textbook and repetition pedagogy (P3, 12/48, 25 per cent). If we combine P1 and P2, they have a distinct edge of at least 8 percentage points over P3 and P7. All other pedagogic forms from P4 to P6 have similar shares (2/48, 4.16 per cent). Since P7 represents significant differences in pedagogies within a school, it means that more than a quarter of schools have such differences and it is most pronounced in the case of MCD schools (11/13, 84.61 per cent). This suggests absence of an institutional pedagogic form in such schools. It has been argued that teaching and pedagogy varies significantly in government schools as it is heavily dependent on individual teachers and varies with them. If this proposition is true, it is worth noting that 2 PUR (PP-SS) schools also fall in P7 category.

Another important observation pertains to P5 and P6 that represent 'progressive' pedagogy. In terms of institutional pedagogic culture, both the P6 schools are MCD schools and of the 2 P5 schools, one

Schools, market and citizenship in Delhi 211

each is from MCD and PUR (PP-SS). More than half (8/15, 53.33 per cent) of the guidebook and drill schools are small PUR schools (PP-MDL), and this is twice the number of such schools from MCD. Textbook culture (P3) dominates government schools as 8 of 12 (6 MCD, 2 DoE) P3 schools are from this group. Textbook and understanding pedagogy (P4) is monopolised by 2 MCD schools. This may point to the prevalence of 'guru' *parampara* (tradition) in some MCD schools where teachers are the sole source of knowledge and other sources of knowledge like textbooks or children fade.

If we attempt to classify the share of each pedagogic form within a school type (Table 8.8), we find that in MCD schools, P7 (11/26, 42.30 per cent) outstrips all other pedagogies and is followed at some distance by P3 (6/26, 23.07 per cent) and P2 (4/26, 15.38 per cent). 'Progressive' pedagogy (P5 and P6) is present in only 3/26 schools (11.53 per cent). It marks a huge difference in its share vis-à-vis class-specific pedagogy in MCD schools. While more than one-third of classes (34.09 per cent) observed in MCD schools were of 'progressive character', at an institutional level, only 1 among 10 MCD schools practises 'progressive' pedagogic forms. Comparatively speaking, no PUR school operating up to the middle level practised 'progressive' pedagogy. Dialogic pedagogy, which aims at developing reasoning, creativity and novelty and signifies the activities to foster higher-order thinking and independent effort among students, is not present in a single PUR school even when it has senior secondary classes. But taken together with P5, 1 in 4 PUR schools of this level has a 'progressive' pedagogic regime. At this moment, an important comparison may be drawn among MCD schools, PUUR schools and PUR schools limited to primary and middle levels. Nine of 11 PUR schools (81.81 per cent) have pedagogic forms (P1 or P2) that are highly teacher-controlled, where learning is conceived as repetition of answers given by the teacher or the textbook and is ensured by rote memorisation. This kind of pedagogic regime with domesticating practices enforced through physical and corporal punishment by unconcerned teachers is found in every 4 of 5 PUR schools and in every PUUR school. In contrast, P2 was present in only 4 of 26 MCD schools, that is, less than 1 of 6 schools. In proportionate terms, this is less than one-fifth of PUR (PP-MDL) schools.

The last set of observations about pedagogies may be made with regard to clientele type (Table 8.9). One-third schools (14/38) attended by Groups 3 and 4 had domesticating and drill types of pedagogies. About one-fifth (8/38) of such schools may be described as practising textbook and repetition culture. More than a quarter of the schools

Table 8.9 Clientele type and pedagogic forms

Clientele \ Pedagogic regime	Domesticating (P1)	Drill and guidebook (P2)	Textbook and repetition (P3)	Textbook and understanding (P4)	Student understanding and experience (P5)	Dialogic, encouraging independence (P6)	Different pedagogies (P7)	No information	Total
Groups 1 and 2	–	–	–	–	–	–	–	1*	–
Groups 3 and 4	2	9	6	1	1	1	7	–	27
Group 4	–	3	2	1	–	1	4	–	11
Groups 1, 2 and EWS	–	–	–	–	1	–	2	–	3
Groups 2 and 3	–	–	3	–	–	–	–	–	3
Groups 1, 2 and 3	–	1	–	–	–	–	–	–	1
Groups 2, 3 and 4	–	1	–	–	–	–	–	–	1
No information	–	1	1	–	–	–	–	–	2
Total	2	15	12	2	2	2	13	–	48

Source: Compiled by the author

* No classes were observed in the school with students from Groups 1 and 2.

attended by these groups had significant differences in the pedagogic forms practised and suggest the presence of distinct individual teacher orientations to pedagogies rather than any systematic pedagogic form. There was also a distinct possibility of students from Groups 3 and 4 experiencing 'progressive' pedagogy (3/38 schools).

Conclusions

This study has shown that the diverse character of schools in Delhi and the increasing share of private schools in the city since 1980s are closely interconnected with the populating of new areas, enterprising activities of private actors and inadequate state provisioning of schools, especially at the middle and secondary levels. Though mapping of class and caste markers of social inequality on to the stratified school system found in this study is not a new finding, the differentiation within public and private schools with respect to space, cleanliness and maintenance dispels any notion that private schools necessarily perform better on these parameters. Rather, in this context, citizenship status is also marked differentially with stamps of privilege and denial. Children of the elite learn and grow in spaces that ensure human dignity with their cleanliness and are spacious, both geographically and symbolically. In metaphoric terms, the cramped nature of school space in the small private schools and a sizeable number of government schools represents the limited nature of citizenship possibilities where the discourse of citizen rights is substituted by the charity of the state and of consumers who avail themselves of private services dependent on their capacities to pay.

The overlap between Hindu and nationalist symbols within state schools may on the one hand be read as reiteration of the geographical, cultural and social boundaries and overlaps that defined who was essential and natural to India and on the other hand, evidence of how the elitist discourse of separation of state and religion and unmarked citizen was undergirded by the Hindu ethos and practices across various state institutions. The demography of Delhi has been changing since the 1980s and especially the 1990s with the rise of Hindutva, when migration of middle-class Hindu trading castes from old Delhi transformed old Delhi into a Muslim area and created Muslim ghettos. Giving this demographic change, the overlap between separation of state and religion and Hindu ethos raises a set of questions about the quality of education in relation to citizenship, but these questions go beyond the scope of this chapter.

A crucial finding of this study relates to pedagogic practices in public and private schools. In contemporary literature, the rent-seeking nature of the permanent government school teachers and their social distance from children from the poor sections of society are explained as causes of their 'apathetic' attitude, disinterest in teaching these children and view of their own effort to teach them as 'wastage' (Mooij, 2009; Banerji, 1997: 2062; Sharma, 2016: 278; Vasavi, 2015: 45). This study shows that government school teachers are not necessarily practising a disciplining pedagogy to produce domesticated, obedient and docile bodies (Vasavi, 2015: 45; Iyer, 2013). Instead, such pedagogic practices are dominant in the unrecognised and small private schools with classes up to the elementary level. Unlike Banerji (1997: 2062), who termed committed government school teachers walking around in the class and talking to children individually as 'unusual', this study found several instances of such empathetic teachers practising progressive pedagogy in their classrooms. But it is quite clear that such pedagogy is largely dependent on a teacher's individual orientation and there is absence of an institutionalised culture for such a practice. At the same time, the presence of such a practice in MCD schools accessed by children from poor skilled and unskilled labour families, in contrast to its total absence in private schools accessed by children from similar backgrounds, points to distinct citizenship possibilities. At a time when state schools are under severe stress with distinct shifts in the urban spaces, such possibilities stand contrary to the discourse about quality, public and private schools being circulated by neoliberal protagonists of the market and the state.

Abbreviations

DoE	Directorate of Education
MCD	Municipal Corporation of Delhi
MDL	Middle
PP	Pre-primary
PR	Primary
PUR	Private unaided recognised
PUUR	Private unaided unrecognised
SEC	Secondary
SS	Senior secondary

Notes

1 Until 2012, Delhi had three kinds of municipal bodies: Municipal Corporation of Delhi (MCD), New Delhi Municipal Council (NDMC) and Delhi Cantonment Board (DCB). Whereas NDMC controls areas of Lutyen's

Delhi, the seat of central government and the diplomatic enclave, DCB has jurisdiction over the army cantonment. In 2012, MCD was trifurcated into South Delhi, North Delhi and East Delhi municipal corporations. At the time of this study, there was one unified municipal corporation.
2 In 2011–2012, there were a total of 5,064 schools comprising 2,782 government schools (54.9 per cent) and 2,282 private schools (45.1 per cent) (Mehta, 2015: 21). At present, MCD, NDMC, DCB and DoE have 1,750, 82, 8 and 924 schools, respectively. There are 43 Kendriya Vidyalayas funded and administered by the central government. The number of private schools aided by MCD and DoE are 44 and 221, respectively, whereas there are 759 MCD recognised and 1,187 DoE recognised unaided private schools in Delhi.
    Source: www.delhi.gov.in/wps/wcm/connect/doit_education/Education/Home/About+Us [accessed 5 April 2015].
3 According to the 2011 census, Hindus constitute 80.21 per cent of Delhi's population, followed by Muslims (12.78 per cent), Sikhs (4.43 per cent), Jains (1.39 per cent), Christians (0.96 per cent) and Buddhists (0.12 percent) (Delhi City Census Data, 2011). Buddhists and Parsis are also notified minority communities in Delhi, but the number of educational institutions established and managed by these communities is too few. Mcduie-Ra (2012: 70) reports that the population of north-east Indians in Delhi is about 200,000, and the majority of them come to Delhi after secondary school.
4 DISE list of schools and the list of recognised schools available on the website of the DoE, GNCT Delhi, were accessed in June and July 2011. This data was used to compare the number of schools across different management types.
5 Besides these unrecognised schools, tuition centres, madrassas, NGO-run educational institutions, *anganwadis* and computer or English-teaching centres were also observed and noted in this study site. This stood in contrast to the DISE State Report Card for Delhi for the year 2011–2012, which had zero schools under madrassas and unrecognised schools category.
6 These seven pedagogic forms are classified as (i) domesticating, (ii) guidebook and drill, (iii) textbook and repetition, (iv) textbook and understanding, (v) student understanding and experience, (vi) dialogic, encouraging independence and (vii) different pedagogies. See report of the study for details of these forms.
7 These 82 classes included 44 in MCD schools, 21 in private unaided recognised (PUR) schools operating up to elementary level, 9 in PUR schools of secondary or senior secondary level, 3 in DOE schools and 5 classes in private unrecognised schools.

References

Balibar, Etienne. (2015). *Citizenship*. Cambridge: Polity Press.
Banerji, Rukmini. (1997). 'Why Don't Children Complete Primary School? A Case-Study of a Low-Income Neighbourhood in Delhi', *Economic and Political Weekly*, 32(32): 2053–2063.

Batra, Lalit. (2002). 'Deconstructing the "World Class" City', *Seminar*, available at www.india-seminar.com/2002/516/516%20amita%20baviskar.htm [accessed 17 February 2015].

Baviskar, Amita. (2002). 'The Politics of the City', *Seminar*, available at www.india-seminar.com/2002/516/516%20amita%20baviskar.htm [accessed 11 February 2015].

Bhan, Gautam. (2009). '"This Is No Longer the City I Once Knew": Evictions, the Urban Poor and the Right to the City in Millennial Delhi', *Environment and Urbanization*, 21: 127–142.

Chakravarty, Surajit, and Negi, Rohit. (2016). 'Introduction: Contested Urbanism in Delhi's Interstitial Spaces', in idem (Eds.), *Space, Planning and Everyday Contestations in Delhi* (pp. 1–17). New Delhi, India: Springer India.

Dalal, Jyoti. (2015). 'The Indelible Class Identity: Ethnographic Examination of a School', *Economic and Political Weekly*, 50(8): 36–39.

Delhi City Census Data. (2011) available at www.census2011.co.in/census/city/49-delhi.html [accessed 27 March 2017].

Ghosh, Archana, et al. (2009). 'A Comparative Overview of Urban Governance in Delhi, Hyderabad and Kolkata and Mumbai', in Joel Ruet and Stephanie Tawa Lama-Rewal (Eds.), *Governing India's Metropolises* (pp. 24–54). New Delhi, India: Routledge.

Government of NCT of Delhi (GNCTD). (2006). *Delhi Human Development Report 2006: Partnerships for Progress*. New Delhi, India: Oxford University Press.

Gupta, Snehlata, and Ahmad, Firoz. (2016). 'Teaching and the Transformative Promise of Public Education: What Went Wrong? Have We Lost Our Way? A Perspective from Two Government School Teachers', *Contemporary Education Dialogue*, 13(2): 266–272.

Gutman, Amy. (1999). *Democratic Education*. Princeton: Princeton University Press.

Iyer, Suvasini. (2013). 'An Ethnographic Study of Disciplinary and Pedagogic Practices in a Primary Class', *Contemporary Education Dialogue*, 10(2): 163–195.

Lok Shikshak Manch. (2012). 'Beware! Danger Ahead', *Reconstructing Education*, 1(3): 27–28.

Mcduie-Ra, Duncan. (2012). 'The "North-East" Map of Delhi', *Economic and Political Weekly*, 47(30): 69–77.

Mehta, Arun C. (2015). *Elementary Education in India: Trends 2005–2006 to 2014–2015*. New Delhi, India: National University of Educational Planning and Administration.

Menon, Radhika. (2014). 'Caught Between "Neglect" and a Private "Makeover": Government Schools in Delhi', in Ravi Kumar (Ed.), *Education, State and Market: Anatomy of Neoliberal Impact* (pp. 114–138). New Delhi, India: Aakar.

———. (2017). 'On the Margins of "Opportunity": Urbanisation and Education in Delhi's Metropolitan Fringe', in William T. Pink and George W. Noblit (Eds.), *Second International Handbook of Urban Education* (pp. 445–467). Switzerland: Springer.

Mooij, Jos. (2009). 'Primary Education, Teacher's Professionalism and Social Class About Motivation and Demotivation of Government School Teachers in India', *International Journal of Educational Development*, 28(5): 508–523.

Mooij, Jos, and Jalal, Jennifer. (2009). 'Primary Education in Delhi, Hyderabad and Kolkata: Governance by Resignation, Privatisation by Default', in Joel Ruet and Stephanie Tawa Lama-Rewal (Eds.), *Governing India's Metropolises* (pp. 135–160). New Delhi, India: Routledge.

Nambissan, Geetha B., and Ball, Stephen J. (2010). 'Advocacy Networks, Choice and Private Schooling of the Poor in India', *Global Networks*, 10(3): 324–343.

Planning Commission, Government of India. (2009). *Delhi Development Report*. New Delhi, India: Academic Foundation.

Saxena, Sadhna. (2013). 'Dilli ke Sarkaree Schoolon Kee Dasha: Ek Baangee' (in Hindi)', *Shiksha Vimarsh*, 15(3): 37–42.

Sharma, Gunjan. (2016). 'Shaping Everyday Educational Vocabulary: State Policy and a Slum School', in Avinash Kumar Singh (Ed.), *Education and Empowerment in India* (pp. 275–291). New York: Routledge.

Srivastava, Sanjay. (2015). 'Politics, Privilege and Post-National Urbanism', *Seminar*, 562, available at www.india-seminar.com/2015/672/672_sanjay_srivastava.htm [accessed 11 October 2015].

Talib, Mohammad. (1992). 'Ideology, Curriculum and Class Construction: Observations from a School in a Working-Class Settlement in Delhi', *Sociological Bulletin*, 41(1 & 2): 81–95.

Tarlo, Emma. (2003). *Unsettling Memories: Narratives of the Emergency in Delhi*. Berkeley: University of California Press.

Tooley, James, and Dixon, Pauline. (2007). 'Private Schooling for Low Income Families: A Census and Comparative Survey in East Delhi, India', *International Journal of Educational Development*, 27: 205–219.

———. (2012). *Private Schools Serving the Poor. Working Paper: A Study from Delhi, India*. Viewpoint 8. New Delhi, India: Centre for Civil Society.

Vasavi, A. R. (2015). 'Culture and Life of Government Elementary Schools', *Economic and Political Weekly*, 50(33): 36–50.

Appendix (to Chapters 7 and 8)
Formation of pedagogy

Padma M. Sarangapani and Manish Jain

Pedagogy is centrally what teachers do. However, it is more than technique or what the teacher is observed to be doing in the classroom. Pedagogy, of course, produces 'learning outcomes' in the form of knowledge states in the child, but it also constitutes the educational identity of the child. This identity is epistemic, social and political – of the child as a learner, a knower and a person – drawing implicitly or explicitly from a learning theory, a social theory and a moral theory.

The pedagogy followed in each school surveyed for this study was characterised based on information from multiple sources. In each case, the processes of teaching and learning that were being followed were attempting to achieve the educational aims of the institution, but also specific educational purposes that teachers intended. An understanding of the distinctive work being carried out in each classroom was characterised by drawing on five dimensions: first, teachers' expectations and intended aims of education for the children that they were teaching and what they expected the children to achieve; second, their expectations of the child's home, particularly support for schooling; third, a 'method' they employed for teaching; fourth, the 'method' that they intended by which students would learn; and fifth, the method of discipline or moral regulation that was prevalent in the school. In order to construct pedagogy, teachers were observed in language/ English, mathematics or science classes. They were interviewed after the class. At least two lessons in class were observed in each school – in primary and middle grades. Additionally, there were observations of the school at various times of day and discussion with the school head. These were drawn on to characterise teachers and schools along the five dimensions. The composite of these five dimensions was reviewed and synthesised into eight broad types of pedagogy. Schools were categorised along these pedagogic forms. Within each aspect of pedagogy,

Appendix: Formation of pedagogy 219

there are variations, some of which are roughly hierarchical in terms of intensity, complexity or abstraction.

Expectations about learning (E)

This aspect of pedagogy refers to the expectations that teachers (and the institution) have of what children would learn. Teachers' expectations refers not generally to expectations of some abstract learner, but more specifically to expectations about what the particular children whom the teacher is expected to teach could be and should be expected to learn. This constitutes an educational aim that informs her or his pedagogic focus and effort. *The range observed varies from expectations that are teacher-referenced to those that are textbook-referenced to finally, those that are society-referenced, that is, they range from the more personal or private expectations to the more public and shared expectations.*

Minimal expectations take the form of teacher-controlled and defined learning of literacy and obedience (E1). The next level is still teacher-centric – children are expected to learn answers as defined by the teacher (E2). The next set of three expectations revolve closely around the textbooks and learning textbook knowledge. At the lowest of textbook expectations are learning textbook answers (E3) in exact form. The next higher is to answer textbook questions and in the textbook language but by finding answers on one's own (E4). Finally, the highest textbook expectation is answering from the textbook knowledge but with conceptual understanding (E5). This range is from exact reproduction of textbook answers to answers that reflect the understanding of concepts and comprehension of the textbook. The final two levels move beyond using the textbook as the reference towards learning that is more widely valued in society – learning of concepts and solving competitive exam papers societally valued (E6) and in a few cases, also the production of reasoning, independence, autonomy, creativity and novelty reflecting the grasp of understanding (E7). E2 to E5 are more memory-based and involve recalling answers, while in E6 to E7, there is an interest in the formation of concepts.

Expectations about home support (H)

Teachers have implicit or explicit understanding of the cultural and economic resources at home that support the child's ability to learn school knowledge. At the lowest end, teachers have no expectations from home and view the child's home circumstances with empathy

(H1). In other situations, a tense relationship prevails vis-à-vis the child's home, particularly where there are difficulties in securing the school fee. In this and in the next type of situation, the home of the child is viewed negatively as contributing to problems that have to be countered in school and where no support could be expected from the child's home (H2, H3). In increasing degrees, there are three types of relationships where the home is perceived as incapable of directly contributing useful things on its own but can be influenced to support the child, and the school and home could together support children towards greater and greater expectations, especially as the economic situation of the home improves and there is greater likelihood of either parent knowing English (H4, H5). In schools that prepare students for competitive examinations, parents are expected to manage children's time at home to a micro level of detail (H6). A last level indicates cultural continuity between the home and school, with the home providing valuable cultural capital – particularly the knowledge of English (H7). *The expectations about home support thus vary on an axis of expecting none in a situation of cultural difference or discontinuity between home and school to full support in a situation of cultural continuity and resource availability.*

Method of teaching (T)

The dominant pattern of teaching in Indian schools is 'whole class instruction', where the teacher engages and addresses the whole class and the entire group of students is basically doing the same things. Also, following a set lesson is the dominant trend. Within this, we can note variations such as the extent to which teachers do or do not give explanations, ask questions of children and expect them to either repeat what was said or articulate in their own words, and expect and allow children to ask questions – moving from mostly silence in children to more dialogic situations.

We observed that *teaching varied from more massified approaches to approaches which focused on individual learners*. In the former, there is little or no differentiation between students and little or no engagement with what children are understanding. Teachers primarily define the objects of learning by marking portions and items to be learnt without any discussion or explanation. The teachers, here, rarely make any eye contact with the children and may ignore them even if they say something (T1 and T2). In approaches where the teaching is more *individuated*, teachers try to monitor the individual child's learning of prescribed knowledge in overall competitive settings

Appendix: Formation of pedagogy 221

(T3, T4). There were many schools, particularly the new corporate managed schools, where pedagogy is scripted and tightly controlled by a centralised office. Here, teachers follow a detailed micro plan and have fixed targets to meet in each lesson. The participation of children in these classes also is a part of a script (T4). There are schools where the teaching seems to demand higher-order thinking from children (T5) and a few which are more dialogic and individualised (T6). Children are often heard saying things on their own and asking questions. It seems that their understanding is appreciated and their independent contributions are valued and incorporated into the ongoing lesson.

Method of learning (L)

Indian teachers are concerned not only with teaching but also 'making children learn', and each teacher functions with an implicit view of how children learn and remember what there is to be learnt or what they have been taught, and how this learning is to be displayed or made visible. *Their theories range from learning by rote – that is, repetition – to learning by thinking and understanding and review.* This feature or aspect of making children learn by spending time in the class on it and of making sure that children have learnt by testing is a part of their pedagogy. In other words, complementing the time and effort in 'teaching' was the time and effort spent on 'making children learn': practice, rehearsal, assessment, review and feedback. This ranges from rote memory-based learning methods in which children are expected to repeat and the teacher made them repeat and repeat and repeat, to making children think and express in their own words, revise and attempt to apply their knowledge to answer new types of questions.

Repetition could be at the alphabet level where children are made to memorise answers at the spelling level (L1) with or without drilling and checks by the teachers (L2). In low-fee paying schools and schools for poor children, sometimes teachers are negligent and do not check students individually or pay attention only sporadically. Teachers sometimes monitor drilling with vigilance and intense personal checking to make sure that individual children have memorised correctly, even while all students repeat in chorus (L3). A significantly larger proportion of time may be devoted to 'learning' than to 'teaching'. In micro planned revisions, frequent testing along with analytics and review of performance over tests and 'scientific' management of test findings are also used (L4). Some teachers and schools favour a more 'practice' approach where children are encouraged to answer in their own words and to review and revise occasionally. Here, 'teaching' is given more time as compared to 'learning', which students are expected to do on their own and to achieve through understanding (L5).

Disciplinary culture (D)

A disciplinary culture is an integral part of pedagogic work; instructional work both assumes and works on moral regulation. Pedagogy and its effects are expected to result in moral learning as well as content knowledge and skill development. The latter follows the former. Thus, pedagogy involves shaping both the moral and epistemic capability and the potential and identity of the student.

Disciplinary cultures vary on the axis of visible to invisible. At the one end, discipline is imposed through very visible forms involving corporal punishment and physical control. This form of discipline usually also extends to and includes psychological violence – labelling, name calling and the use of insulting language (D1). There may be the use of guilt and conveying inadequacy arising out of moral failure: being lazy, dishonest or playful. While there is no physical punishment, this discipline is also very visible and involves fear (D2). As the disciplinary cultures moved towards more invisible forms, they could take the form of micro control through rigorous timetabling and control of the space and time of the student, in some cases for very extensive hours from the early hours of the morning until late at night (D3). Religion and religious values may also be invoked in establishing the invisible controls and normative frameworks that students are expected to draw upon to self-regulate (D4). In a few cases, control may be expected to take the form of self-control through the use of reason and developing autonomous judgement (D5). *The axis of variation is from visible – external control of the body – to invisible – internal control through reason.*

Classrooms and schools were characterised along the dimensions of and the variations in these qualities of expectations of learning and home, methods of teaching and learning and disciplinary cultures.

Pedagogic forms

Each school was assigned its characteristics along the five dimensions. The characteristics were found to be more or less common in a given organisation, with very little variations between teachers in that organisation. The characteristics were then resynthesised into eight broad forms of pedagogy. These pedagogies were then assigned to each school as its dominant pedagogical character. Needless to say,

Appendix: Formation of pedagogy 223

there were variations and minor distinctions, so the fit is approximate and not exact. In a few schools, there was wide variability in pedagogic form between teachers, and this is in itself a key aspect of the pedagogic characteristics of some schools. Figure A.1 indicates the combinations that lead to the formation of pedagogies.

Domesticating pedagogy: Learning objectives are the very basic skills of literacy and numeracy, obedience and at most, learning the teachers' answers. There are no expectations from children or home, and the home is tolerated. Where fee collection is involved, the relationship is tense and one of distrust. The main methods of teaching are to mark out or write out what needs to be learnt – children are to copy and repeat in order to learn. Children's voices are not heard in the classroom, except when they are permitted to talk by the teacher. Instructions are monosyllabic or short phrases that are barked out in the vernacular or in English. The focus is mostly at the alphabetic, spelling and exact reproduction levels. The supervision by teachers is mostly negligent and sporadic. The discipline culture generally involves corporal or physical control or abusive and insulting language involving name calling and aimed at producing fear and obedience.

Rote: The learning objective is to reproduce exact answers as provided by the teacher or the textbook. There are either no expectations from home or expectations of negative influences from home, specifically, a general lack of support and neglect from home. The relationship with the students' homes is mainly built around fee collection. Teaching is very brief, with the focus on questions and answers to be written up and marked. Children's voices are not heard, or they are permitted to talk only in response to questions. Learning involves rote memorisation, with occasional sporadic checking by teachers. But teaching and learning is, on the whole, massified. It takes the form of tutoring groups of students in the multigraded settings, where portions are marked out during 'teaching' and then students are expected to repeat and rehearse them individually. Discipline is physical or guilt-based, individualised, with work being checked while holding and twisting the child's ear for mistakes or pinching and slapping.

Drill: The learning objective is production of textbook or guide answers and learning English. The home and the school co-operate for the child's learning – the child is a 'moral project'. (Complaints are exchanged between parents and teachers, and the child is exhorted to exercise more discipline and self-control.) Alternatively, the home is to be educated and influenced to support and meet school requirements and monitor the child's punctuality, supervise the homework and other tasks. Teaching is through brief explanation followed by

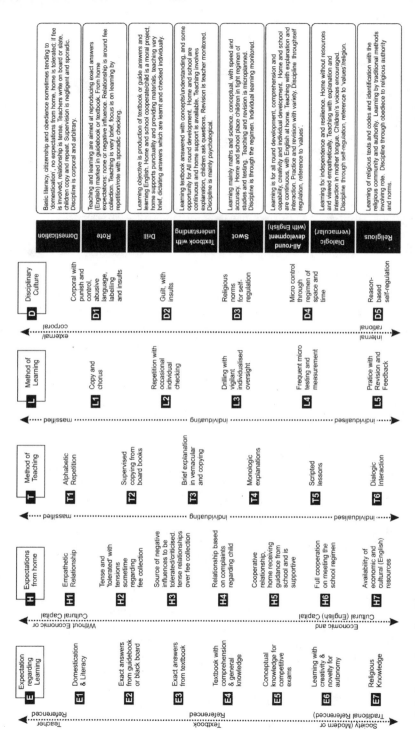

Figure A.1 Formation of pedagogy
Source: Authors

question-answer sessions and may occasionally involve longer teacher monologues and answers dictated and checked. Learning is by repetition and drill, with monitoring by the teacher.

Textbook-based with understanding: The learning objective is production of textbook-referenced answers with understanding of concepts. The home and school environments are continuous, and home support is generally available. Teaching involves explanations and teacher monologues. Children ask and answer questions, but on the whole, learning is textbook-oriented. Revision is monitored by the teacher. Discipline is mainly psychological.

Swot: Learning objective is speed and accuracy of reproduction of information learnt from textbooks and guides, with competitive exams in mind and with the focus mostly on maths and science. School and home co-operate to place children in a tight regimen of disciplined study. Lessons are all micro planned and controlled. Revision is micro planned involving repeated testing. New expanded curriculum may or may not be followed, but it is based on the micro curriculum. Discipline is through strict regimen controlling space and time.

All-round development (English): The learning objective is comprehension, capability, reasoning and creativity. The school and home are continuous, and there is home support for all school requirements as well as for English and cultural capital to draw on. Teaching is dialogic and interactive; children's voices are heard and encouraged. The teacher acts autonomously. Practice and revision involve variety and independent thinking. Discipline is through self-regulation, with appeal to reason or to normative frameworks drawn from religious or national values.

Dialogic and child-centred (vernacular or mother tongue): Learning is for independence and self-reliance. The teacher aims for higher-order thinking and reasoning skills, self-expression and self-confidence. Teaching involves elaborated explanation and is dialogic and in the vernacular or the students' mother tongue, with children asking questions. Revision involves variation and positive feedback and encouragement. There are no expectations from home, and home is viewed with empathy. Discipline is self-directed and reason-based or may involve appeal to reason (and sometime to religious norms).

Religious learning: Learning of religious texts and codes is at the core. Identification with the community and religious authority is central. Methodologies of teaching involve traditional methods of repetition and reading from the text, with a focus on memorisation.

Discipline is brought about through regimen and religious values and can include corporal punishment. Home is usually not expected to provide any support to school learning. 'Modern' education outcomes of literacy (vernacular or English) and numeracy, state curricula and examinations and certification are secondary and in some instances may not even be available.

9 Curriculum as a dimension of quality

Its production and management in schools in Hyderabad

Sakshi Kapoor

Introduction

The work presented in this book arose from the authors' shared concern that everyday understanding of quality of education is inadequate. We, therefore, took a fresh look at the ever-evolving landscape of schools in India, particularly re-examining government and private school provisioning and the quality differential between them. Results from empirical studies carried out in Delhi and Hyderabad, as presented in Chapters 7, 8 and 9 of this book, highlight the diversity in schools and the vast variation in education quality. Given this diversity, Sarangapani in Chapter 7 of this volume argues that, the 'calculus' operating in the production of quality education is based on the consideration that schools now occupy 'multiple niches in the market ecosystem' rather than whether they are private, aided or government schools. She makes the case that diversity of schools and their quality can be better understood by 'unpacking the categories of "private" and "government"'. In this chapter, I present a way to do this.

The basic argument I make in this chapter is that the production and management of 'quality' is not a function of the type of school management – that is, government, aided or private – but a function of the type of school ethos and the practices emanating from it. Examining a school's ethos reveals processes, activities and practices in the everyday 'life world' of a school, which adequately describe how different dimensions of quality, as delineated in a framework in Chapter 6 of this book, are operationalised. This chapter explores and discusses these processes and practices, problematising a commonly held claim that government schools are 'poor quality' and private schools offer 'good quality' education (Tooley and Dixon, 2005; Muralidharan, 2006; Tooley, Dixon, and Gomathi, 2007). I postulate six types of school ethos, which explain the quality differential in different categories of schools. Building on this, I further argue that methodologically, 'school ethos' is a useful concept to understand 'quality' in education.

The research context

This chapter draws on a yearlong engagement with 10 different categories of schools in Hyderabad, which were selected from the census of schools undertaken for the study described in this book (see Chapters 7 and 8). These schools were a mix of government high school, government primary school, private unaided school affiliated to state board, private unaided school affiliated to central curriculum board, aided school, low-fee private (LFP) school, private unaided unrecognised school and what is commonly known in Hyderabad as corporate school – thus representing all types of schools that exist in the selected geographical area. Table 9.1 gives a brief profile of the selected schools.

In these selected schools, in-depth interviews were conducted with principals, vice principals, senior members of the school management team (like director and correspondent) and a senior teacher each from the primary and secondary sections. In addition, observations were conducted of key school processes – parent–teacher meetings, school management committee (SMC) meetings, morning assembly, classroom teaching and school inspection. Through these interviews and observations, an attempt was made to examine, in each of the selected schools, some important aspects of a school's everyday functioning – admission procedures, scholastic and co-scholastic activities, procedures for making timetables, selecting textbooks, recruiting teachers, reporting and management structure, examination and assessment routines, school's interaction with external stakeholders, procedures concerning fee and finances and the nature of teachers' and school management's work.

School ethos

Many educationists and researchers have theoretically and empirically developed the concept of school ethos (Hogan, 1984; Donnelly, 2000; Smith, 2003; McLaughlin, 2005). The concept tends to be used in relation to subjective, less measurable features of the school environment, such as the relationships between people and the values and principles underlying policy and practice and may also refer to the core values of the school, which are deep and fundamental in its life and work (McLaughlin, 2005). An ethos is 'manifested in many aspects of the

Table 9.1 Basic profile of selected schools

Features	GP	GH	KT	S	GV	N	B	Z	KE	M
School type	Govt	Govt	Aided	Pvt unaided	Pvt unaided	Pvt unaided	Pvt unaided	Pvt unaided	Pvt unaided	Pvt unaided unrecognised
Established	1948	1948	1930	1989	2003	2005	1990	1983	2001	2011
Classes	1 to 5	6 to 10	1 to 10	1 to 10	1 to 10	1 to 10	1 to 10	1 to 10	1 to 10	1 to 7
Pre-primary (PP)	Yes	No	No	Yes	Yes	Yes	Yes	Yes	Yes	Yes
PP enrolment	22	–	–	330	157	64	75	108	184	23
Other class enrolment	273	531	249	1,596	625	959	198	627	414	58
Total school enrolment	295	531	249	1,926	782	1,023	273	735	598	81
Co-ed	Yes	Yes	Yes	Yes	Yes	Yes	Yes	Yes* ()	Yes	Yes
No. of teachers	10	18	12	95	41	84	13	40	19	7
Curriculum	State board	State board	State board	CBSE	State board	State board	State board	State board	State board	State board
Medium of instruction	English, Urdu, Telugu	English, Urdu, Telugu	Telugu	English	English	English	English	English	English	English
Fees (annual, range, in rupees)	–	–	–	25,200 to 33,600 (8,400 to 11,200 per term, 3 terms)	17,000 to 24,000	24,000 to 47,000	4,800 to 9,000	6,300 to 9,000	3,600 to 8,400	1,800 to 3,600
Clientele	Lower income families	Lower income families	Lower income families	Middle to upper middle income families	Middle to upper middle income families	Elite and upper income families	Lower income families	Heterogeneous population	Lower income families	Lower income families

Source: Author's field notes, 2011 and 2012

Note: First row of the table are the pseudonyms of the selected schools.

* Separate sections for boys and girls from class 3 onwards.

entity in question' and in the context of schools, it 'comes up for assessment in terms of the extent to which it embodies and facilitates educative influence' (McLaughlin, 2005: 311–312). Additionally, ethos is not a static phenomenon. It depends on the values and attitudes of the key actors involved as well as on the social and political culture. Ethos is a negotiated process since it can do two different things: one, constrain people to follow rules and regulations and adapt their behaviour in ways that fit with those who hold positions of power or authority and two, challenge established hierarchies in instances when school members do not submissively accept the status quo and act on their own initiative to strongly resist the directions of those in authority (Donnelly, 2000).

The term 'ethos' also has strong connections with the term 'culture' and Bourdieu's 'habitus'. Donnelly (2000) writes that the term 'ethos' is more specific and located and subsumed within the concept of culture, elaborating that, 'school ethos refers to formal and informal expressions of school members and these expressions tend to reflect the prevailing cultural norms, assumptions and beliefs' (Donnelly, 2000: 136–137). Smith (2003), on the other hand, points out that it is unclear whether habitus as an attribute of individuals can also be an attribute of an institution. He treats ethos as a special case of habitus, 'as a complex dynamic interaction of continuous construction and re-construction of individuals' and institutions' habituses' (Smith, 2003: 466).

Thus, school ethos may be understood as an aspect of a school's everyday life that is unquantifiable, intangible and defined by a central feature distinguishing the school. Such a central characteristic may be represented in fundamental values espoused by the school, or it may be embodied in individuals in the school or it may manifest through routine practices of the school.

With this understanding of school ethos, my focus in this chapter is to show that it is the characteristics of the school ethos and the ensuing practices that explain the quality differential amongst various categories of schools. Of the six dimensions of quality mentioned in Chapter 6 of this book – aims of education, provisions, curriculum, pedagogy, standards and accountability – I illustrate in this chapter, production and management of curriculum. Six types of school ethos are identified and are attributable to strong school leadership, managerialism, affiliation to a centralised curriculum board, school run as small-scale family business, complacent school staff and a particular ideology. The ethos explains how curriculum as a dimension of quality is produced and managed in the selected schools. These attributable factors characterise the school ethos and are a binding factor or a common denominator that explains why and what practices schools employ to operationalise quality. In other words, a group of schools exhibiting a particular kind of ethos show similar manifestations of quality compared to schools exhibiting a different kind of ethos. This provides a better explanation of educational quality and diversity.

Production and management of curriculum as a dimension of quality

Very broadly, I take curriculum to be an overarching frame within which students' experiences occur during an educational process. The specificities that make this frame are contingent upon educational aims, which are constantly negotiated based on a society's priorities. To provide for students' educational experiences, curriculum is transacted through specific academic content and co-scholastic activities. It is in this wide scope – educational experiences and specific content and activities – that I discuss the production and management of curriculum. Of the six dimensions of quality, I chose curriculum since it is a central and a wider dimension that also reflects or holds other aspects of quality like the aims of education, pedagogy and standards. Six types of school ethos, each of which is attributable to a unique feature of the school, ensue practices that produce and manage the curriculum, explaining why quality differs across different types of schools.

The ethos of the corporate school N is defined by centralised planning and organising, centralised mechanisms of monitoring and control, tight performance specifications, emphasis on teachers' accountability to parents and the principal working as a manager to implement predetermined plans. All this is to coach students for competitive exams. This results in specialised and differentiated curricula for which students are sorted through systematic procedures.

In government high school GH, private trust-run school KE and private unaided GV, the school leader and his or her leadership shape the ethos. These leaders build a vision, identify key goals for the organisation, have high performance expectations, provide individualised support, build productive relations with families and communities, connect the school to the wider environment, staff the programme and provide teaching support, monitor school activity and buffer the staff from distractions in their work. Given the school head's active leadership, state prescribed curriculum is enriched with additional programmes and resources.

232 Sakshi Kapoor

In private unaided school S, the school's affiliation to CBSE board shapes the school ethos. This means that all requirements mandated by CBSE with respect to infrastructure, fees, staff and service conditions, teaching and learning, examination and assessments are followed in school S, giving its ethos a distinct character. The curriculum therefore is rich and diverse, with a range of scholastic and co-scholastic activities.

The ethos of private unaided LFP school B and private unaided unrecognised school M derives from these schools being operated as a small-scale family business unit. As such, implementation of curriculum is about employing practices that retain the clientele, thus assuring sustainability of the family business.

In aided school KT and government primary school GP, the school staff, having written off the school's clientele, is complacent towards their work and as such the school ethos is characterised by a lack of desire to put appropriate efforts into the activities of the school. The implementation of curriculum in these schools is about doing the minimum – limited to transacting the textbook and completing the syllabus.

Lastly, the ethos of private unaided school Z is shaped by aims espoused by a particular ideology, which the school upholds. The ideology is to nurture a modern and Islamic citizen and as such the state-prescribed curriculum is supplemented by *Islamiat* curriculum. Since space does not allow for a detailed presentation of all types of ethos, I have selected three (in no particular order) – managerial ethos, strong school leadership ethos and ethos attributable to a particular ideology – to illustrate that production and management of curriculum or any other dimension of quality may be explained by the characteristics and the ensuing practices of a school's ethos.

Managerial ethos (school N)

This ethos is distinct for it reveals itself through a kind of school management that is modelled as a corporate business. Locally referred to as 'corporate schools', schools like N are characterised by managerial practices such as hierarchically organised management and centralised mechanisms of monitoring and control. This in school N is to obtain a single objective – train students for competitive entrance examinations to engineering and medical colleges. I use Hoyle and Wallace's (2005) conception of managerialism to describe the ethos of school N.

Hoyle and Wallace note,

> Managerialism, on the other hand, is leadership and management in excess. It transcends the support role of leadership and

management and in its extreme manifestation becomes an end in itself. Underpinning the hyperactivity of managerialism, the constant creation of new tools for organising work, is an ideology which holds that not only *can* all aspects of organisational life be controlled but that they *should* be controlled.

(Hoyle and Wallace, 2005: 68, emphasis in original)

Coming in the wake of New Public Management (NPM), the idea of managerialism that all aspects of an organisation should be controlled arose from the belief that managerial practices of the private sector, particularly business enterprises, can be learnt and applied to public service activities like education. While NPM, more broadly, proposes features like large-scale privatisation, customer-driven provision of services, decentralisation and processes to ensure cost-efficiency, managerialism is about 'hands-on, professional management; explicit standards and measures of performance; managing by results; value for money' (Green, 2011: 18–19).

The application of these management practices is found in school N. School management is hierarchically organised – chairperson, vice chairperson, governors, directors, zonal heads, academic regional coordinator, principal, vice principals, subject heads and then teachers – and the relationship amongst colleagues is on the lines of manager-subordinate. Pattern of governance is such that planning and organising, monitoring and control are centralised and done systematically by tools such as a micro schedule that lays down what teachers should do hour by hour and a micro planner that tracks a teacher's progress against the micro schedule. There is 'tight coupling' between the office of the principal and the teacher's work. Accountability is emphasised. The principal describes himself professionally as an 'executor' and his job as 'meeting the demands of the customers'. A team from the school's central office regularly conducts inspection to fix accountability at all levels – teachers' accountability to management, teachers' to parents and managements' to parents. The impact of managerialism is emphasis on performance. There is tight performance specification and various kinds of tests measure outcomes. For example, for maths and science, one set of tests assesses students for analytical understanding and logical reasoning and another assesses them for 'concepts, definitions and formulae'. These specialised tests are over and above the unit or assignment tests and the term exams that are conducted in most schools. Through tools like 'error lists', students' performance in specialised tests is tracked on each question and on the overall scores in these tests; branches are ranked on league tables. The curriculum that is delivered in such an ethos is specialised and tightly monitored.

Specialised, differentiated curricula and technologised system to 'sort' students into curricula

School N is affiliated to the state board but, in addition, provides specialised curricula. Curricular programmes called 'olympiad', 'e-genius' and 'genius' are offered from classes 6 to 10 and vary in level of difficulty. All these are 'integrated' curricula for which the syllabi prescribed by different curriculum boards (CBSE, ICSE, IB and SSC)[1] is put together. The curriculum in the e-genius programme is pegged at a level two years higher than what is required for a given class. The olympiad programme covers syllabus that is still '25 per cent' larger in comparison with e-genius. The genius programme is similar to SSC but with a focus on coaching students for competitive exams. The aim of the school management in providing these programmes is to present the school as an educational institute offering coaching for engineering and medical entrance exams along with the mandated state curriculum. The principal and the vice principal of school N claimed that top rank holders in the olympiad and e-genius programmes are certain to succeed in the Indian Institute of Technology Joint Entrance Examination (IIT JEE). Textbooks published in-house are used to teach these curricula. Based on an assessment, students are sorted into these curricula and at the end of an academic year, based on performance in specialised tests, parents are advised to move their child from genius to e-genius or vice-versa. Using an analogy of appetite for food, the principal justifies the school offering different curricula to suit the student's appetite. He said,

> that appetite may not be satisfied with *idli*. So that I should go for something else. Even the brain. It requires the same feel what our belly feels. So I am a dull student. I may not capture, I may not work hard and hard and hard. So I generally prefer a relaxed programme like genius. If child is very intelligent, bright, whatever you are giving he is very much interested to take still still. That child cannot be stopped with little knowledge. His quest of knowledge is not fulfilled. Then he needs to go for e-[genius].
>
> (13 September 2012)

The principal was of the view that there was no 'force' or compulsion involved as the students became motivated to take these difficult courses and tests,

> We are only giving way to the child. We make the child walk only four steps by holding the hand, then we are showing that this is the way to walk. After that he goes on walking, then he runs, he wins. This is the only way we are giving; it's not that we are dumping.
>
> (4 July 2012)

Production of curriculum in school N, therefore, is by offering specialised and differentiated curricular programmes, and this is managed tightly by monitoring teachers' work against a predetermined teaching plan and by closely analysing and tracking students' performance especially in maths and science.

Strong school leadership ethos (schools GV, GH and KE)

A strong and active school leader heads schools GV, GH and KE. The leaders are the principal in government school GH, appointed by the Department of Education; the principal in private unaided school KE, appointed by members of the trust which runs the school; and the director in school GV, appointed by the owner of school GV. They are strong and active leaders. I note this difference to point out that it is not the appointed or the self-appointed feature of the leadership that contributes to this ethos but the specific leadership practices of these leaders that results in quality materialising in ways different from those in other schools.

The heads of these schools undertook leadership practices like 'staffing the programme, providing teaching support, monitoring school activity and buffering staff from distractions to their work to improve teaching and learning' (Day et al., 2011). The principal of KE was very clear about recruiting teachers who are good learners and those who can adapt to the needs of the student population being served by the school. When such teachers were not professionally qualified, she trained them on the job but did not compromise on her criteria for selecting teachers. The director of GV, on the other hand, ensured that teachers were happy while at work in his school. He created service conditions whereby teachers got financial benefits like provident fund and gratuity and also employed sufficient support staff so that teachers were not overburdened. As a result of this, attrition rate in school GV was low, with some senior teachers serving in the school for more than 18 years.

The leadership of these schools also instituted practices to monitor school activity. The principal of KE maintained a notebook with month-wise syllabus written for all the classes, and against that, she regularly mapped the progress made in each class and by each teacher. The director of GV held informal discussions with students to gauge their academic progress and also interacted with teachers and parents to understand how new initiatives like the 5-day week timetable were being received. The headmaster of government school GH fixed dates of a month to scan randomly selected notebooks from each class, for each subject. Based on a directive from the Department of Education, students in GH were tutored after school hours by a local NGO. The headmaster took the lead in actively engaging with the NGO's tutor to ensure that these extra tutorials augmented the regular teaching and were not merely followed as another official directive.

The leadership of these three schools also provided teaching support by building an '"academic climate" and providing resources in support of curriculum' (Day et al., 2011: 30). While the headmaster of GH actively sought external donors like charitable foundations and local business entities to provide funds to buy additional teaching learning material (TLM) like blackboards, the principal of KE encouraged teachers to teach maths and science in the mother tongue and the director of GV gave teachers enough autonomy to teach in ways that supported learning.

Another leadership practice that immensely impacted production and management of quality was the leaders' proactiveness in buffering teachers from distractions to their work. By prioritising work, principals of GH and KE protected their teachers from excessive departmental work. The principal of KE also buffered her teachers when parents unfairly blamed teachers for their child's low academic performance. The director of GV, on the other hand, shielded his teachers and principal when they were forced to give in to unlawful activities during public examinations. All this not only helped teachers to focus on their teaching but, with the school head's support, they were motivated to put in additional efforts. Thus, a strong school leadership ethos is shared and common amongst private unaided school GV, government school GH and LFP school KE.

School leaders augment the state-prescribed curriculum

The director of school GV introduced new activities in the timetable to enrich the curriculum. He decided to initiate a 5-day week school timetable for the academic year 2012–2013 to be able to schedule educational trips on Saturdays and to enable students to enrol in co-curricular activities outside school. Every Saturday, students from some sections go on trips to places like a chocolate factory, aviation academy, museum, brass factory and so on, while other students are encouraged to enrol in co-curricular activities like skating, badminton and music. The director, in collaboration with a local NGO, also initiated a programme whereby students of his school travel to a nearby village to meet, interact with and learn along with their peers in the village government school. In a conversation with the director and the principal, these initiatives are discussed at length,

PRINCIPAL: [varied experience] which they normally will not happen. Okay, see, parents' awareness also is less. So they cannot appreciate this much, but now maybe after some time they will understand. The children are going to do the project work, they are going to write about it . . . give them a certificate. [. . .] So it may help them in the long run to have a hobby [. . .] No, it helps you see . . . now some children of our school, they are going for higher education to other countries, so there they ask them, what is your extra co-curricular hobby. So they want those certificates. If they do not participate, we tell we don't give anything. [. . .] So that's why we made attendance compulsory. [. . .] And parents won't take them to such places or if they take them also they cannot tell them the education aspects also. It is under archaeology [students were taken to see sandstone scripts]. These are . . . these exposures are important for children. This is also the part of education.

DIRECTOR: No, no, it is only beginning. Children who are in 4th and 5th, by the time they leave our school, they will see so many places. [. . .] Result of [this], definitely two years you will see [. . .] Another thing they . . . those two days they stay with the parents; quality time with parents [. . .] So, give them a space instead of just dumping, dumping dumping like that [. . .]. In every exam . . . like quarterly is there, 20 marks are allotted for this. [. . .]

PRINCIPAL: So, naturally they will become more keen and it will help them in the long run. People don't have that awareness . . . that is the problem because they have seen a very closed . . . this thing atmosphere; like ok get marks.

(30 August 2012)

This episode highlights several leadership traits – the director's vision of setting direction by broadening the scope of the education that the school imparts, providing resources to augment the curriculum and building an academic climate that does not restrict learning to the textbook.

Likewise, the head master of government high school GH, in collaboration with the Indian Air Force, initiated NCC classes for students of classes 8 and 9 to expose them to technical knowledge in aviation as well as to guide them about a career in defence. Also, the principal in KE, through her social network, called upon resource persons to address students on various topics so that students could connect textbook knowledge with their everyday life experiences.

School ethos attributable to a particular ideology, in this case nurturing a 'good Muslim' (school Z)

In school Z, the school ethos is guided by an ideology that aims to nurture a 'good Muslim' who is worthwhile for his or her community. The school ethos thus results in practices that incorporate modernity but not at the cost of 'Islamic values' that are central to the community's identity. These values pertain to everyday aspects of life and derive from school members' belief in and understanding of prescriptions in the Quran. I enumerate below key features of school Z, which are in accordance with Islamic values and shape the school ethos.

Separate sections for boys and girls: Although school Z is registered as a co-ed school, there are separate sections for boys and girls from class 3 onwards. These sections are housed in different parts of the school building so that boys and girls do not come in contact with each other during school hours. Teachers, both male and female, however, are common and they move between these separated parts of the school. The correspondent of school Z said, 'Quran says there should be separation,' explaining, 'other than marriage, all relationship is harmful.' As such, girls and boys are segregated so that they are not 'distracted from studies'. School, therefore, is considered as an appropriate site to 'control' for situations where students may experience 'distress [. . .] in the name of friendship'.

Teachers' time in school: School Z is an Islamic institution and follows norms 'as per [the] religion' and as such, a teacher's time with her or his family is valued. Teacher trainings are not conducted during holidays, and teachers are not asked to take extra lessons or put in extra hours after regular school timings. This is so because of certain values prescribed in the Quran, which state that the relationship between a husband and wife will break 'if third force (school job in this case) enter between them'.

Content of TLM: The school does not prescribe any TLM with content that is against Islamic values. When certain content is objectionable, the correspondent corresponds with the publishers to suggest changes that may be made in the textbook. The correspondent narrated an instance when he did not allow a facilitator to use big charts sent by the Ministry of Health and Family Welfare because the charts had nude pictures of an 18-year-old boy and girl. Such content, the school correspondent said, would 'generate curiosity' amongst students 'before time', which would distract them from their studies. This feature too highlights how Islamic values are embedded in everyday aspects of school Z. Decisions like these are reasoned on certain dos and don'ts stated in the holy book, that is, these are particular to Islamic values and not simply a result of generic cultural beliefs.

Dealing with students who fail: Students in school Z who fail in the annual exam are not rejected because the school staff follows the principle prescribed in the holy book: The 'sinner' may 'repent any time' and 'god may accept the repentance.' The school thus follows the practice of making such students attempt the question paper again during the holidays and a test is conducted on the first day when the school reopens. This is done to 'put a hurdle' in students' path, thereby instilling in them the value that success can only be attained through hard work.

As a result of these characteristics, school Z has a fixed clientele. The principal informed that parents who want Islamic education for their children prefer school Z, especially non-resident Indian families who return from West Asian countries. Other attractions for Muslim parents are separate sections for boys and girls, school offering time for afternoon prayers and high school girls compulsorily having to wear *hijaab*. Parents, according to the principal, 'like' these features of the school.

Curriculum to nurture a modern Islamic citizen

A manifestation of school Z's ethos is the Islamiat curriculum offered in addition to the state-prescribed curriculum. This curriculum is taught by especially trained teachers and delivered through oral sermons up to class 4 and through 'supplementary books' from class 5 onwards. The medium of instruction in Islamiat classes is Urdu, and there is a shared understanding in school that for such learning, 'mother tongue is best.' Islamiat classes are scheduled twice a week.

In a conversation, the correspondent explained the content of this curriculum,

CORRESPONDENT: Mostly morals we teach them and we do not give them extreme teachings . . . moderate teaching. We want to make them very good persons in life; practical.
ME: Do they come up with certain hard hitting questions; especially the older children? Considering the exposure to news and information that we have. . .
CORRESPONDENT: Before that, we clarified everything to them, what real Islam is. We have been teaching to them since their childhood days. We give very much importance to morals, ethics and how good person should be, how a good Muslim should be with his parents, with his neighbours, with his teachers and all those things.
ME: But there are lot of misconceptions that children may. . .
CORRESPONDENT: Yes. Sincerity, honesty everything and when there was 9/11 incident in USA, we explained to them what exactly *Jihad* was during the time of Prophet Mohammed. He did not attack anybody. When people attacked him, he defended, that too after he underwent long period of persecution. We told them all these things. Harming . . . life is very important, most precious thing on the face of the earth [. . .] So we must protect it. Human blood is very respectable, we cannot shed it as you like. All those things we inculcated in them . . . real teachings of Quran and Prophet's life. [. . .] And, for example, if I go to girls section, I will tell . . . now you are a small girl; one day you will become full-fledged lady. Your roles will be different . . . you will marry, you will do so many things in life. So you should be very devoted in life, very good daughter-in-law, very good person . . . all those things. What is happening in the society we have to study all those trends and we have to give them better knowledge, correct knowledge.
(17 July 2012)

In addition to this, 'all types of *duas*[2]' are taught. According to the correspondent, the controlled environment of a school is the 'best place' to impart such teaching because 'main age' of students' lives is spent in school. In addition to the state-prescribed curriculum and the Islamiat curriculum, students participate in internally organised events like exhibition of 'best out of waste things', sports day, debate, elocution, essay writing, story telling and recitation and in external events like inter-school competitions and science exhibitions organised by the Department of Education. Unlike in school S where the school's ethos, deriving its characteristics from CBSE by-laws, results in teachers making conscious efforts to open such events to all students so that learning, as mandated by CBSE, is not limited to scholastic subjects, in school Z, only 'good students' or students 'who study nicely' or 'A+ students' are selected for these activities. The criterion is not just meant to select a student who is better placed to win but also to select someone who is the most appropriate representation of the school's communitarian ideology – a 'good Muslim' who is 'good' in both modern and Islamiat education. Teachers and the correspondent in Z also seek out opportunities whereby students participate in events organised by entities imparting Islamic learning. These events are 'Islamic competition, recitation of Quran, recitation of some songs and hymns'. During a visit to the school, I observed that a few students, in preparation for an inter-school competition organised by an Islamic organisation, had built a model of a ship and were rehearsing to explain the destruction of the *Titanic* according to relevant verses in Quran.

In school Z, therefore, curriculum as a dimension of quality is produced by supplementing the state-prescribed curriculum with Islamiat curriculum. This practice emanates from and at the same time reinforces the school's ideology of producing a 'good modern Muslim'.

Conclusion

In this chapter I have attempted to show how a dimension of quality – curriculum – is produced and managed in different categories of schools. Based on empirical data, I presented that the curriculum in a school unfolds through ensuing practices of the school ethos. Three different types of ethos attributable to strong school leadership, managerialism and typical ideology explain the multiple practices through which a curriculum is implemented.

This exploration unambiguously implies that quality in education is not simply a function of the type of school management. 'Private' schools are of 'good quality' and government schools are not is an oversimplified position that not only overlooks the complexity which characterises a concept like 'quality' but also bypasses the minutiae in a school's daily functioning. This yields a few implications.

First, it problematises viewing quality in education through the government–private binary by showing that 'private' is not a homogeneous category to describe the nuanced practices which unaided schools undertake in the name of quality education. Although all are classified as private, the leadership of schools KE and GV, the business-like management of school N and the vision of a certain kind of individual in school Z resulted in very different practices and manifestations of curriculum, though the state curriculum is prescribed in all these private schools.

Second, it highlights that the production and management of quality does not only occur within the confines of a classroom but the nature of school's engagement with its external environment also has a bearing on the practices of quality. While the principal of a government high school (school GH) proactively engaged with external stakeholders, thereby augmenting resources that supported the curriculum, the correspondent of an unaided school (school Z) 'controlled' sources of knowledge that were considered to be against the grain of the school's ideology. This supports the idea that an examination of quality should consider the site of a school as a 'system', which is in interaction with and impacted by the external environment. Sarangapani, in Chapter 6 of this book, argues that a 'system of education' contains all the characteristics discussed under the concept of quality 'and not the unit of the school per se'.

Third, methodologically, the way to understand 'quality' in education lies in uncovering the school ethos. It cannot be reduced to binary variables of government–private, good–bad (pedagogy), more–less (provisions), high–low (standards). The use of a concept like school ethos allows for a comprehensive analysis in a way that is not always possible by the common categorisation of schools into government and private. An exploration of school ethos revealed, for example, that three schools – very different with respect to type of management (a private unaided school (GV), a government school (GH) and an LFP trust run school (KE)) – had similar manifestations of quality because these schools exhibited the same type of ethos – an ethos attributable to strong school leadership. In a traditional analysis of government versus private schools, these schools would not be analysed together.

The use of the concept of school ethos, in other words, makes us recognise that there is much more to production and management of quality than limiting the analysis to type of school management. While the type of school management may be used as the first cut of analysis, an investigation into a complex concept like education quality needs a dynamic frame like school ethos. By highlighting different types of school ethos, this chapter has attempted to bring forth the complexities and multiplicities involved in delivering quality education. School ethos is a dynamic concept that can capture minute details that characterise the 'life world' of schools and help to identify a common denominator that explains this life world and the production and management of quality in it. In the main, this chapter has provided empirical evidence that an investigation to understand 'quality' in the Indian school education system needs to depart from simply associating 'state' with 'poor or low-quality schooling' and market with the catch-all term 'private'.

Notes

1 CBSE – Central Board of Secondary Education; ICSE – Indian Certificate of Secondary Education; IB – International Baccalaureate; SSC – Secondary School Certificate.
2 *Dua* – In the terminology of Islam, the word means 'to call out' or 'to summon' and is regarded by Muslims as the core of worship.

References

Day, C., Sammons, Pam, Leithwood, Ken, Hopkins, David, Gu, Qing, Brown, Eleanor, and Ahtaridou, Elpida. (2011). *Successful School Leadership: Linking with Learning and Achievement*. England: Open University Press.

Donnelly, C. (2000). 'In Pursuit of School Ethos', *British Journal of Educational Studies*, 48(2): 134–154.

Green, J. (2011). *Education, Professionalism and the Quest for Accountability: Hitting the Target but Missing the Point*. New York: Routledge.

Hogan, P. (1984). 'The Question of Ethos in Schools', *The Furrow*, 35(11): 693–703.

Hoyle, E., and Wallace, Mike. (2005). *Education Leadership: Ambiguity, Professionals and Managerialism*. London: Sage.

McLaughlin, T. (2005). 'The Educative Importance of Ethos', *British Journal of Educational Studies: Values, Ethics and Character in Education*, 53(3): 306–325.

Muralidharan, K. (2006). 'Public-Private Partnerships for Quality Education in India', *Seminar*, (565).

Smith, E. (2003). 'Ethos, Habitus and Situation for Learning: An Ecology', *British Journal of Sociology of Education*, 24(4): 463–470.

Tooley, J., and Dixon, P. (2005). 'An Inspector Calls: The Regulation of "Budget" Private Schools in Hyderabad, Andhra Pradesh, India', *International Journal of Educational Development*, 25: 269–285.

Tooley, J., Dixon, Pauline, and Gomathi, S. V. (2007). 'Private Schools and the Millennium Development Goal of Universal Primary Education: A Census and Comparative Survey in Hyderabad, India', *Oxford Review of Education*, 33(5): 539–560.

10 Management of home–school relationship

Role of school principals in low-fee private schools

Poonam Sharma

Introduction

The first section of this book has drawn attention to the emergence and growing significance of low-fee-paying private schools in the educational landscape of urban India. Offering English medium education at fees that are affordable to an emerging lower middle class, this sector of schools has begun to receive attention as serving the needs of the poor. In recent discussions of the ability of the market to meet the demand for quality education, this is the sector that is presented as offering us the live model of how market discipline, brought about by consumers exercising choice, voice and exit, can produce quality and efficiency (Tooley and Dixon, 2006; Tooley 2007; Fennell, 2012).

This chapter adds to the small but growing literature that has begun to look into low-cost private school and its management, providing us with insights into how management works and also examining the extent to which and how various market logics play out in this space. Given the difficulty in accessing these spaces as they are closed and not obligated to allow the presence of researchers, detailed accounts of the inner life in these institutions are few. Srivastava (2007, 2013) notices the lack of any evidence that suggests market-based engagement of the household with these schools has translated into more equal power relationships. She claims that these schools are accessed by the lower middle class and working class, who make immense sacrifices to access them but are not the most disadvantaged, not belonging to the poorest of the poor. This is counter to the claims of affordability of these schools. She also reveals that these schools are segmented by class and that the concept of affordability bypasses the aspects of exclusionary factors. In addition, these schools are also noted to engage in malpractices for attaining government recognition.

Lall's study (as quoted in Nambissan, 2013) is among the few studies that looked closely into the quality of teaching learning process in these schools. She highlights the monotonous pedagogy of these schools. Unlike the observations made by Tooley, she found there was nothing beyond copying text from the board and the textbooks and enormous amounts of homework. This was coupled with the presence of untrained teachers and high expectations of managers from teachers to produce signs of learning English in the children. Teachers worked under stress and corporal punishment was common in these schools. She writes that these schools are content to offer only minimalistic primary level schooling with the promise of good-quality English medium education.

This chapter, examines and provide insights into how the image of the school and the relationship between parents (as consumers) and the school are managed by the school management to ensure that the relationship cannot be cast in the straightforward consumer–supplier mould. Cultural models and market principles interact in complex ways to shape the relationship of these schools with the families.

The chapter is based on my doctoral ethnographic field work conducted between July 2011 and June 2012 in the town of Kasimpur[1] located on the northern fringe of the metropolitan city of Delhi near the Haryana border. The town had a total of 22 schools, which included 5 government and 17 private schools. Children from this town attended these local schools, and some attended schools outside the town. The study involved exploration of the relationship between families and schools and the children's agency. I studied four families, three of which were from the other backward castes (including one Muslim family) and one was a dalit family. Of the 12 children who were a part of my study, 8 studied in the two private schools in the town. I visited these schools several times in the course of my field work, and have observations spread over 120 days at these two schools. In addition to observations in the school ground as well as classrooms, I had access to the room of the school owners, 'principal-sir' as they were referred to, where I made several observations and had conversations, formal and informal, with them. I was able to observe their interactions with parents, teachers, children and other visitors. This chapter draws on my analysis of this data and brings the focus on the owners of the two schools: the two 'principal-sirs'.

The schools and their owners

The first school was Uday Model School founded and run by Mr Jitender from a local *jat* family. The jats are the dominant caste in this region. The second school was Lovely Public School run by Mr Balvinder, a *baniya* whose parents had migrated to Kasimpur about 35 years ago. The principal-sir of Uday Model School had a reputation of not taking Muslim students and of making disparaging remarks about Muslims in public. Thus, although the school was near an area of Muslim population concentration, Muslim parents avoided sending their children to the 'jat school'. This school largely received children from jat families and other caste groups who were the original inhabitants of Kasimpur. 'Principal-sir' was the manner of referring to the defacto principal of the school – the school's owner. In both the schools, the principals' wives had the necessary qualifications and were designated as principal, and they did have a role in managing the school. However, it was their husbands who looked after the school business.

As the baniya family had migrated to Kasimpur, Lovely Public School was known as 'the school established by outsiders' *(bahar ke logo ka school)*. The clientele of the school was largely migrant workers but also included children from a few families of the original inhabitants of the town, a few lower-caste families and a few jat families who were economically better off. The jat school was referred to as 'the school established by the villagers' (*gaon ke logon ka school*). Both the schools were recognised by the Municipal Corporation of Delhi as primary schools (standards 1 to 5). But both had nursery and kindergarten classes and included standards 5 to 8. Both the schools were located in the dense residential areas of the town. They charged fees ranging from Rs. 150 to Rs. 500 per month (depending on the standard). These schools competed with each other for clientele and were quite similar in the way they dealt with families.

Managing 'Impression'

In both private schools, the official principals were women, but it was their husbands who were actually the 'principals-in-action'. Officially, these men occupied the post of school manager. But in fact, they oversaw all aspects of the school, both the business side and the academic side. They were effectively the 'principal', a fact well recognised and understood by the teachers, the parents and the children. The instructions of 'principal-sir' were final in any circumstance of confusion. Both the men were deeply involved in town life and politics in various ways, and their extended social networking was an essential part of their work and their school business.

Mr Jitender spoke the regional language Haryanvi. Mr Balvinder largely used Hindi and garnished his speech with English. Both came from patriarchal joint families and were deeply rooted in the traditional culture of the area (Sarangapani, 2003; Maan, 1979). Both men had a large circle of friends whom they met every day in the town.

A description of their office in the schools is important as it was the site where not only were academic and administrative decisions made but also power politics between the parents and the principal was played out. The principal-sirs themselves told me that their room was deliberately located at the entrance to the school as a way of establishing their authority and command over the school processes. No one could enter or leave the school without being seen from this office. This space was the action site of the principal-sirs; they were continuously busy doing one thing or the other or in asserting their authority over children, parents and teachers in various ways.

The principal-sirs were involved in impression management (Goffman, 1956). They made continuous efforts to create and manage an impression of the school in the minds of others. Their room was the stage for this performance. This room was the space for marketing and showcasing to the parents the qualities and achievements of the school. Trophies and shields from competitions and photographs of school children receiving awards were displayed prominently. The principal-sir sat at a huge office table on which were kept files and registers and records. Often, when parents visited, the principal would not offer them a seat and would start the conversation that was sub-texted with the power equations. This set-up of the room seemed to state the authority of the school principal.

Often, in the presence of parents, they could be heard questioning, correcting and instructing the teachers on their ways of teaching and disciplining the children. Rarely did any teacher in either of the schools object to these instructions. Parents sometimes did, but the principal-sirs manipulated these objections and devised ways to assert their views and ideas about parenting. They frequently drew on the examples from school, and their own experiences as children and as parents.

Both the principal-sirs monitored every small detail of the classroom on a daily basis. For example, there was a ritual in the LPS school: a register was circulated every morning to record absent children. Parents were then expected to communicate with the principal-sir rather than the child's class teacher for leave application. The principal-sirs felt proud of the fact that they kept such a close watch over the work of their teachers and students. This oversight of their teachers' work and student's attendance, they believed, was the secret of the success of their school. They contrasted this with the government school, saying this was a reason why government schools were doing so badly.

Principal-sir and the parents – relationships of obligation

Before discussing the principal's relation with parents, it is useful to understand some of their beliefs about the parents. Both men had very low opinions of the capacities of the parents because the parents had very little formal education and belonged to the town. When I asked Mr Balvinder why he started the provision of day boarding[2] in his school, he responded by highlighting the word 'illiterate parents'.

> It's been two years now. As it is, we only had to take care of this work [homework]. These are illiterate parents; they never bother about their children. They say 'Sir, you only please take care of these children, take a few extra rupees – 100 or 200 – and you only make them do their homework here.' What will they [parents] do; they don't even know which school is recognised and which is not recognised.
> (Mr Balvinder, 12 March 2012)

Mr Jitender shared:

> The kind of parents we receive in our school, we have to do double work for them. Not only we have to teach the children, but we also have to tell the parents how to bring up their children. They will feed the child with omelettes every morning and send them to school. The other day I had a child in school, he vomited early in the morning. I called the mother immediately and told her what a good diet is for a child in the morning. We have to keep on doing such things. These parents do not have time for their own children and then they expect that school should do everything for them.
> (Mr Jitender, 2 February 2012)

Their view of the 'incompetence' of parents justified the extent of their involvement in the business of parenting. It was presented as an obligation they felt necessary to make for the good of the children. Both the principal-sirs put most parents under a general umbrella of 'illiterate (*unpadh*)'. Both schools had illiterate as well as educated parents, even cases where both father and mother were college graduates. There were also children from families who were landowners and who were financially well-off but less educated (studied up to 8th or 10th class). The principal-sirs had very different ways of dealing with these groups. Parents without schooling who were well-known shopkeepers in the town were treated differently from parents without schooling who worked in factories. Factors like education level, land ownership, being shopkeepers or traders, being factory workers with graduation, government jobs and political affiliations seemed to be factors that entered into the calculations and influenced the way the principals treated parents and their children. Parents, in addition to providing the fee which financed the school, also brought resources (material and social networks) which were drawn upon to improve the profitability of the school enterprise in various ways. The principal-sirs labelled these parents as 'profitable parents' (*kaamke ma-baap*). On the other hand, factors such as being uneducated, having poor financial backgrounds, both working parents or being migrants were viewed as social liabilities as these parents influenced the perception of others of the school. The principals viewed these parents negatively and labelled them 'waste parents' (*bekarke ma-baap*). As Mr Balvinder put it, 'I develop relationships based on their potential *(Mai matha dekh kar tilak karta hun)*'.

The principal-sirs cultivated a sense of obligation among parents in various ways. They helped the town people and parents on occasion, and also carried out very personalised transactions of goods and favours in exchange for special attention to be given to particular children. The principal-sirs' performance with and treatment of different sets of parents differed based on their assessment of the family background and whether the parents would be of some benefit to the school. 'Profitable parents', parents coming from resourced backgrounds, were able to gain more attention of the principals for their child in return for various favours they were asked for. Even while asking for these favours, the principal-sirs skilfully managed the situation so that it seemed that they were doing the parents a favour, making them feel obliged to the principal-sirs in the process.

The following excerpt is Mr Balvinder's side of a phone conversation, a call he made to a parent who owned an electronic shop in Kasimpur.

> Hello, yes brother, how is the child now? What had happened? . . . Oh no! You should now take a medical policy; next time whenever you go to Stephen (hospital), you should buy. It is good for children . . . No, there is no need of panel in medical. If it is an emergency case, papers get cleared immediately. Now I have a little problem here, though we should not have disturbed you at this time. We bought a machine from you. Now it is giving problems. What do I do? Whom can I contact? (notes down a number) . . .

Don't worry about the exams. Once the child is well, we will take care of the exams. We are not like big selfish schools. You take care. Bye.

(Mr Balvinder, 19 March 2016)

In this conversation, Mr Balvinder was able to gain the favour of repairing a machine in exchange for postponing the exams for this particular child. He also took care to convey that this concession was a good feature of his school, unlike other 'money making' big schools that were not very concerned about the interests and issues of the children and parents. The parent in this case was a resourced parent. The 'waste parents' generally did not receive much attention and time of the principal-sir unless they had something that could be of advantage to the school. The following episode illustrates the treatment meted out to a non-resourced parent. In this case, a father came to Uday Model School to ask about admission for his son in standard 2. The father was concerned about what may happen after completion of standard 5 in the school.

FATHER: I want to admit him into the government school in 6th class. Will they take admissions from your school?

MR JITENDER: Why shift him in class 6? Let the child study in our school up till class 9. Then in 9th class, the child can be sent to government school from our school. We will do all the running around for paper work; you don't have to do anything. And if at that time, your son decides to go to the private school (further study in another private school), then he will have to compete for admission.[3] How much he is able to achieve. If you find problems with the coverage of syllabus while he is studying with us, you let us know. I don't think he needs to change his school in 6th class. When he reaches 9th class, we will get it done on our own.

FATHER: Can you guarantee his admission in government school after he passes out from your school?[4]

MR JITENDER: Yes, I am telling you.

(UPS principal, 24 March 2014)

This father was not a resourceful father. He was the senior member of a joint family. The children of his younger brother were to join the school next year. Mr Jitender anticipated these children's admission to his school. He tried to win the trust of this father and promised the admission of his child into a government school after passing out from his school. He did this because the other two children of the family were in the pipeline for admission in his school next year. Whether he will give admission or not was a separate matter, but this performance was to increase the number of applications to his school, which would feed public perception of the school.

In another case, the parents of a *dhobi* family (washer folks, low caste) were sending their child to Uday Model School. The principal-sir arranged that he would waive the fee of Rs. 350 per month in exchange for the family ironing their clothes for free. It was a permanent arrangement with the family. In case there was any fee amount to pay over and above the washing bill, that was to be cleared on the last day of every month. The mother was grateful for this gesture. The principal-sirs' relationship with parents was certainly that of a seller and buyer in which the entrepreneur took care to maintain and increase his customer base. However, as these episodes show, parents were viewed not only as customers but also as owners of resources that were useful to the school. Maintaining these relationships was useful and contributed to the overall profitability of the venture. Parents with these additional resources were aware that they could gain additional favours and attention for their children, giving them small advantages over others. These low-fee-paying schools also projected their local character and accessibility as giving an advantage to parents as opposed to 'big schools' that were more anonymous and bureaucratic. Both the school principal-sirs and the parents were involved in these transactions for mutual gain, and the school principals managed to couch the negotiations in ethically acceptable ways, ensuring that they always held the upper hand.

The expert authority on children and child rearing

Negotiations and bargains were made in the principal's room. While talking to parents, the principal-sir made sure that teachers, if they were present, supported his arguments so as to give more strength to his point. They used other office material to present themselves as experts who worked hard to handle the children in the school.

Schools had expectations as regards the participation of parents in the schooling of the child. They communicated these expectations to parents from the position of professionals with expert authority on education as well as child rearing. Neither the principal-sirs nor teachers nor parents imagined the parental role as having to do with academic work or teaching the child at home. Though the family background of the child was frequently brought up when the performance of the child was being discussed, what the teachers actually meant by 'home support' was not assistance given to the child in academic work. During my observations, I realised that although the teachers and the school principal always talked about the need for parents to provide support to the child at home, in fact, they rarely expected and seldom allowed the parents to interfere with the subject work of the student. They did not want parent's style of teaching and ways of writing (formal letters, word problems, etc.) to interfere with or contradict what they were doing in school. Also, it was a commonly held belief that parents were not likely to be aware of the current formats of writing and the teachers were since they belonged to this profession and were responsible for knowing the current status of knowledge. Many parents also held the view that 'if we have to teach the children at home, what is the use of sending them to school?'

In the European context, mothers have been found to be academically engaged with the child (Reay, 1998). Also, some researches in India have found that in upper middle class families, mothers are heavily invested in academic school-like work with the child at home (Donner, 2006). However, in Kasimpur, academic work was the main responsibility of the school, and there was no conflict of understanding between the school and teachers regarding the parental role. They expected parents to support the school by sending a 'resourced teachable child' to school. Teachers made comments about the parents for not sending the child dressed properly to school, making the child sleepy in class because the child was up late, not providing proper lunch (giving fast foods like instant noodles) or not equipping the child with proper stationery material and letting the child bring torn notebooks to class. Teachers expected parents to pack books and the notebooks according to the class timetable.

The principal-sirs continuously told parents about what was expected from their parenting. Their office room was the space where they theorised about children and parenting while conversing with parents. Both the principal-sirs communicated their own authority using two lines of argument, depending on the parental socioeconomic and educational position.

1. 'You are incapable or without resources or your approach is inferior.' This was an approach used mainly with parents with less schooling and of lower economic status. In their conversation, the principals' main aim was to explain to the parents that they could not sufficiently support the child since they lacked money and the knowledge of subjects in the school. And so, they must obey school instructions as to how parenting should be done.

2. 'You are capable and resourceful, but you are investing effort in the wrong direction; your parenting style needs alteration.' This approach was used for parents who were well-off and also had moderate schooling. The main aim in these conversations was to establish that parents did not know how to do good parenting and therefore they needed guidance by the school.

To parents in the first category, a frequently cited best practice advice was 'At least sit with the child for some time and have a look at his notebooks, sit and paste them with him at home.' For the parents of the second category, 'You need to show interest in the things yourself and then he will be interested, like watching Discovery channel.' The principal-sirs knew almost each of the families well; they were familiar with family circumstances and drew on this when they advised on parenting.

Many interactions between the principals and the parents involved lectures on how to do good parenting so that the children could be the right kind of 'school child'. This included all kinds of advice from disciplining children to what should be given to them for meals and what television programmes they should be allowed to watch and for how long.

> Principal (to me): In fact, even basic things we have to teach their mothers, like how to send them to school clean and hygienic . . . They should send them with clean clothes, that they need to iron it. . . . Shoes should be polished; their nails should be cut at least once in a week. We are not getting that kind of support which urban schools get; they don't have to teach them [the parents] these basic things, so their time and energy are utilised in other activities.

Both the principals never missed the opportunity to make suggestions of discipline and moulding the child's behaviour. Hidden under these suggestions was an aspiration towards the middle-class childhood in which the child was imagined in a psychosocially protected space away from the events in the lives of adults. The principals constantly emphasised a romantic emotional bond between mother and child. Their own parenting was held up as the model to be emulated.

> PRINCIPAL: Why did you send him in the torn pant? Why did you not get him the other pant?
> MOTHER: Sir, we belong to village; the other pant was not washed.

PRINCIPAL: No . . . no, I will not take this excuse. The child has first of all come in a torn pant. Why? First of all, you stop beating him. Have you heard yesterday's news? First sit with him and treat him as your son (*Pahle ise apna beta banao*).

. . .

PRINCIPAL: Take him to the market a few times, buy him something, and keep him emotionally. . .

MOTHER: We do buy things for them . . . His younger brother is there; he never tears his book. But this one, he is indeed naughty.

. . .

PRINCIPAL: This means he needs more of your attention, and you do not give that attention. When you know that the child does tear the books, sit with him, open his notebooks every second day, start pasting with him. One time, you sit with him and paste. The next time, you ask him to do it on his own; find ways. You will have to do it; this child is not very old.

. . .

MOTHER: What shall I do? No parents like to do this to the child, but still. . .

PRINCIPAL: I am telling you, this child needs more of your attention. He wants that his mother should ask him daily, 'Has anything of yours torn (notebooks); let me fix it.' Also see, the more the classes will increase, the load of studies will increase, and he is not weak (*kamjore*) in studies.

MOTHER: Yes, that is so.

. . .

PRINCIPAL: This is called carelessness (*laparvahi*), you have to work with him and finish it. I have told you the way, to sit with him every Saturday and make him do things. When he will see mummy is wasting my time every Saturday, he will on his own stop doing that. I am giving guarantee to you.

(LPS principal, 15 February 2015)

This mother was quite assertive with her interpretation of her son's problems. But the principal-sir did not give in. He spoke on behalf of the child to argue his version of what was needed. (There were no instances where the principals counselled the child on behalf of parents.) There was often reference to the efforts that parents were making to send their children to the private school, and children were often chastised roughly for not performing well and wasting their parents' efforts.

The idea of partnership was proposed as essential for the success of the child, which was eventually connected with the success of the school, as evident in the following statement after a parent–teacher meeting:

> So now you take him home and fix up all his notebooks. And you [to the teacher] tell her which notebooks she needs to work on. If you and we will work in collaboration, then only the child will succeed. And when the child will succeed, then our school will gain fame, you will go and tell ten more people that our school is good.
> (LPS principal, 15 February 2015)

This explicit acknowledgement of the role of parents and of the need for children's efforts clearly partitioned the achievement of school success in three ways: between the school, the parents and the child. It was clearly not presented as something that the school would guarantee on its own. The extensive attention paid to the issue of parenting by the school ensured that the school could not be held responsible for the children's failure or lack of success.

Brand building

The following is an episode where a mother came for the admission of her child and her sister-in-law's children to the UPS. Mr Jitender quoted an admission fee which she thought was much too high. When she negotiated on that, the principal-sir explained the qualities of his school, establishing it as a brand.

RAHUL'S MOTHER: All our three kids will come, you see (tries again to bargain down the admission fee).
MR JITENDER: Beta, you decide and bring your children. (continues his work) Our ways of dealing with children are very different. We just don't start beating, we first tell the child with love. Find out what is the problem he is facing and then we work accordingly. None of my teachers touch the children [no physical punishment].
  Meanwhile, one of the school teachers visits the principal's room.
MR JITENDER: Rita madam, you tell her, she wants to admit her children.
RITA MADAM: We teachers give a lot of focus on children; that is the main quality of our school. We not only pay attention to academics but also have so many competitions, medical camps, computer,

visits. Like this year, children went to Nehru Planetarium. You will yourself realise the difference.

...

RAHUL'S MOTHER: Isn't it too much?

MR JITENDER: Beta, the kind of work I am doing with children, I am not taking from you that much. You don't worry. If you wish, you can just let your child study in our school for a month. In one month, you will get to know. We can make some adjustments if you can't pay all together. After all, we are from this village only; we are not forcing you for paying once in all.

RAHUL'S AUNTY: One of mine (son) already studies here.

MR JITENDER: Good, then, are you satisfied or not? (expecting an obvious 'yes' answer)

Later, the mothers are conversing outside his room.

RAHUL'S MOTHER: This principal talks politely. They teach computer from the beginning, from class 1 itself. Here, they don't scold children. And after all, they are from our village; they are our own people. They never force to submit the entire fee in one go. There are a lot of good things for the child.

(UPS principal, 2 April 2012)

In this episode, not only did the principal advertise the school himself, but he also involved the teacher in doing so, and brought up his belonging to the town as a measure of his trustworthiness. The teacher showcased various events organised by the school, which were valued by the parents. During one event of independence day celebration, Mr P said: 'It is important to be in the talk of people. The public must keep on talking about your school, whether you teach or not, at least create the buzz around it.' Every independence day, the school organised a big event where children performed and small competitions were arranged. The whole programme was video recorded. Later on, the videos were made available to the parents for Rs. 50 each.

A lot of effort was put in building the brand of the school not only by the school diary, school books or school dress but also by training the children in certain qualities. These principals were very consciously moulding the personalities of the children who were the products of their school. They were observing and telling teachers their next step in making into 'good children' the children that belonged to their 'brand school' and could easily be spotted outside the school on account of the qualities that the school claimed to have inculcated in them. Mr Balvinder liked to teach the children and also the teachers to behave with *sabhayta*, or good manners. As he said in the following example just after morning assembly:

> Mr Balvinder: . . . but it is important to make children fearless (*bhay kholna*). Your presentation should be like soothing to eyes (*najroon me bas jae*). You look at my kids; Sudha talks very maturely. We have to pay attention on this matter in whole school.
> . . . you all make a 15-point format, which children must know. All teachers come together and make an opinion. So that even if anyone talks to our children outside, people can recognise these are children of our school. Like to talk politely (*aram se*), issues them books like good children (*acche bacche*, books from Hindu publisher Gita Press). In the feedback of class 4–5, it has come that children are being aggressive on parents. You work on this. Stand on stage and without hesitation, they should be able to talk. Even in co-scholastic activities (circular from MCD)[5] it has come 'attitude towards parents, teachers and companion is important.'
> (LPS principal, 6 December 2011)

In this way, the two school principal-sirs positioned themselves as social reformers and social workers rolled into one and perpetuated in the school culture their personal ways of thinking and beliefs about the children and their home backgrounds. They regularly cited and reiterated the examples of their own children while instructing the teachers. They often shared their ways of dealing with children to teach the teachers and parents how to discipline the school children.

This chapter highlights the active role of the school principal in impression management of the school. However, it does not suggest that the parents and teachers did not exercise any agency. This has been discussed in other papers (Sharma, 2017). In the given circumstances, where the principals were mostly engaged in the publicity of the school, they had unofficially appointed a teacher for their support. This teacher is in reality managing the job of the school principal, including the setting of curriculum, admissions formalities and evaluations. This person was a little above the position of the teachers and mostly worked from the school principal's room, handled the school's documents and set the timetable. She was called upon for teaching also in case of teacher absenteeism. She was incharge of organising the school trips, collecting money for that and managing the school academic life.

Conclusion

The focus of this chapter is the work of low-cost private school principals in managing the impression of their school and in influencing the family and school relationships. The school culture that is considered to be a modern space can be thus seen as shaped by the individual ideologies of the school owners. Through various examples, I have tried to show how the principal, through his talk and school activities, tried to oblige the parents and the teachers and posed to them the significance of their attachment to the school.

The school principals were making significant contribution to the public image of the school. All their efforts, including informal conversation with parents, training the teachers, organising events in school, were targeted at "creating the buzz" around schooling. In doing all these, they operated according to their personal beliefs about teaching and parenting and traditional power relationships between men and women. These beliefs were rooted in the middle-class imagination of childhood and parenting. The principals' own children and parenting style, which resembled the middle-class Eurocentric view of parenting and childhood, were portrayed as the role models for parents. And parenting was always assessed with this as a reference point. Through this in-depth study of the everyday work of the school principals, it can be concluded that the home and school relationship in the case of the private school is not only a simple customer and service provider relationship as described by the economic theories of the education system. This relationship is embedded in more than one way in the belief systems of the school staff, in this case specifically, of the school principal.

Notes

1 Schooling in this town was studied by Sarangapani (2003) in 1993–1994.
2 Day boarding is the two hours after school that children spend in school to complete school work and other activities.
3 Private schools in this village and around conducted tests for admissions.
4 Parents attached greater value to children studying for class 10 and 12 at government schools as the government school certification was considered to have higher value.
5 Municipal Corporation of Delhi.

References

Donner, H. (2006). 'Committed Mothers and Well-Adjusted Children: Privatisation, Early Years Education and Motherhood in Calcutta', in H. Donner (Ed.), *Modern Asian Studies 40*. Cambridge: Cambridge University Press.

Fennell, S. (2012). 'Between a Rock and a Hard Place: The Emerging Educational Market for the Poor in Pakistan', *Comparative Education*, 48(2): 249–261.
Goffman, E. (1956). *The Presentation of Self in Everyday Life*. Edinburgh: University of Edinburgh, Social Science Research Centre, Monographs no 2.
Maan, R. (1979). *Social Structures, Social Change and Future Trends*. Jaipur: Rawat Publications.
Nambissan. (2013). 'Low-Cost Private Schools for the Poor in India: Some Reflections', in IDFC (Ed.), *India Infrastructure Report 2012*. New Delhi, India: Routledge.
Reay, D. (1998). *Class Work: Mothers' Involvement in Their Children's Primary Schooling*. London: Taylor and Francis.
Sarangapani, P. M. (2003). *Constructing School Knowledge: An Ethnography of Learning in an Indian Village*. New Delhi, India: Sage.
Sharma, P. (2017). 'The Family and the School: An Exploration of Children's Educational Experience', Unpublished Ph.D. thesis. Tata Institute of Social Sciences. Mumbai.
Srivastava, P. (2007). 'For Philanthropy or Profit? The Management and Operation of Low-Fee Private Schools', in P. Srivastava and G. Walford (Eds.), *Private Schooling in Less Economically Developed Countries: Asian and African Perspectives* (pp. 153–186). Oxford: Oxford Studies in Comparative Education Series (Symposium Books Oxford).
———. (2013). 'Low-Fee Private Schooling: Issues and Evidence', in P. Srivastava (Ed.), *Low-Fee Private Schooling: Aggravating Equity or Mitigating Disadvantage?* Oxford: Oxford Studies in Comparative Education Series.
Tooley, J. P. (2007). 'Private Schools and the Millennium Development Goal of Universal Primary Education: A Census and Comparative Survey in Hyderabad, India', *Oxford Review of Education*, 33(5): 539–560.
Tooley, J. P., and Dixon, P. (2006). '"De facto" Privatisation of Education and the Poor: Implications of a Study from Sub-Saharan Africa and India', *Compare: A Journal of Comparative and international Education*, 36(4): 443–462.

11 School quality

Parent perspectives and schooling choices

Eleanor Gurney

Introduction

The fostering of parental school choice is one aspect of what the editors of this volume identify as the new discursive regime that has come to shape educational ideas in India in recent decades. Predicated on assumptions of greater efficiency, accountability and equity via increased competition between schools, consumer 'choice' has taken on new significance as a mechanism to ensure quality education. However, policy discourse that frames parents as consumers who work to make the 'best' choices for their children often fails to consider varying parental definitions of school and educational quality.

Equally, for most parents, quality preferences are only part of the story with respect to school quality and schooling decisions. For example, financial constraints to school access and school-level bureaucracy may impede parents' ability to enact their choice of school in practice (Srivastava and Noronha, 2016). Parents' ability to exercise either 'exit' or 'voice' in response to school quality failings is also not straightforward (Srivastava, 2007; James and Woodhead, 2014). As such, how parents make sense of constraints that impede their ability to access quality education for their children is relevant to understanding the relationship between school choice and quality.

Empirical studies of school choice in India are few in comparison to those in developed countries and have tended to focus on choice outcomes (most particularly the choice of private schooling) rather than choice processes.[1] However, in-depth accounts of how parents understand differences between schools and how in turn this influences their schooling decisions are significant to an understanding of broader issues of educational quality and purpose. In this chapter, I draw on data from interviews with parents living in three lower income communities in Delhi to examine both their conceptions of school quality and how non-quality factors intertwine with such conceptions to produce eventual schooling decisions. The analysis suggests that parents' quality perceptions are influenced by different educational and non-educational aims, informal information networks and the socio-cultural contexts of choice-making. The distinction between quality preferences and choice outcomes also illuminates the significance of different forms of capital (economic, social and cultural) for parents when they seek access to quality education.

Methods

This chapter draws on data collected for my doctoral study of how the education market in India works at the micro level, with a focus on how low income households navigate the decision-making process for elementary education.[2] Forming the heart of the wider study, data presented here are drawn from 58 semi-structured interviews with parents from across three slum squatter sites (*jhuggi jhopri* clusters) in south and east Delhi that took place between September 2014 and February 2015 (Table 11.1).

The two main case study sites (Locations A and B) in south Delhi were selected based on: (1) researcher knowledge of the areas; (2) the concentration of lower income families residing in each locality; and (3) the range of schools and school types within the immediate vicinity (within a 1 km radius of each community). Across the two study sites, schools with an elementary section included government schools managed by the South Delhi Municipal Corporation (SDMC) and the

Table 11.1 Number of parent interviews by location

Interviewees	Case study site			Total
	A	B	C	
Mother	13	15	3	31
Father	2	12	2	16
Other family member (main caregiver)	2	0	1	3
Joint (parents)	2	2	2	6
Joint (parent with another family member)	1	1	0	2
Total	20	30	8	58

Source: Author's data

Delhi Directorate of Education, private aided schools and several private institutions that varied by cost and recognition status. Reflecting the diversity of institutions captured by the empirical study detailed by Jain in Chapter 8 of this volume, schools were also found to differ by medium of instruction, co-educational versus single sex status and religious affiliation.[3]

A small number of parents were interviewed from the third site (Location C) in east Delhi. This site was selected for its higher proportion of Muslim households in comparison to Locations A and B. Lower income Muslims are known to experience inequalities of access to education (Government of India, 2006; Sarangapani and Winch, 2010). In addition, as with Locations A and B, the local education market in Location C included a range of government and private institutions.

Parents living in each selected community with children of elementary school age (ages 6 to 14), or with children currently accessing elementary schooling, were eligible to take part in the study. In part because of the study focus on the local contexts of choice-making, recruitment was conducted at the community level. The recruitment strategy initially involved approaching people in public areas of the community (the main walkways, outside shops or areas where a few people were sitting), explaining who I was, what the study was about and asking if they would be willing to be interviewed. From an early stage, I found that my obvious outsider status (I am a white, British woman) had an unexpected benefit: people were naturally curious about who I was and why I was there, so often approached me directly. This gave me a much-needed 'in' to starting initial conversations; in time, contacts with other potential participants developed through snowballing.

Interviews took place at interviewees' homes or within the local area at a place of the interviewee's choosing and lasted an average of 45 minutes. Most interviews were conducted in Hindi,[4] with the support of research assistants, who also assisted with the interview transcription and translation. Using an interview schedule as a guide to allow topical trajectories to be followed when appropriate, parents were asked about the schooling and other education services they were accessing for their children (if any) and their reasons for these choices. This included questions concerning parents' opinions about the characteristics of a 'good' school and what they saw as the wider purpose(s) of education. In general terms, parents who agreed to be interviewed were open to discussing their children's schooling and the factors that they perceived as having shaped their decisions in this respect. Some parents did show some hesitation in sharing their opinions with respect to school quality, questioning whether they could judge this given their own relative lack of formal education. While this is an interesting finding in and of itself, most parents did express more detailed views as interviews continued, possibly as they became more relaxed or because of lines of questioning that helped parents to express their ideas and experiences in more detail.

Findings and analysis

Aims and outcomes

As Winch notes in Chapter 2 of this volume, to understand how education quality may be defined and assessed by parents, it is necessary to consider the aims of parents in seeking education for their children. Parents discussed various motivations for enrolling their children in school that encompassed both educational and non-educational objectives.

In terms of educational aims, outcomes with a social good orientation, such as being able to 'help others' and being a good citizen, were mentioned by a small number of parents in interviews. However, specific skills such as literacy and numeracy were the most common aspects that parents hoped their child would acquire through schooling. For some parents, this was related to relatively everyday activities, such as being able to read bus numbers and to complete forms. For others, as existing studies of schooling in India have identified (Chopra, 2005; Srivastava, 2006), the perceived value of at least a basic level of education in the marriage market was a key driver behind the decision to enrol their daughters in school:

> In this community, it is better that a girl is educated. Everybody wants an educated girl these days.
> (Ganika, mother of seven, ages 6 to 21; government schools)[5]
> Interview, 18 December 2014, Location A

In addition, English and, to a lesser extent, computer skills were key educational outcomes that several parents understood as conferring advantages within the competitive employment market and which largely, although not exclusively, were meant for boys. For example:

> When he [her son] grows up, I understand that if he studies in an English medium school, it would be easier for him to have a job

[. . .] We are sending him to an English medium school so that he is able to compare better in the future.

(Aishi, mother of two, ages 9 and 18; private school and government school)[6]
Interview, 10 December 2014, Location B

Whilst the empirical evidence is limited, men in India with minimal English-language skills have been identified as earning an hourly wage up to 13 per cent higher than their non-English-speaking counterparts (Azam, Chin, and Prakash, 2013). Thus, whilst the desire for English reflected broader social aspirations than may be captured by reference to the labour market alone, parents' focus on English medium schooling could be understood as a strategic decision in view of the potential for relative financial gains.

Equally, the findings suggest that the association between English medium schooling and social privilege, the historical context of which Jain outlines in Chapter 1, enhanced the desirability of English for some parents in meaningful ways. For example, one mother, Garima, noted what she perceived as the social value of English within the wider society:

These days, nothing else matters but the knowledge of English; you only have to speak in English and people think nothing else matters, no other knowledge [. . .] English is required everywhere; who speaks in Hindi these days?

(Garima, mother of one son, age 8; private school)
Interview, 15 February 2015, Location B

Given that neither Garima nor many other local residents spoke English, Garima's question of 'who speaks in Hindi these days' is revealing in the implication that it is not herself or her immediate acquaintances to whom she refers. This indicates the strategic nature of Garima's choice of English medium schooling for her son in seeking to build the right kind of 'cultural capital' (Bourdieu, 1977) that will provide access to a different social stratum than the one the family currently occupies. The attentiveness to indicators of social privilege, in this case English, also draws attention to the role of non-educational aims in shaping parents' schooling choices, an issue to which I return later in this chapter.

School quality indicators

The knowledge of English as a key educational outcome, associated with both employability and social prestige, was found to shape parental schooling choices and quality perceptions across all study sites. Indeed, parents almost always referenced English in response to questions about 'good' schooling, with English operating in effect as a proxy quality indicator. For example:

> [Name redacted] is a good school; its medium of teaching is English.
> (Janvi, mother of two, ages 2 and 8; government school)
> Interview, 28 November 2014, Location A

> [RA: [Eleanor] wants to know what you liked about the school when you saw it for the first time?]
> First of all, we liked that not only the teachers of the school but even the students were speaking in English. So, we thought everyone here, including the teachers, are talking in English which doesn't happen in other schools. We thought it would be good for our child.
> (Varshil, father of two, ages 3 and 6; private school)
> Interview, 18 February 2015, Location A

At the same time, it is important to note the close association between English and private schooling, which was promoted by private schools across all study sites. The majority of private schools in each area advertised themselves as 'English-medium' explicitly on school signs or suggested this by using English for notices and in reception areas. However, while parents may associate English with private schooling, the extent to which this may be borne out in practice is not always clear (Majumdar and Mooij, 2011). School visits and informal conversations with teachers during fieldwork revealed that English was not a functional language within some schools at the lower end of the fee spectrum.

Despite this, parents continued to associate private schools with English, whilst government schools as a broad category attracted criticism from parents for failing to teach English effectively:

> [Good education] means the skills that one should have after passing [Class] XII, the skills or ability that a new job seeker must have. The command over English language that one should have is not there in someone passing out from a government school.
> (Rakesh, uncle of three, ages 11 to 15; private schools)
> Interview, 15 January 2015, Location B

Parents also made broader criticisms of government schools, pointing to what some felt was widespread failure within the government system. For example, several parents asserted that there was a complete absence of any teaching and learning in government schools:

> The teachers do not turn up; the kids do not study. They do not teach anything in these government schools.
> (Sai, father of two, ages 5 and 11; private and private aided schools)
> Interview, 12 February 2015, Location B

As exemplified by the above extract, teachers were the subject of particular criticism from parents, with poor teacher attendance, lack of care and inadequate supervision of children forming part of what was seen as a wider disregard for children's learning within the government sector.

Complaints with respect to school quality were not restricted to parents who were accessing private schools. For example, one mother in Location C explained that she felt that there was a lack of care and adequate supervision from teachers at the government schools that her children attended, as well as a failure to connect pedagogical activities with children's learning:

> It happens often that students are sitting in one class and teachers in another; I mean they don't give enough attention to the children. All they do is to sip tea throughout the day in the staff room [. . .] The children in the classroom need to concentrate. All that a teacher does is to write on the blackboard. Whether the children are able to understand the concepts or not, they don't care.
> (Adena, mother of six, ages 6 to 15; government schools)
> Interview, 26 January 2015, Location C

However, it is also important to note that not all parents who were interviewed were so critical of government schooling and drew distinctions between institutions. For example, several parents in Location A spoke favourably of the nearest Kendriya Vidyalaya (KV), which a small number of children from the community were attending, and drew explicit comparisons between this school and SDMC schools in the area.[7] Whilst these comparisons tended to be quite general (one father referred to the KV as of a higher 'standard'), some parents noted that the school was English medium but less costly than nearby private schools.

Another father, Krishnan, whose children were attending a private aided school in Delhi, also spoke favourably about what he saw as the better quality of government schooling available in Tamil Nadu, where he himself had attended school:

> A balance between sports and studies is struck, so that the kids do not get bored. They have long periods there. I mean kids get engaged in the activities at schools so much that they forget about any issues that their households may be facing, tensions and anything else at all about their households. He feels at home in school.
> (Krishnan, father of three, ages 13 to 17; private aided school)
> Interview, 12 February 2015, Location B

It is notable that the ways in which Krishnan characterises good education are focused not on learning outcomes, but the processes involved in producing these, namely, engaging children effectively in learning, the provision of extracurricular activities and children feeling comfortable in the school environment. Thus, whilst Krishnan was not accessing government schooling for his children currently, his perspective does add nuance to the widespread discourses of failure surrounding government schooling.

With a similar focus on children's well-being, other parents who were accessing government schooling for one or more of their children tended to focus on effective communication with parents and the care of children in their accounts of quality within the government sector:

> They have the mobile numbers of all parents so there is no problem; they call us if there's a problem [. . .] It often happens that the teacher calls in case the child is not feeling well or has been absent. So that makes us feel good that the teachers look after the children.
> (Sandeepan, father of three, ages 1 to 11; private and government schools)
> Interview, 26 February 2015, Location C

Thus, discussions of government schooling drew attention to a varied range of school quality indicators that were found to contribute to some parents' overall conceptions of good education, as well as the varied experiences of parents who were accessing government schooling for their children. At the same time, interview data reflected what other researchers have identified as the 'culturally hegemonic language around the failure of government schools' (Subrahmanian, 2005: 69) and a perception of the superior quality of private schools, sometimes despite a lack of direct personal experience (Majumdar and Mooij, 2011; Kaur, 2017). For example:

> [RA: What do you think is the difference between education in a government and a private school?]
> There is a lot of difference in a private school. Private school is much better [. . .] Private schools cannot be the way government schools are. We do want to educate our children, but we don't have the required money. We want to send them to private schools.
>
> (Neeti, mother of two, ages 7 and 13; private aided school)
> Interview, 10 December 2014, Location B

Parents drawing quality comparisons between government and private provision at a very broad level were common across interviews and suggested the function of management type as a proxy indictor, associated closely with English. The (re)production of such discourses at the community level is explored in the following section.

'Hot' knowledge and government school failure

In the absence of formal information in the public arena in the form of league tables or exam results, informal networks were the primary source of most parents' information about schools in each area, with most describing speaking to their neighbours, relatives and in some cases employers for information and advice about schooling. For example:

> When it comes to their education, I speak to my elder brother and a friend, [name redacted]. There are two or three more friends whom I ask about good schools.
>
> (Varshil, father of two, ages 3 and 6; private school)
> Interview, 18 February 2015, Location A

Some parents who had attended school also drew on what they presented as their 'first-hand' knowledge to support their perspective of government school quality failings. For example:

[RA: Why and how have you come to feel that the level of education in government schools is so low?]

That's because we ourselves have studied in government schools. We exactly know what happens there. Teachers come to schools, they gossip around, someone is knitting a sweater, someone [pause] You must know it all [by now]. No one is concerned about kids' education, whether they are studying or not; no one bothers with that.

(Rakesh, uncle of three, ages 11 to 15;
private schools)
Interview, 15 January 2015, Location B

The relationship between personal experience and quality perceptions illuminates one aspect of the relationship between parental biography and choice, with biography an important but often overlooked influence on parents' schooling decisions (Drury, 1993). Equally, the above extract reveals how individual experiences may feed into a broader narrative of government school failures within communities. Rakesh does not present his school experience as isolated, for example, but as typical within the government sector.

Personal experience is also one aspect of what Ball and Vincent (1998) term 'hot' knowledge, or the unofficial information that is exchanged within informal social networks. In contrast to official, 'cold' knowledge, 'hot' knowledge includes emotional responses, rumour and gossip (Ball and Vincent, 1998). In this way, the significance of hot knowledge to quality conceptions could also be identified in unsubstantiated narratives about schools that arose in interviews with parents. One mother's account of her reasons for choosing a local private school for her son, for example, captures some of the local gossip concerning safety failures at government schools:

Students of government schools run away from there during half break [. . .] I felt my child cannot even talk properly, he doesn't know how to speak to people, and if someone takes him away, what would I do.

[RA: So students run away from government schools?]
Yes, they do that during half break.
[RA: This problem exists in all government schools nearby?]
Yes, in all of them. Children scale these walls and run away.

(Ridika, mother of one son, age 5;
private school)
Interview, 22 February 2015, Location B

To classify Ridika's account as gossip is not to conclude that children running away from schools at break time was not an issue in the area. However, such examples do draw attention to 'the power of the negative story, the destructive anecdote' (Ball and Vincent, 1998: 379) in discourses surrounding government school quality.

In addition, researchers in other national contexts have identified that hot knowledge consists of information concerning the social composition of school spaces (Ball, 2003; Kosunen, Carrasco, and Tironi, 2015). Whilst very few parents whom I interviewed referred to class or caste directly when discussing their children's schooling, comments concerning children's cleanliness and behaviour suggested an attentiveness to the social backgrounds of children attending different schools. For example:

> The children complained about the atmosphere of that school. The other boys there were dirty, and they didn't like it. They only stayed for two days; within two days, we realised that it was not good, so we went to [private school].
> (Kayaan, father of two, ages 12 and 15; private aided school)
> Interview, 11 January 2015, Location B

Discourse concerning the social composition of different schools may thus feed into broader 'discourses of derision' (Ball, 1990) surrounding government schooling and, in turn, may contribute to parental conceptions of 'good' and 'bad' schooling options.[8] At the same time, the attempt that some parents made to draw distinctions between their own children who were going to private schools and those accessing government schooling illuminate the significance of schooling for parents as a strategy of social differentiation (for further discussion of these issues see Gurney, 2017).

Non-educational aims, indicators and schooling choices

In addition to social status perceptions and associated schooling decisions, other non-educational aims and associated indicators were found to play a role in shaping parents' schooling choices. In particular, the findings suggest that parents were influenced by their own social identities with respect to regional and religious affiliations. For example, a group of parents in Location B who had migrated to Delhi from Tamil Nadu described their rationale for enrolling their children at a Tamil medium, private aided school outside of the immediate locality in terms of pride in regional identity. As one father, Siddharth, explained:

> It is a Tamil school. They teach Tamil, Hindi and English there, which is good. I am Tamil and I am proud to send my children to a Tamil school.
>
> (Siddharth, father of four, ages 15 to 21; private aided school)
> Interview, 10 November 2014, Location B

Later in the interview, Siddharth was also explicit about the comparative significance of quality indicators and social identity in relation to his choice of school:

> *[RA: Do you think it is a good school?]*
> Compared to others I think it is OK. But it is not a good education [. . .] The principal is not good. There is no order there; children just sit around and do not work.
>
> (Siddharth)

Thus, learning outcomes and other educational aims were not necessarily the only factors that parents considered when making schooling choice for their children, nor was 'good' education with respect to quality indicators necessarily prioritised. This illustrates the social justice implications of the role of parents as proxy consumers in market spaces (as Winch notes in Chapter 2) by drawing attention to the various interests that contribute to parents' schooling choices beyond outcomes focused on the child in question.

In addition, the role of sociocultural factors in shaping choices was also apparent in gendered patterns of school enrolment. In addition to cost, which has been identified by other researchers as a meaningful issue with respect to school access for girls (Maitra, Pal, and Sharma, 2014), gendered conceptions of safety were also significant to parents' schooling choices. Whilst this was not the case across all households, single sex schools close to the family home tended to be prioritised for girls over all other choice criteria. Within the context of the study sites, this restricted options substantially both geographically and to government schools.

Quality compromises

A common assertion by many parents was that their ability to access quality schooling was dependent on financial resources. Almost every parent who was interviewed referenced budget considerations as playing a role in shaping their decision-making processes and access to good or better quality schooling. For example:

> I don't dare to think about good schooling because I don't have the capacity to pay for it. I don't have the money, so why think about these schools and about sending them there? Why think about it?
> (Sanjana, mother of one son, age 7; private school)
> Interview, 19 November 2014, Location B

Moderating aspirations with respect to school quality was a common strategy adopted by parents in the face of significant disadvantages within the education market. Financial resources as the key determiner of the ability to access quality schooling was accepted as part of the status quo, with one father implying his perception of a direct relationship between cost and the quality of teaching and learning:

> No, their studies do not go well. Nor are they made to understand properly. In accordance with the fees, studies get done.
> (Neel, father of three, ages 4 to 8; government and private schools)
> Interview, 1 February 2015, Location C

Other parents also described quality compromises in non-academic aspects of school quality, such as a constructive relationship between teachers and parents. For example:

> [RA: What do you get fined for?]
> Well, one thing is if a boy urinates. Parents are called and asked to clean that. We are paying fees for cleaning, but are called when a small child has urinated. 'Your child has done something, you have to clean it.' This is humiliating for us. It makes me so angry! This is discriminating against us! It also happened to a relative of mine; they also called her about this.
> (Minakshi, mother of one son, age 5; private school)
> Interview, 19 November 2014, Location B

As is apparent from this extract, Minakshi was very angry at the discriminatory treatment that she felt that she and others in her family experienced from school authorities. Despite this, and examples she gave of the bullying her son experienced from teachers and other pupils, Minakshi continued to send her son to this particular school. Thus, a trade-off between well-being and learning outcomes was the quality compromise that Minakshi felt that she had to make in view of affordability constraints and what she perceived as the relatively better academic aspects of quality within the school.

In fact, very few parents reported having exited a school because of quality concerns or having raised complaints with school authorities or teachers. For example, Arjun, a father of two, describes why he felt reluctant to complain about his sons' private aided school:

> I did not go for making a complaint. When everyone is facing this problem, then why should it be just us who complain about it? A meeting would be conducted, and he [the teacher] would lose his job. So we did not go for complaining. It's a government school, not a private one that is taking charges for educating the kids. Had it been, we could have said something. We don't have to pay money in government schools. Education is free there. They would say, are you paying anything? This is what we would get to hear.
> (Arjun, father of two sons, ages 15 and 10; private aided school)[9]
> Interview, 10 November 2014, Location B

However, whilst in the above extract, Arjun suggests that he would have felt able to raise a complaint in a private school because the payment of fees would lend greater consumer power, this was not borne out in reports from parents who were accessing private schooling. For example, Minakshi, despite her unhappiness with significant aspects of her son's schooling, characterised the parent–teacher association (PTA) meetings as one-sided with apparently little, if any, constructive discussion between parents and teachers:

> [RA: Do you have any PTA meetings or a time when you can speak to teachers?]
> We are called to school for the parent-teacher meetings, but only the teachers speak, you just keep silent. We are only called to pay a fine or to correct bad behaviour.
> (Minakshi)

Thus, the response of parents to poor quality was not necessarily voice or exit. Loyalty to the school itself does not seem to explain the actions of Minakshi or Arjun, for example, who chose to keep their children in their current schools despite serious quality concerns. Nor does it seem adequate to label either parent an 'inert client' (Hirschman, 1970), as both were quality conscious but had made the deliberate decision to remain. Instead, I want to suggest that Bourdieu's concept of habitus may be useful in illuminating the apparent resignation to poor quality provision that several parents expressed.

Bourdieu (1977) loosely defines habitus as the set of dispositions that 'produces practices in accordance with the schemes engendered by history' (p. 82). By emphasising the active role of the social agent in the construction and navigation of social reality (Strand, 2001), Bourdieu (1977) proposes habitus as 'the strategy generating principle enabling agents to cope with unforeseen and ever-changing situations' (p. 72). For parents who participated in the current study, the moderation of quality expectations within heavily constrained circumstances may thus be understood as a rejection of higher-quality options that anyway are not available to them:

> The most improbable practices are therefore excluded, as unthinkable, by a kind of immediate submission to order that inclines agents to make a virtue of necessity, that is, to refuse what is anyway denied and to will the inevitable.
>
> (Bourdieu, 1990: 54)

Therefore, schools regarded as better quality were considered impossible to access and were excluded from the choice landscape, with a complaint resulting in effective change regarded as equally unlikely and unachievable.

Gaining access: resource leverage

Lack of available funds and budget restrictions are, of course, a clear barrier to acquiring goods in any market setting. However, the bureaucratic systems that parents encountered in school spaces that were not of their own design could operate as barriers to school access. Power dynamics in the form of hierarchies between school staff and parents also constrained parents' ability to adopt consumer behaviours within the education market.

For example, a few other parents were apparently trapped in a complicated cycle of school admission 'lucky draws', illuminating the distinction between making a choice and actually gaining access to a desired school:

[RA: Why did you choose [private school] for your son? Why did you admit him there?]
RAJIV: Actually, we filled forms at two to three schools. But our number did not turn up there.
[. . .]
MISHKA: He was not getting admission anywhere, so we had to admit him in this school.
RAJIV: We tried in a number of schools! But nothing worked out.
[. . .]
RAJIV: We can't take the chance of sending him here till Class V, because then his number may not come in other schools. So, we are thinking of admitting him to some other school this year itself, in Class III.
[RA: Do you have any school in your mind, where you would like to admit him?]
MISHKA: We will fill forms in two to three schools this time around.
(Rajiv and Mishka, parents of three children, ages 1 to 8; private school)
Interview, 6 December, 2014, Location A

The bureaucratic challenges involved for parents in entering such 'lucky draws' or other admission procedures should not be underestimated; requirements such as a birth certificate, or legal affidavits, and English-language admission forms not only necessitated additional expense and time, but also some administrative 'know-how'. This was also true for parents who ventured into private school spaces, where the admission process was also often described as frustrating, characterised by compromise rather than the exercise and empowerment of choice:

> This was not our first choice. I had visited [higher-fee private school] at first, which is located in [name redacted]. But they refused admission. They wanted recommendations, [an] approach and other things too. We did not have any choice.
> (Garima, mother of one son, age 8; private school)
> Interview, 15 February 2015, Location B

Such accounts illuminate not only the emotionally stressful nature of the admissions process for many parents but also the general perception that both financial resources *and* social contacts were a requirement to gain admission to 'good' schools, even when parents were in theory able to pay the fee or were exempt through the RtE Act.

Indeed, the findings indicate that families with 'know-how' or other forms of capital were better able to utilise specific strategies for gaining admission to desirable schools, including through the RtE Act 25 per cent reservation. Indeed, simply knowing about the reservation should be understood as a considerable advantage within the market, given that most parents who were interviewed were not aware of the reservation, although some expressed a general awareness of government schemes to support school access.

Across the data set, 5 of the 58 households interviewed were identified as having gained access to a school under the 25 per cent reservation (3 in Location A and 2 in Location B). However, it was notable that 3 of these households described receiving some additional 'assistance' in this process, typically through a social contact who could enable parents to bypass regular admission procedures. For example:

> *[RA: And how did you get admission for him at [name of school]?]*
> I have a contact with a member of parliament of New Delhi, and I asked him to help me get admission. He did not help me. I also know the driver of [government official] who has admitted his child in [name of school], and he helped me.
> *[RA: So was there a lottery or anything like that for admissions?]*
> No lottery, there was an interview with the principal, and then he was admitted.
>
> (Sachin, father of one son, age 9; selective government school)
> Interview, 16 November 2014, Location A

The school that Sachin refers to is one of the schools that Rajiv and Mishka had tried and failed to secure access to through the admission lottery and were planning to do so again in the next round. This illustrates the significance of social capital in facilitating school admission and the strategic use of such capital by some parents, as well as illuminating the variation in experience between different parents. In addition, admission under the reservation did not in all cases result in free education as per the terms of the RtE Act; 2 of the 5 households reported paying additional fees for school expenses, making similar schooling choices unaffordable for other parents from across the study sites (see Srivastava and Noronha, 2016, and Mehendale, Mukhopadhyay, and Namala, 2015 for discussion of similar issues with respect to the implementation of the RtE Act).

One father (Ritvik) also acknowledged explicitly that he had used false documents, organised through a work contact, to gain admission for his younger daughter at a local private school in Location B under the 25 per cent reservation. This was only disclosed at the end of what was a long interview, perhaps when Ritvik felt more comfortable in sharing this sensitive information when trust had been established between us. However, despite having essentially benefited from being able to use economic capital to secure school admission by a 'back door' route, Ritvik still felt unhappy about what he perceived as the unfair treatment his family had received when seeking admission at other schools in the nearby area:

> You take admission in four or five schools, and then they release the wait list, [but] we don't get to know about it.
> [*RA: Did you speak to anyone when you went for admissions that you could ask about this?*]
> You don't see a face! You just get the form and go.
> (Ritvik, two children, ages 6 and 8; private and private aided schools)
> Interview, 23 November 2014, Location B

Ritvik's assertion that school admission could only be secured through payment may be partly to justify his own decision to pay for false documents, framing this decision as a reasonable course of action within a market context where financial resources are definitive. The frustration that some parents felt over the lack of transparency of school admissions may thus result in parents deciding to subvert prescribed procedures through the justification of necessity.

Conclusion

Within this chapter, I have tried to capture some of the diversity in parents' conceptions and experiences of education and school quality that was evident within the wider data set. Regarding overall conceptions of school quality, communication with parents, appropriate supervision and effective teaching and learning were all aspects that parents cited during interviews. However, parent perceptions of the education landscape were found to be shaped by two dominant ideas: the poor quality of government schooling and the desirability of English medium, private schools. In the former, widespread discourses of derision surrounding government schooling were found to circulate through informal information sharing networks that took the form of personal experiences, rumour and gossip. In the latter, desirability of English may be understood as a response to labour market demand, as well as a reflection of associations between English, fee-paying schools and broader social advantages. Nevertheless, despite narratives of government school failure, it is also important to recognise nuances that were noted between government schools, as well as more positive accounts of government school quality.

In addition, very few parents expressed satisfaction with the school that their children were attending currently, and even fewer described having exercised either voice or exit in response to quality concerns within a specific school (as opposed to the decision to reject the government sector entirely). Parents who stayed in what they perceived as poorly performing schools were not inattentive to school failures, but described moderating their quality expectations and aspirations in view of structural constraints. Together with the function of non-educational aims in shaping school selection identified in the findings, for example in relation to gender, such quality compromises illuminate some of the social justice implications associated with the role of parents as proxy consumers within the education market. The findings thus point both to the complexity in seeking to define quality from the perspective of parents and how 'choice' as a policy mechanism for quality improvement may be problematic in practice.

Notes

1 Exceptions include Srivastava (2008), who explores school choice amongst households accessing two low-fee private schools in Uttar Pradesh; Hill, Samson, and Dasgupta (2011), who detail the dynamics of school choice in one village in Rajasthan; and James and Woodhead (2014), who focus on the decision-making processes of frequent school movers within a broader, longitudinal study into children's lives in Andhra Pradesh.
2 This work was supported by the Economic and Social Research Council (ESRC) under Grant ES/J500057/1.
3 The number and location of schools in each area was developed through household interviews, field observations, District Information System for Education (DISE) data and secondary household survey data accessed via a Delhi-based NGO.
4 Other languages spoken by interviewees during interviews were Bhojpuri, English and Tamil.
5 Note that all names used throughout are pseudonyms.
6 Aishi's daughter was attending a Hindi medium government school. Her son attended an English medium private school.
7 Two parents with a child attending this school were interviewed as part of the current study. Both were attending the school under the 25 per cent reservation, as stipulated in the Right to Education Act, 2009 (RtE Act). However, other parents in the area also discussed the school and its perceived quality at some length in interviews.
8 See Hill, Samson, and Dasgupta (2011) and Kaur (2017), who also identify the significance of caste to parents' schooling decisions.

9 Whilst not free, the fees at this private aided school were minimal (reported as Rs. 150 per annum). All parents who were accessing the school referred to it as a government school in interviews.

References

Azam, Mehtabul, Chin, Aimee, and Prakash, Nishith. (2013). 'The Returns to English-Language Skills in India', *Economic Development and Cultural Change*, 61(2): 335–367.
Ball, Stephen J. (1990). *Politics and Policy-Making in Education: Explorations in Policy Sociology*. London: Routledge.
———. (2003). *Class Strategies and the Education Market: The Middle Classes and Social Advantage*. London, New York: Routledge.
Ball, Stephen J., and Vincent, Carol. (1998). '"I Heard It on the Grapevine": "Hot" Knowledge and School Choice', *British Journal of Sociology of Education*, 19(3): 377–400.
Bourdieu, Pierre. (1977). *Outline of a Theory of Practice*. Cambridge: Cambridge University Press.
———. (1990). *The Logic of Practice*. Cambridge: Polity Press.
Chopra, Radhika. (2005). 'Sisters and Brothers: Schooling, Family and Migration', in Radhika Chopra and Patricia Jeffery (Eds.), *Educational Regimes in Contemporary India* (pp. 299–315). New Delhi, India: Sage.
Drury, David. (1993). *The Iron School Master: Education, Employment and the Family in India*. New Delhi, India: Hindustan Publishing Corporation.
Government of India. (2006). *Social, Economic and Educational Status of the Muslim Community of India* (The Sachar Committee Report). New Delhi, India: Cabinet Secretariat.
Gurney, Eleanor. (2017). 'Choosing Schools, Choosing Selves: Exploring the Influence of Parental Identity and Biography on the School Choice Process in Delhi, India', *International Studies in Sociology of Education*, 26(1): 19–35.
Hill, Elizabeth, Samson, Meera, and Dasgupta, Shyamasree. (2011). 'Expanding the School Market in India: Parental Choice and the Reproduction of Social Inequality', *Economic and Political Weekly*, 46(35): 98–105.
Hirschman, Albert O. (1970). *Exit, Voice, and Loyalty: Responses to Decline in Firms, Organizations, and States*. Cambridge, MA: Harvard University Press.
James, Zoe, and Woodhead, Martin. (2014). 'Choosing and Changing Schools in India's Private and Government Sectors: Young Lives Evidence from Andhra Pradesh', *Oxford Review of Education*, 40(1): 73–90.
Kaur, Satvinderpal. (2017). 'Quality of Rural Education at Elementary Level', *Economic and Political Weekly*, 52(5): 58–63.
Kosunen, Sonja, Carrasco, Alejandro, and Tironi, Manuel. (2015). 'The Role of "Hot" and "Cold" Knowledge in the Choice of Schools in Chilean and Finnish Cities', in Piia Seppänen, Alejandro Carrasco, and Mira Kalalahti (Eds.), *Contrasting Dynamics in Education Politics of Extremes: School Choice in Chile and Finland* (pp. 139–157). Rotterdam: SENSE Publishers.

Maitra, Pushkar, Pal, Sarmistha, and Sharma, Anurag. (2014). 'What Explains the Gender Gap in Private School Enrolment? Recent Evidence from India', available at SSRN http://ssrn.com/abstract=2673817 [accessed 9 March 2017].

Majumdar, Manabi, and Mooij, Jos. (2011). *Education and Inequality in India: A Classroom View*. London, New York: Routledge.

Mehendale, Archana, Mukhopadhyay, Rahul, and Namala, Annie. (2015). 'Right to Education and Inclusion in Private Unaided Schools: An Exploratory Study in Bengaluru and Delhi', *Economic and Political Weekly*, 50(7): 43–51.

Sarangapani, Padma, and Winch, Christopher. (2010). 'Tooley, Dixon and Gomathi on Private Education in Hyderabad: A Reply', *Oxford Review of Education*, 36(4): 499–515.

Srivastava, Prachi. (2006). 'Private Schooling and Mental Models About Girls' Schooling in India', *Compare*, 36(4): 497–514.

———. (2007). *Neither Voice nor Loyalty: School Choice and the Low-Fee Private Sector in India*, Occasional Paper, 134, National Center for the Study of Privatisation in Education, Teachers' College, New York: Columbia University.

———. (2008). 'School Choice in India: Disadvantaged Groups and Low-Fee Private Schools', in Martin Forsey, Scott Davies, and Geoffrey Walford (Eds.), *The Globalisation of School Choice? Oxford Studies in Comparative Education* (pp. 185–208). Oxford: Symposium Books.

Srivastava, Prachi, and Noronha, Claire. (2016). 'The Myth of Free and Barrier-Free Access: India's Right to Education Act – Private Schooling Costs and Household Experiences', *Oxford Review of Education*, 42(5): 1–18.

Strand, Torill. (2001). 'Paradoxes in Bourdieu's Practice of Theory', *Nordisk Pedagogik*, 21: 197–213.

Subrahmanian, Ramya. (2005). 'Education Exclusion and the Developmental State', in Radhika Chopra and Patricia Jeffery (Eds.), *Educational Regimes in Contemporary India* (pp. 62–82). New Delhi, India: Sage.

12 Teaching because it matters

Beliefs and practices of government school teachers[1]

Niharika Sharma and Padma M. Sarangapani

The last 20 years have witnessed the downfall of the image of Indian government school teachers. They are widely perceived as dysfunctional, non-productive, low-performing and ineffective employees and the ultimate cause of the failure of the educational enterprise to provide quality education to all and in particular to the children of the poor. The popular image of the government school teacher as discussed above is often on account of a perspective which views education, teaching, learning and performance of teachers as reducible to measurable outputs. The finding that children of the poor have low learning achievement levels leads to the conclusion that their teachers are ineffective (Kremer et al., 2005). A frequently cited remedy is adopting contractual arrangements of hiring teachers (like para teachers) to be able to demand better performance through stricter control mechanisms and accountability akin to the private sector.

Kingdon and Teal (2007), who examine the impact of higher pay and performance-related pay on student achievement levels, claim that performance-related pay for teachers in private schools in India does improve student performance and relative pay is effective at eliciting greater effort, as monitoring teacher effort is difficult. They draw comparisons between private school wage structures based on performance-related pay as compared to the permanent nature of government school teachers' jobs and suggest that flexibility of managers to set wages and dismiss lax teachers could act as an incentive lever to enhance teacher incentives and as a motivating device.

Jain (this volume), on the other hand, provides a contrasting view to the new managerial perspectives on teachers as 'indispensable labour' who can be 'controlled' through application of strict management strategies and argues that teaching is more than a service delivery and teachers' own beliefs about learners, learning, educability, aims of education and their own sense of professional identity is at the core of what constitutes what they do and don't do.

The research presented in this chapter takes the view that the claim that government school teachers are ineffective is an overgeneralisation growing out of a failure to notice the lived culture of teachers' work and the failure to notice that there are within the system government school teachers who are dedicated and able to engage children in meaningful learning. These are teachers who have developed engaging and socially responsive pedagogies to work with children with various disadvantages, and they have done this through their own experience and efforts. Avalos (1986), in her monograph 'Teaching Children of the Poor: An Ethnographic Study in Latin America', draws attention to the influence of teacher attitudes on schooling outcomes of children who come from a low socioeconomic background, primarily on account of their position of enormous power and control over classroom events. The drabness of many of the teaching contexts and the difficulties produced by the 'official' pejorative treatment of teachers has led many to despair of actions to counteract these conditions and to feel justified in neglecting the quality of their teaching. This study also provides evidence and examples of some good and different teachers, like Senora Rosa, who were different from the rest in their teaching of children from deprived backgrounds by enabling meaningful learning, respecting their learning needs and personality traits, without holding their backgrounds of poverty as detrimental to their performance while also understanding that poverty does create limiting conditions.

Avalos suggests in the study that there is a need to know more about both the 'majority' and the 'Senora Rosa' kind of different teachers, about their ways of thinking, their practical philosophies or ideologies and how these are formed, particularly among teachers in the lower school levels of poor environments. Negating Senora Rosa kind of teachers and their work will be negating any new possibilities of change and reform in the education of poor children that can be brought about by systematically studying the work of such teachers and bringing it to the forefront. The teacher working in a government school is the only institutional worker of the educational enterprise who works with children from underprivileged backgrounds closely and directly on a day-to-day basis and as the only direct channel through which the purposefulness of educating children can be realised both for children and their parents and also the educational institutions. For a deep understanding of the pedagogic practices of such teachers, it is essential to engage with the purposes, meanings, messages and values that underlie their pedagogic decisions and the dilemmas of the ideal and circumstance which teachers deal with daily.

To understand the pedagogic practices of teachers, along with the beliefs and theories which inform it, Bruner's (1996) framework of folk psychology and folk pedagogy is useful. Bruner (1996) proposes that the everyday intuitive theories about how our own mind and the mind of others work provide pedagogical theories and are present in all practical and educational decisions. It is important to take into account these folk pedagogical theories which guide classroom discourse because any innovation has to compete with, replace or otherwise modify the old theories that already guide pupils and teachers. The teacher's conception of the learner has a direct bearing on the form of instruction that he or she employs.

The study on which this chapter is based aimed to shed light on the teachers whose practice challenges the stereotypes of the unmotivated and disengaged government school teacher. The study was designed to engage deeply with the pedagogies and beliefs of some of the government school teachers who represented educationally valuable pedagogies and who were engaged with teaching in order to achieve higher educational outcomes for their children. It also aimed to understand how these government school teachers perceive, understand and explain their own pedagogy. In this study, these teachers are referred to as 'effective' teachers. Pedagogy in the study has been understood as:

> [T]he observable act of teaching together with its attendant discourse of educational theories, values, evidence and justifications. It is what one needs to know, and the skills one needs to command, in order to make and justify the many different kinds of decisions of which teaching is constituted. This definition requires two subsidiary and complementary frameworks, one dealing with the 'observable act' of teaching, and the other with the 'knowledge, values, beliefs and justifications' which inform it.
> (Alexander, 2008)

The study was located within 'The Baseline Survey of the Schools Scenario in India' (Sarangapani et al., 2013)which has been reported in Chapters 7 and 8 and formed a part of the Delhi schools survey (Manish Jain, this book Chapter 8). From the observations of the pedagogic practices in 23 government school classrooms, seven teachers were identified whose pedagogy qualified as 'effective' – they moved beyond the textbook in dialogic processes with children and emphasised construction of meaning. They made a lot of effort with the children and had affectionate and respectful relationships with them. They emphasised higher-order thinking and imagination and paid attention to individual learners and active participation. They encouraged children to relate their learning to their everyday life, to share experiences, argue, think and counter-question them. Five of these teachers agreed to participate in the study and gave time to be observed and interviewed in-depth on their work and their lives. Data was gathered in 2011–2012. Based on the analysis of approximately 100 pages of observations of their classrooms and pedagogies and 150 pages of interviews with them conducted in Hindi and translated into English by the first author, this chapter presents finding on four key themes: their understanding of the context of disadvantage, their educational aims, their methods of addressing inequalities and the metaphors they used to construct the teacher–pupil relationship.

The five 'good' teachers and their schools

The five teachers, four women and one man, were between 33 and 52 years of age. Four of them were married. They all had different academic and professional qualifications, which included BEd from different universities, including Delhi University, DEd and BElEd. One of them was highly qualified and had a doctorate in fisheries. Table 12.1 provides a summary of information about these teachers. Most had a very good reputation in the school in terms of ownership they take with children in their classrooms. Ramesh, the only male teacher, also had a very good reputation in the community – he has worked in the same school for a very long time. The others had worked in the same school for over 10 years (except Malini who was new to the school).

Their schools were all run by the Municipal Corporation of Delhi (MCD) and located in east Delhi. One, which was a model girls' school, had good facilities and infrastructure and was better maintained. It had colourful displays for children and a quiet atmosphere. The others were generally poorly maintained and swept but never mopped. Garbage from the neighbourhood was frequently dumped on the school premises. The classrooms tended to have no furniture and poor to adequate lighting and ventilation. Three of the schools had a strength of about 250, one was about 900 and the model school had a strength of about 600. The parents of the children were mostly unskilled daily wage workers – rickshaw pullers, vegetable vendors, factory workers and domestic workers. They were all migrants to the city.

Table 12.1 General profile of teachers

S. No	Name	Gender	Age	Marital status	Year of joining MCD	Year of joining present school	Academic qualifications	Professional qualifications
1	Sulekha	Female	38	Married	1993	1999	BA and MA, history, Delhi University	BEd, Delhi University
2	Surita	Female	37	Separated	1997	1997	BCom, Delhi University	DEd, Delhi DIET
3	Suresh	Male	52	Married	1988	1988	BA, Uttar Pradesh	BTC diploma, Uttar Pradesh
4	Malini	Female	33	Married	2006	2009	BElEd	BElEd, Delhi University–affiliated college
5	Reema	Female	42	Married	1997	2001	BSc, MSc, PhD, fisheries; NET qualified in fisheries	BEd, Bhopal University–affiliated college

Source: Author's own work

Findings

The context of socioeconomic disadvantage: The teachers talked about different kinds of challenges they faced while teaching children, which made their everyday circumstances of teaching quite complex and difficult to deal with. This was due to the poor socioeconomic background of the learners, resulting in many disadvantages that teachers or students had to cope with. Teachers emphasised the need for them to understand the background of these children as it affects them in different ways.

> There is one girl who is very mischievous and doesn't show any interest in studies. She doesn't have both the parents and is staying with her grandmother. She doesn't get love, so as a result, she keeps fighting with everyone in the class and doesn't take any interest in what is being done. How much can a teacher do? She cannot fulfil everything that is missing in her life. Even if I love her, pamper her, but still the impact of home environment will be there on the child.
> (Surita, from Interview 2, 14 December 2011, New Delhi)

Teachers believed that a child's behaviour in the class is an indicator for them to inquire, know and understand the circumstances that the child might be dealing with outside school or at home. According to them, this helps them in dealing with children's problems in a better way. While talking about a girl who remained extremely quiet, Malini said:

> Children get impacted by harsh life situations like with this girl, she has lost her father, and her mother is now all the time busy in earning because she has to take care of the children alone. So parents not being there for them could also impact them and the loss of the father too. There could be many other life situations that they face daily, which can affect children emotionally and psychologically.
> (Malini, from Interview 2, 20 December 2011, New Delhi)

These teachers were aware of the various challenges that the home circumstances posed for the children. Lack of parental aspirations to become something in life, lack of involvement in, support for and participation in children's education due to lower educational levels in parents resulted in children having limited realisation of the importance of education. Poor conditions required both parents to earn, leaving them with no time to spend with the children. Children were burdened with responsibilities of household chores and care of siblings. There was violence in the home – wife-beating and alcoholism, use of abusive language and frequent fights – which affected the children psychologically. There was also material deprivation of even basic needs such as pencils, erasers and notebooks. Children lacked motivation to study.

> Parents also have their own compulsions (*majboori*) to feed their family, for which earning becomes the first priority for them to survive. They also don't have any option because their economic condition is such. They leave home early in the morning and come back late at night after work. By the time they come, children sleep, and in the morning, parents leave for work before children get up. There is no time left for children. Here, children dress up themselves in whatever ways and come to school. There is no one to dress them up properly at home or to check their uniform, arrange their bags like we do for our children. So many of them even come on an empty stomach to school because their mothers also leave early in the morning for work. So they have to do everything on their own.
> (Surita, from Interview 2, 14 December 2011, New Delhi)

Teachers saw themselves as supporting the children in dealing with these challenges and also felt that they were the main node through which children could access education. They believed in providing as many learning opportunities to children as they could during the limited time that the children were in the school. They said that they had to constantly reiterate the relevance of education and constantly work towards the idea of 'becoming something' in life with children as this was missing in the home environment.

Although most of the teachers sympathised with parents for not being able to provide all the above-mentioned conditions due to their own genuine problems, teachers also talked about their discontentment with parents. Views ranged from seeing them as being irresponsible to non-serious and casual about their children's education. But this didn't stop the teachers from taking responsibility to compensate for what they saw as lacking in children's homes to the extent that they could. According to Surita, curriculum and syllabus was something that came later, but what came first was the mental and emotional well-being of the child, which she saw as a pre-condition for any kind of learning to take place. She felt that she had to handle these kinds of issues before she could even get children to study.

Surita gave an example of a girl from the class who was observed to be sleepy, and when asked the reason, answered that her father had beaten up her mother the previous night due to which she could not sleep the whole night. Surita explained that 'it affects the psychological state of children so much and even the next day gets spoilt and the child loses out on studies completely.'

The teachers' own socioeconomic background and positioning in society served as a reference point to understand the disadvantages that their learners and their parents faced or might be dealing with. They drew parallels with their own children and how they themselves participated in their children's education, their own everyday lifestyle and the material conditions in which their own families lived, all of which were missing from the lives of the children they taught. This comparison was used by the teachers to understand what was missing in their learner's backgrounds, and they tried to compensate for these disadvantages.

Educational aims: Teachers' pedagogy seemed to flow out of a variety of aims and objectives of education that they held. Some of the aims had a social orientation, such as 'become a good citizen', 'preparing children for adult life by making them good persons who can contribute positively in society'. This included moral and socioemotional development – respecting elders, honesty, not fighting, habit of sharing things, listening to others and personal cleanliness, habits like wearing washed and neat clothes, dressing up neatly and washing hands. Others related to the development of specific abilities such as literacy and the development of cognitive abilities of imagination, questioning, reason, argue and problem solving.

There were many commonalities evident in the aims, but the teachers differed in the way they articulated them and in their understanding and perception of their importance for the children. Some of the aims seemed compensatory and reflected their understanding of the children as having disadvantages on account of their economic positioning and family.

Suresh aimed at building positive attitudes in children along with building a sense in them to be able to judge good habits from bad habits and things that are right to do from things that are not right to do, as he said that these children were mostly exposed to negative things.

Reema believed in having high academic and behavioural expectations from children. For her, it was not only important to enable children to acquire literacy but also to acquire higher-order literacy skills such as different genres of writing.

> They should be knowing the difference between poet and a writer. If the child doesn't know the difference, then what is the use of studying. They should know is it a poem *(kavitaa)*, story *(kahaani)* or an essay or an article. If we don't tell them this difference, then they will all be same for the child whereas they are different. Like there is a different way of reading a poem, and there is a rhythm in a poem, and an article is read. Poem is small and article is long, and the way they are written is also different. If they have Hindi book, they should be able to know what the type of chapter is. If they know the difference, then they will tell themselves that whether it is poem or an article or what.
> (Reema, from Interview 1, 12 January 2012, New Delhi)

Having aspirations to 'become something in life' and developing basic routine habits like dressing neatly, taking a bath every day, eating something before coming to school would have been a given for children coming from well-to-do families. But for this group, teachers felt these were also aims, and they worked towards instilling routines and aspirations in children's lives. Developing the ability to think, reason, question and argue, which each of these teachers intended to develop in children, was important in their view as these were capacities and tools which would help children to deal with and think beyond their present circumstances and disadvantages. For example, Suresh extensively spoke about developing imagination in children being a significant aim. According to him, it is very important to develop imagination in children as it helps children to look at things in a creative way and is also important for children to be able to progress.

> The aeroplane has been made using imagination by someone; otherwise, it wouldn't have got made. So I really think that it is very important to develop imagination in children, and we as teachers have to colour their imagination in such a way that the child goes beyond the boundaries and is able to think and imagine.
> (Suresh, from Interview 1, 8 December 2011, New Delhi)

Engendering equality: The nature of aims held by the teachers for this group reflected that they intended to help children move beyond the limitations of their home context and took responsibility for enabling children in a manner that would help them to widen the horizon of thinking, finding opportunities and making choices. For example, Sulekha addressed gender discrimination experienced by girls in one of the lessons. She felt that girls face a lot of discrimination at home, and she aimed to make girls aware that there is nothing that they cannot do in comparison to boys and encouraged them to pursue what they want to do in life. She also regarded this as being important to be able to bring out their personality and potential. The teacher saw the hope of some change, as she believed that children's thinking is mouldable and less rigid as compared to adults, but at the same time, she felt that change was a gradual process that is influenced by what children see and experience at home and outside school.

> Actually, these girls also get to see this kind of discrimination at home front. Many parents tell these girls not to play outside as they are entering into a young adolescent age. So I wanted to know from them only whether they face it in their lives. Their grandparents also do it when they go back to villages. I wanted to connect their experiences of facing such discrimination and wanted to then relate it to making them conscious that there is nothing that you cannot do and that you are no less than boys. Actually, it is difficult to change the attitude of adults towards discrimination because they become rigid about their ideas, but it is good to start with children as their thinking can still be moulded. I have tried to discuss with them a lot about it, but I really don't know how much it is going to affect them and stay with them . . . hmmmm . . . change comes gradually . . . we can only try
>
> (Sulekha, from Interview 1, 16 November 2011, New Delhi)

Teacher–student relationship: The teacher–student relationship that the five teachers shared with their students was a highly significant aspect of their pedagogic practice. Each relationship had its own unique quality marked by a feeling of care and concern for children and a need to see them succeed. They seemed to all feel an institutional, professional and moral responsibility to work towards the development of children. There was a feeling of ownership of this responsibility, which the teachers took positively, and it became evident in their relationship with the children. I have discussed the unique aspects of their relationship using metaphors which either the teacher themselves used or I identified: the companion teacher, the instructor teacher, the mothering teacher, the guide teacher and the guru teacher.

The *sathi* (companion) teacher relationship was structured around being a 'buddy' to whom children could feel close. The teacher aimed at bridging the physical, emotional, psychological distance, and students were able to freely express themselves to her and around her without any fear or hesitation. She thought that appreciation is very effective in bringing a change in children as it helps them to understand and establish a connection with what the teacher wants them to do in studies and behaviourally. This relationship worked on the teacher's belief that teachers can also learn from students and there should be an acknowledgement by the teacher of this openness to learn. The teacher openly asked for co-operation from children and believed that this is needed by the teacher to be able to do different activities and things for children's learning and to make it a fun-filled process.

> I keep telling them that alone I cannot do anything, but if you are with me, then you will also learn so many things with enjoyment and I will also feel like doing different things with you. I also tell them that you also teach me so many things and tell them very openly if I don't know something. Like I told them that there are so many different ways in which you have made the tortoise, which I didn't know. So they also feel good that they can also teach me. I also tell them that I will also learn from you what I don't know, and you also learn from me what you don't know, but more important is to learn. I want to be their companion [*sathi*] in learning and in fun both. That is why I always participate with them in the activities and even when they play games in the playground.
>
> (Sulekha, from Interview 1, 16 November 2011, New Delhi)

The 'instructor teacher' seemed to be in complete control of the class, with children being the ones on whom, and for whom, her authority rested. The teacher was the epistemic, moral and functional authority in the classroom who maintained and regulated everything in the classroom. But this regulation was subtle and not overt. The nature of interaction between the teacher and students was largely limited to doing things according to the instructions given by the teacher. The boundaries of the relationship looked clearly defined with no child attempting to cross those boundaries. Underlying this strong structured and formal frame was the teacher's concern for children and their learning. The achievements of children who had benefited from this formal structure was evident in her class that was performing well. The control that she exercised in her class was not used by her to suppress children in unproductive ways, but rather she regulated that control to make them perform in desirable ways, which was different from the authority of some of the other teachers.

The 'mother teacher' saw her relationship with the students as extending to mothering. She believed that young children need somebody in school whom they can relate to as to their mother and someone with whom they feel a closeness (*apnaapan*). Her relationship was filled with affection, respect, love and freedom for children. This teacher was highly affectionate towards children, and similar affection and attachment was visible in the behaviour of children as well. They were quite comfortable in touching and holding the teacher, and often, one could see children hugging her as well. She believed that this leads to children becoming more open with her in sharing their thoughts and feelings. Scolding and beating was something that she disliked, but at the same time she stressed the need for being firm when required.

The relationship of being a 'guide' was built based on the teacher's belief that children have the capabilities and potential to learn through self-learning and peer interaction. She saw her own role as being a 'guide' who could give the right direction and opportunities and explanations to children to learn from time to time, rather than teaching them everything. She believed that learning needs to be a two-way process where children themselves actively participate, and she believed in creating a friendly atmosphere in the class.

> I think it is good if children were coming and asking me about their doubts freely because there should be no fear in children to ask something or clarify their doubts. What is the use of the teacher otherwise because if children will not ask freely, then it will affect their learning. Teacher needs to clarify the smallest doubts of the children.
> (Malini, from Interview 2, 17 January 2011, New Delhi)

While these were the metaphors of the women teachers, the metaphor that best applies to Suresh is that of 'magician-guru'. He described himself as *jaadugar* (magician) who takes the children on a trip into the world that he wants to show them. Children would listen to him in the class mesmerised by his ways of talking and teaching as he actually taught the lesson with a mixture of excitement, thrill, suspense, fun, humour, twists and turns, questions and opportunities to think and express. This teacher also believed that teaching is selfless, sacred work. He stressed the importance of having a friendly and emotional bond, without which there can be no learning. In the classroom, he was the ultimate and unquestioned authority, and children did not even try to disobey him. They were scared of his disapproval but at the same time, seemed quite comfortable and fond of him. They would touch his feet in the morning and while going back home and would share their home stories with him. This teacher held the idea of a teacher being intimate with his students so that they experience that the teacher is their partner in sorrow and happiness.

These metaphors bring out the multiple unique ways in which teachers built relationships with students, within which they were able to engage with positive and responsive pedagogies for their development. These relationship forms allowed and even facilitated the work that they were doing in the context of the children's socioeconomic disadvantages.

Discussion

The pedagogies of these government school teachers drew from their beliefs and perceptions about learners and their socioeconomic backgrounds, learning and aims of education, and each had a unique expression of professional identity which shaped and drew from their pedagogic practices. Teachers constructed the indispensable and critical nature of the role that they believed they could play in the education of the children of the poor, by transforming the relationship that exists between them and the schools. Their work was complex. It required teachers to be sensitive and understanding towards the life situations of children and the issues they deal with, while at the same time enabling children to cope with home circumstances and remain engaged with school. They were constantly and simultaneously focused and oriented towards not letting these circumstances of disadvantage derail the learners' capacity for meaningful engagement at least for the period that they were in school. Teachers believed that the school could intervene and disrupt the cycle of one kind of disadvantage leading to another kind of disadvantages – of not being able to learn and participate in learning in the classroom in turn leading to further disadvantages.

The teachers were engaged in more than mere teaching of the content to children. These teachers acted as the channels through which children could access the relevance and worthwhileness of education that these teachers created with them. In them, children gained access to a concerned individual who held aspirations for them whether it was to perform in the present or becoming something in the future. Even though these teachers believed that children's background affected their participation in learning in different ways, they did not reduce these children as 'ineducable' and limit their work. They believed in the need for schools and teachers to 'compensate' for the material and psychological disadvantages in students' homes. They made efforts during the process of teaching and learning to avert failure, or the feeling of failure, in children, safeguarding them from feelings of inferiority resulting from any kind of labelling or inability to perform. Children were respected as individuals with their own personality traits and differential learning needs by attending to them individually and scaffolding so as to enable them to perform.

The teacher–student relationship that these five teachers shared with their students was a highly significant aspect of their pedagogic practice. Each relationship had its own unique quality marked by a feeling of care and concern for children and a need for them to succeed. They seemed to all feel an institutional, professional and moral responsibility to work towards the development of children and it was evident in their relationship with them. In the metaphors to describe the relationship, the ideas of a good teacher as mother, didact or guru have strong cultural and traditional roots (Sarangapani, 2003), while the teacher as companion or guide are more modern and associated with progressive pedagogies taught in the pre-service teacher education (PSTE) programmes of the University of Delhi (BEd and BElEd) where these teachers had acquired their professional training. Interestingly, it was these two teachers who also spoke about how the PSTE had prepared them for their role; the others had either found PSTE not adequate for the current challenges or had no special recollection of PSTE training. Rather, they drew on their own autobiographical experiences supported by cultural resources to develop their metaphors and their roles.

The teachers' empathetic knowledge about the circumstance of poverty of the children, the aims they had for the children and the educational aims they held for them reflected an 'ought to be' imagination that was not constrained by the present disadvantages of the context of the children. Rather, their aims reflected a belief in the possibility of teachers' work, the transformational nature of education to change personalities, attitudes, behaviours and dispositions of children, and the possibility of transcending the constraints presented by their immediate surroundings and context. Despite the children's disadvantageous backgrounds, the teachers envisioned children as being capable of changing their own lives and also being capable of productively contributing towards the social change. The deprivation of socioeconomic and cultural capital in children did not restrain these teachers from holding aims that would provide access to the children to this capital. They did not practise a restricted functional education of 'coping' alone, delivering a restricted and limited version of education quality of achieving basic aims and learning outcomes alone (Avalos, 1992; Connell, 1994; Sarangapani, 2010). On the contrary, these teachers along with the curricular aims and objectives, worked on forming the mental aptitudes considered to be powerful, such as confidence, questioning, reasoning, arguing, logical thinking, analysing, putting forth one's perspective, considering the perspective of others, and dispositions, attitudes, habits, behaviours and values which are necessary for negotiating in all realms of life, be it individual, sociopolitical, economic or cultural. They saw these qualities as much more important to develop in children than content knowledge alone because they saw that these potentials could help children deal with the struggles of their present life and would also enable them to participate, negotiate and contribute in the larger world outside of their immediate context. This supports the observation made by Sarangapani (Chapter 7, this volume) regarding education in the mother tongue offered by some government teachers and charitable institutions for the poorest of the poor. The teachers in Hyderabad seemed to value these capabilities as life skills because they were not expecting the children to continue in formal education or even complete elementary school.

Kumar (2010) also thinks education has a transformative role as was reflected in the aims that teachers held for children and brings out the role and capacity of education to enable the less enabled, less competitive or less brilliant of today to acquire the characteristics that would make them more competitive as social categories in the course of time. The range of aims that teachers worked for acted as a broad framework of reference, and within this, it seems that these teachers could be more responsive and spontaneous to the immediacy of the context of teaching and learning in the classroom. Elaborating on educational quality, Kumar (ibid.: 16) mentions that 'educational quality requires that the learner retains some control in his or her own growth and the teacher remains autonomous enough to respond to the learner rather than to orders from above or demands that emanate from parents or the market'.

The understanding of the disadvantageous background of children and the demotivating environments that children come from did not lead teachers to develop a theory of 'multiple childhoods' (Sarangapani, 2016) in which they could be guided by alternative norms of what to expect from children and what to work towards. For all the teachers, their own lives and children formed the 'norm' against which they looked at the children and their families. They were compensating for what the students' homes could not provide. But this did not lead them to have lower expectations from the children or doubt their 'educability'. These teachers were unique also as they were not focused on the success of only a handful of children in their class or of only a select few. Rather, they were focused on making all children feel successful in different ways through their responsive pedagogies and by averting failure in children. They saw themselves as the only channels through which the 'self' of the child could be addressed, to build confidence, self-esteem, mutual respect and self-worth in children. This became crucial for teachers specifically in the context of teaching girls due to their awareness of the constraints that the highly gendered environments put on the personality of girls. For example, Sulekha addressed the issue in her class through a lesson about girls not being any less able than boys, being able to play games that boys play and aspiring to become anything they want to become in their lives. She actually conducted a match with girls where they played kabaddi.

Kumar (ibid.) argues that the quality of education needs to be defined in a way that is relevant to each of the social categories that demarcate inequality like caste, class and gender. Such a treatment is necessary because quality as an experiential aspect of education is likely to pose challenges to the children belonging to diverse social categories suffering from inequality, for which he lays quite a lot of responsibility on the school as a provider of educational experiences. Schools should include curricular and pedagogic devices to address deeper sources of inequalities so as to enable children's freedom from restraining influences. The teacher's autonomy in making professional judgements is central to this. These five teachers show us that it is possible to expect to find such stellar examples of autonomous practice producing valuable education within the government school system.

Note

1 This chapter is based on the MPhil study of the first author carried out under the supervision of the second author titled 'An Exploration of Teachers' Beliefs and Understanding of Their Pedagogy', unpublished MPhil dissertation submitted to the Tata Institute of Social Sciences, Mumbai, 2013.

References

Alexander, R. J. (2008). *Education for All, the Quality Imperative and the Problem of Pedagogy*. CREATE, Brighton: University of Sussex.

Avalos, B. (1986). *Teaching Children of the Poor: An Ethnographic Study in Latin America*. Canada: International Development Research Centre.

———. (1992). 'Education for the Poor: Quality or Relevance?' *British Journal of Sociology of Education*, 13(4): 419–436.

Bruner, J. S. (1996). *The Culture of Education*. Cambridge, MA: Harvard University Press.

Connell, R. W. (1994). 'Poverty and Education', *Harvard Education Review*, 64(2): 125–149.

Kingdon, G. G., and Teal, F. (2007). 'Does Performance Related Pay for Teachers Improve Student Performance? Some Evidence from India', *Economics of Education Review*, 26(4): 473–486.

Kremer, M., Chaudhury, N., Rogers, F. H., Muralidharan, K., and Hammer, J. (2005). 'Teacher Absence in India: A Snapshot', *Journal of the European Economic Association*, 3(2–3): 658–667.

Kumar, K. (2010). 'Quality in Education: Competing Concepts', *Contemporary Education Dialogue*, 7(1): 7–18.

Kumar, K., and Sarangapani, P. M. (2004). 'History of the Quality Debate', *Contemporary Education Dialogue*, 2(1): 30–52.

Sarangapani, P. M. (2003). *Constructing School Knowledge: An Ethnography of Learning in an Indian Village*. New Delhi, India: Sage.

———. (2010). 'Quality Concerns: National and Extranational', *Contemporary Education Dialogue*, 7(1): 41–57.

———. (2016). 'Schooling in Contexts of Cultural Diversity: Difference or Deficiency?' Unpublished paper presented in the Philosophy of Education, Bangalore: Azim Premji University.

Sarangapani, P. M., Jain, Manish, Mukhopadhyay, Rahul, and Winch, Christopher. (2013). 'Baseline Survey of the School Scenario in Some States in the Context of RTE: Study of Educational Quality, School Management, and Teachers (Andhra Pradesh, Delhi and West Bengal)', Unpublished report submitted to the Sarva Siksha Abhiyan, Ministry of Human Resources Development, New Delhi, India.

Index

accountability 5, 8, 9, 17, 18, 35, 104, 105, 106, 110, 112, 119, 124, 126, 129, 132, 133, 134, 140, 142, 143, 144, 145, 147, 147, 148, 149, 153, 154, 162, 176, 184–186, 189, 230, 231, 233, 260, 281
aided school(s) 4, 40, 43, 46, 55, 56, 107, 163, 165, 167, 168, 178, 182, 185, 186, 187, 228, 232; grant-in aid 49, 55
aims/aim (of education/educational) 6, 9, 14, 15, 16, 17, 18, 19, 20, 23, 71, 72, 80, 83–103, 125, 129, 132, 134, 143, 144, 145, 147, 147, 149, 153, 154, 156, 162, 176–177, 187, 188, 218, 219, 230, 231, 234, 238, 261, 263–264, 271, 278, 281, 284, 288–290, 293, 294, 295; curricular 16, 295; individual 85, 87–88, 98; national/state 17, 77; non-educational 261, 263; political (and/or) economic 1, 15, 144; public (and/or) private 14, 15, 54, 59, 60, 68, 84, 116, 117; social 16, 147, 148, 154
Alexander, R. 124, 146–148, 283
assessment/learning outcomes (of students/learning) 1, 6, 108, 129, 134, 146, 148, 149, 152, 170, 183, 221, 228, 232, 234, 249; large scale 9, 71, 72, 77; of quality 139, 145, 147, 153; tests and measures of 68, 69, 233

autonomy 33, 35, 60, 71, 129, 147, 187, 188, 219; provincial 39; teacher 145, 236, 296

Bourdieu 230, 264, 274
brand 21, 163, 255–257
Bruner, J. S. 125, 283
budget/low-fee school(s) 7, 11, 21, 107, 161, 47, 1, 2, 4, 6, 11, 23, 4, 69, 105, 106, 116, 163, 165, 166, 168, 173, 174, 177, 183, 187, 228, 244–259, 278; accountability in 184, 185; pedagogy in 180, 182, 221
business 11, 32, 63, 77, 108, 172, 176, 199, 233, 236, 241, 246; corporate 232; entrepreneurs 188; family 21, 230, 232; plan 170, 172; small 173; of the state 81

caste 15, 32, 36, 40–43, 45, 48, 50, 52, 54, 56–57, 59, 80, 83, 95–96, 132, 154, 162, 167, 198, 213, 245–246, 251, 270, 278, 296; see also social inequality
charitable (schools/trusts/ institutions/foundations) 20, 108, 165, 176, 187, 188, 136, 295; charity/ies 175; family run 170, 171, 179
christian(s)/christianity, missionary 38, 41, 44, 47, 43, 165; education 176; see also religion
citizenship 20, 34, 83, 90, 124, 180, 181, 187, 191–226

Index

client/clientele 18, 19, 20, 21, 156, 162, 168, 170–176; 198–200; claims of 119; clientelism 78; client-vendor relationship 173
coaching 57, 163, 165, 168, 179, 234
compulsory education 46, 83–84, 88, 92–93
corporate schools 177; management 170
cost effective/efficient 126, 127
culture/cultural/traditions/indigenous 37, 38, 48, 50, 50, 59–60, 91, 93, 127, 128, 93, 147, 21, 37–38, 50, 247; tradition culture and society 90–97
culture of school 12, 20, 184, 187, 214, 257, 258, of education 146, 154
cultural capital 11, 69, 76, 79, 80, 162, 183–184, 206, 210, 220, 225, 261, 264, 276, 295; social 69, 75, 79, 80, 124, 261, 276
Curriculum framework (national/state) 86, 95, 98
curriculum (quality dimension) 143–144, 146–149, 153–154, 162, 170, 179–180, 227–243

discipline/disciplinary/punishment 180, 182, 183, 218, 222–226, 257

educability 131–132, 281, 296
Education for All/Universalisation of Education 10, 12, 88, 90, 140
efficiency 1–24, 47, 55, 57–58, 60, 61, 111, 116, 126, 127, 129, 134, 140–142, 144–145, 147–149, 233, 260
English medium 11–12, 20, 163, 167, 176, 181, 183, 187, 194, 197, 205–206, 263–265
entrepreneur, entrepreneurial, entrepreneurship 48, 58, 170–172, 177, 179, 182, 187–188
equality *see* social inequality
examinations competitive 163, 177, 179, 181, 231, 234; school tests 176, 233

fee 62, 57, 55, 41, 57, 74, 108, 113, 155, 163, 166, 168, 169, 170, 171, 172, 173, 175, 176, 177, 182, 183, 188, 220, 228, 232, 246, 249, 273, 276, 278; collection of 187, 188, 223; spectrum 265; unpaid 185; waiving 251

goods/bads (public, private) 44, 67–81
Government schools 12, 167, 173, 176; enrolment in 11, 107, 192; facilities 75, 178, 193; pedagogy in 180; quality of 4, 227, 241, 266–278

high-fee school(s) 11, 57, 75, 165, 166, 168, 169, 172, 173, 183; accountability in 184; pedagogy in 177
Hindu(s)/Hinduism/Hindutva 40–44, 167, 168, 187, 197, 198, 213, 257; *see also* religion
home-school/support 182, 219–220; concerns regarding 205–206; –school relationship 224–259, 286–288; *see also* religion

ideology 170, 179, 185, 230, 232–233, 238
Islam/Islamic/Islamiyat/Muslim 43, 165, 194, 197–198, 213, 232, 239–240, 262; *see also* religion

Kumar, K. 38, 127, 145–147, 295

labour dignity of 53; market 73, 264, 277; teachers' 281; wage 32, 206
local 36–37, 39, 42–43, 46, 48, 52, 55–59, 61; neighbourhood 173

market (education) 14, 18, 20, 109–110, 133, 161–189, 191, 261–262, 272, 274, 278
marketisation as commodity, education 67–74, 118
medium of instruction 20, 45, 155, 229, 239, 262

Naik, J. P. 17, 50, 55, 139–142, 144, 145, 149
New Public Management (NPM) 8, 17, 110, 126, 134, 233; managerialism 21, 230, 232–233, 241

parent/parenting 245–258; 247–248, 252–253, 255, 258; expectations from 180, 182, 185, 187; mothering 291–292; perspectives of 260–279
parent-teacher associations/meetings 273, 255
pedagogy/ies/gic/teaching 124, 125, 146, 152, 204, 206–211; 213–214; 218–226, 230–231, 242, 245, 283, 288, 293; all-round development 225; culture 206, 210, 282; dialogic and child-centred 225; domesticating 223; drill 223–225; folk 124–125, 127–129, 132; formation of 218–226; forms 180–184, 206–213; forms 20, 222–226; method of learning 221–222; method of teaching 220–221; progressive 184, 210–211, 213–214; rote 223
power of state 33, 36, 78, 114, 116; colonial 36, 51, 52; consumer 273; hierarchies of 274; private 56
private unaided schools 5, 11, 40, 108, 196, 228, 232, 235, 236, 241, 242
provisioning of physical space, of school 75, 78, 79, 172, 177, 178, 192, 200–213, 270, 274; religious/nationalist symbols in 196–198, 213; size 168, 196, 197, 199, 200
profession/professional (of teaching) 123–135; identity 17, 125, 127, 131, 133, 282, 293
provisioning (quality dimension) capacity 144–145, 148–149, 152; space 177–179, 292–293, 197, 200–204, 205, 208, 213
public–private/government–private/state–market 1–23, 31–63, 67–81, 107–109; colonial history of 35–52
public–private partnerships (PPPs) 4, 12, 109, 161, 194
purchaser (of education) 69, 71–74, 76; –beneficiary split 74, 76, 79

quality, concept of 17, 67–68, 124, 140–154; assessing 70–72; framework 148, 227 in Kothari Commission 54–58; history of 149–152, dimensions of 176–186; metrics 149, 152; production and management 227–243; proxy indicators of 265, 268, 271, 278; regulating 115–116; unit of analysis 172–154

regulation/regulatory framework 5, 6, 10, 12, 32, 70, 75–79, 91, 123, 130, 155–156, 185, 192, 197; decentred regulation 112, 117; defacto deregulation 115, 117, 118
religious affiliation 262, 270; symbols 198
right to education, 89, 92, 196; RTE Act 5, 58, 78, 79, 114, 116, 106, 109–114, 116, 275–276
Rights child 10, 86–87; human 86–88, 90

school choice 5, 22, 47, 194, 260–279
school, ethos 18, 21, 228–243; managerial 232–235
school inspection 43, 46, 49, 116, 228, 233
school leader/leadership, principal 230, 232, 236–238, 224–259
school management (types of) 170–173, 187, 198–213
school, types of 165–170, 196–198
small schools 168, 170, 172, 187; stability of 168, 187–188
social class 9, 10, 11, 12, 34, 38, 52, 54, 57, 58, 107–108, 128, 149, 156, 162, 173–176, 177, 180, 186, 187, 193, 198–200, 206,

244, 252, 253, 258; *see also* social inequality
social inequality/disadvantages/stratification 1, 6, 8, 11, 12, 40, 42–44, 48, 50, 52, 58–59, 70, 95, 96, 112, 132, 145, 154, 162, 174, 186, 198, 205, 213, 244, 264, 270, 282, 286–288, 293–296
social mobility 11, 12, 37, 42, 48, 59, 118, 128
standards (quality dimension) 141–145, 147–150, 153, 156, 162, 230–231, 233, 242

teacher(s): absenteeism 2, 5, 150–152; accountability 3–9, 22, 142; autonomy 145; beliefs and practices of 281–297; costs of/pay of/salaries of/service conditions 3–5, 57, 108–114, 163; education/preparation 98, 108–114; entrepreneur 187–188; as guru 291–292, 294; management of 21, 108–114; nature of work 17, 22, 97, 146–154; para-teachers 3–4; profession of 123–135; quality of/qualification 74, 108–117, 140; –student relationship 128, 290–294; tuition 171–172, 179, 182
textbook 207–212; culture 187, 211
Tooley, J. 151, 161, 194, 244–245

unrecognised schools 174, 192, 194–197, 200–203, 208, 210

voice 12, 107, 244, 260, 273, 278; exit 8, 12, 107, 244, 260, 273, 278; loyalty 273

Winch, C. 6–7, 14–15, 17, 139, 140, 142–145, 147–148, 155, 161